Australian Queer Screens

Australian Queer Screens

Diversity and Social Change in Film and TV

Rob Cover, Whitney Monaghan, Stuart Richards, Scott McKinnon and Tinonee Pym

BLOOMSBURY ACADEMIC
NEW YORK • LONDON • OXFORD • NEW DELHI • SYDNEY

BLOOMSBURY ACADEMIC
Bloomsbury Publishing Inc, 1359 Broadway, New York, NY 10018, USA
Bloomsbury Publishing Plc, 50 Bedford Square, London, WC1B 3DP, UK
Bloomsbury Publishing Ireland, 29 Earlsfort Terrace, Dublin 2, D02 AY28, Ireland

BLOOMSBURY, BLOOMSBURY ACADEMIC and the Diana logo are trademarks of
Bloomsbury Publishing Plc

First published in the United States of America 2026

Copyright © Rob Cover, Whitney Monaghan, Stuart Richards, Scott McKinnon and
Tinonee Pym, 2026

For legal purposes the Acknowledgements on p. vii constitute an extension
of this copyright page.

Cover design by Megan Wilson
Cover images (from left): Still of Louise Lovely in *Jewelled Nights*, 1925 © NFSA;
Still from *Silks and Saddles*, 1921, via BestDomainVidz on YouTube; Still from *Silks
and Saddles*, 1921, via BestDomainVidz on YouTube; Still from *Jewelled Nights*, 1925
© NFSA; Still from *Silks and Saddles*, 1921, via BestDomainVidz on YouTube

Bloomsbury Publishing Inc does not have any control over, or responsibility for, any third-
party websites referred to or in this book. All internet addresses given in this book were
correct at the time of going to press. The author and publisher regret any inconvenience
caused if addresses have changed or sites have ceased to exist, but can accept no
responsibility for any such changes.

Library of Congress Cataloging-in-Publication Data
Names: Cover, Rob | Monaghan, Whitney author | Richards, Stuart James author |
McKinnon, Scott author | Pym, Tinonee author
Title: Australian queer screens : film and TV diversity and social change / Rob Cover,
Whitney Monaghan, Stuart Richards, Scott McKinnon, Tinonee Pym.
Description: New York: Bloomsbury Academic, 2026. | Includes bibliographical
references and index.
Identifiers: LCCN 2025029015 | ISBN 9798765128428 hardback | ISBN 9798765128435
paperback | ISBN 9798765128459 pdf | ISBN 9798765128466 epub
Subjects: LCSH: Motion pictures–Australia–History | Television–Australia–History | Sexual
minorities in motion pictures | Sexual minorities on television | LCGFT: Film criticism |
Television criticism and reviews
Classification: LCC PN1993.5.A8 C68 2026 | DDC 791.430994–dc23/eng/20250724
LC record available at https://lccn.loc.gov/2025029015

ISBN: HB: 979-8-7651-2842-8
PB: 979-8-7651-2843-5
ePDF: 979-8-7651-2845-9
eBook: 979-8-7651-2846-6

Typeset by Deanta Global Publishing Services, Chennai, India
Printed and bound in the United States of America

For product safety related questions contact productsafety@bloomsbury.com.

To find out more about our authors and books visit www.bloomsbury.com and sign up for
our newsletters.

Contents

List of Figures   vi
Acknowledgements   vii

1   Introduction: The Renaissance in Australian Queer Screen (Studies)   1

Part One   Histories and Formations

2   The Politics of Film Representation   21
3   Australian Queer Television   39
4   Framing Politics: Filmgoing and Activism   57

Part Two   Australian Queer Film Production

5   Motivation and Impact among LGBTQ+ Screen Stakeholders   73
6   The Australian Queer Film Festival   89

Part Three   Reading the Australian Queer Text

7   Australian Queer Screen Criticism   105
8   Gender-Diverse, Trans and Emergent Identity Frameworks in New Screen Contexts   119
9   Historical Reception Practices, Policing and Community Change   137

Part Four   Audience, Identity and Culture

10   Australian Queer Screen Audiences: Place, Time and Memory   151
11   Young Audiences, Mental Health and Identity   167
12   Queer Screens and Social Change   185
13   Queer Australian Screen Futures and Affordances   209

References   211
Filmography   231
Index   239

Figures

2.1 One of Australia's first tomboys on screen in *Silks and Saddles* (1921). *Silks and Saddles* directed by Robert F. Hill © Universal Pictures 1929. All rights reserved   22

2.2 *Sunshine Sally* directed by Lawson Harris © Austral Super Films 1922. All rights reserved   23

2.3 A poster for a screening of *Witches and Faggots, Dykes and Poofters* (1980)   34

7.1 Issue 1 of *Lesbians on the Loose*, January 1990   113

Acknowledgements

The authors acknowledge the many film and television producers, creators, actors, avid fans and casual viewers, collectors, archivists, researchers and project research participants whose conversations, information and insights have contributed significantly to this research.

We particularly thank Olympia Barron and the Australian Film Institute Research Collective, Nick Henderson and the Australian Queer Archives, Sydney's Pride History Group, and Silke Bader at the State Library of New South Wales for access to, and support in, navigating, research materials and archives. We thank also Paula Hamilton, Susan Luckman, Jess Pacella, Beans Goodfellow, Damien O'Meara and Saige Walton.

Research for Chapter 3 was funded through a 2019 AFI Research Collection Fellowship (held by Whitney). Research for Chapter 9 was funded through a State Library of New South Wales Nancy Kessing Fellowship (held by Scott). Chapters 5, 8, 10, 11 and 12 draw on data gathered and anonymized interviews undertaken for the project *Representation of Gender and Sexual Diversity in Australian Film and Television, 1990–2010* ('AusQueerScreen') which was funded by the Australian Research Council Discovery Programme (DP180103321, led by Rob). We especially thank Mona Chatskin and Duc Dau, who worked as research associates on the AusQueerScreen project.

This book was written on the unceded lands of the Wurundjeri, Taungurung, Boonwurrung, Ngunnawal, Ngambri and Kaurna peoples, the traditional owners; we pay our respects to the elders past, present and emerging.

Introduction

The Renaissance in Australian Queer Screen (Studies)

Introduction

Although it is sometimes said that queer people have until recently been absent from our entertainment screens, Australia – like elsewhere – actually has a very rich history of representing LGBTQ+, gender- and sexuality-diverse characters, stories and themes in film and broadcast television. When we stop to think about it, many of us of all ages not only recall some of that media representation, but remember how important it was to see it. Or we remember our critical responses to it. Or we recall the conversations and discussions we had about it with family, friends and colleagues about what might have been done differently, how a depiction could have been better, or what made a particular queer character particularly significant. Indeed, we might say that the tendency to forget these important queer screen stories, depictions and readings is not because we did not encounter them, but because a particular kind of journalistic, community and activist discourse encourages a false belief in the relative absence of sexuality and gender diversity – a discourse that in itself is important when we also acknowledge that despite this rich history there has not been quite enough inclusivity in Australian media so far.

This book brings together research on the history, significance, production, content and cultural reception practices of Australian queer screen media. It is not intended as a 'celebration' of Australian queer screen depictions, even though there is much to celebrate. Rather, it is a critical engagement with queer representation in Australia: how it came about, what its trajectories have been, how producers and creative practitioners talk about what is meaningful, and how audiences engage critically with the texts to find personal and community utilities, whether for pleasure, well-being, knowledge or the production of identity.

To take such an approach is to actively 'queer' queer media histories and scholarship. The term 'queer' remains contested at times, sometimes because it refers to complex theoretical approaches, sometimes because it is a term that continues to inscribe shame for some people (Munt 2007). Nevertheless, we actively embrace the term as having continued purchase for powerfully describing a diverse and complex field of study, and, more generally, as capturing a perspective and a politics that remain deeply valued by many. Although queer originated as a term of derision for homosexual men in the nineteenth century, it was 'reclaimed' in the late 1980s with a more positive interpretation and application. In fact, it was reclaimed more than once at the same time: In one domain, the term queer began to be used to describe the particular ways in which poststructuralist theory was being applied to topics related to gender and sexuality, to critical and literary practices and to sociological enquiry (Epstein 1996, Stein and Plummer 1994). Unrelatedly, but at about the same time, the term queer was being deployed in North America among the activist work of Queer Nation, an off-shoot of HIV activist organization ACT-UP – an unrelated but productively interesting intersection with the first meaning (de Lauretis 1989). From a queer screens' perspective more than three decades later on the other side of the world, this productive juxtaposition remains valuable, because it speaks not only to how we might read queerness into a range of film and television texts, but also because it reminds us that there is an activist element to queer on-screen representations that create public stresses of the kind that may help produce social change, tolerance and acceptance of gender and sexuality minorities.

Not long after these two parallel reclamations, the term queer was quickly adopted as an easy 'umbrella' shorthand for describing the growing points of coalition and intersection across lesbian, gay, bisexual and transgender politics and community. This use of queer drew on an ironic deployment by Gay Liberationists in the 1970s and 1980s (Gay Liberation Front 1970) 'reclaiming' the language formerly used by bigots as a positive community self-descriptor (Stewart 1995). Internationally, queer came to operate alongside other ways of communicating the idea of a shared politics and community outside of normative sexualities and genders, first as 'lesbian and gay', then as LGBT, and then having its own letter added on to create the acronym LGBTQ. The intention here was to provide space within the whole for those whose sense of sexuality and gender subjectivity did not fit easily into lesbian, gay, bisexual and/or transgender conceptualizations, but who nevertheless experienced these aspects of their lives in ways that were marginalized from normative representations and structures. Now, the Q remains a feature of those umbrella acronyms, while other letters have been added to extend the acronym to LGBTQIA+ or varieties of this. Again, the tensions involved in a term that both serves as an umbrella for gender and sexuality diversity, a coalitional approach, but also, at the time, a generational distancing from particular perceptions of gender and sexuality identity, has pragmatic possibilities for thinking about Australian queer screen media.

Indeed, these various tensions open a number of important questions – ones we embrace in this book but do not seek to give definitive answers – including some of the following: *What is an Australian queer screen text?* Is it anything with a clearly defined LGBTQ+ character, such as *The Adventures of Priscilla, Queen of the Desert* (1994) or texts where same-sex attraction is implied, such as *The Getting of Wisdom* (1977) or can it include films and series where metaphors of marginalization and resilience can be read as representative of queerness like *Muriel's Wedding* (1994)? Is it an *Australian* queer screen text if it is filmed in Australia, such as *The Sum of Us* (1994) or *The Secret Life of Us?* (2001–5)? Or do the actors, producers and screenwriters need to identify as gender- or sexuality-diverse Australians for it to be an Australian queer text? Is the widely panned 1980s film *The Pirate Movie* (1982) an Australian queer text because it was filmed around Victoria and its principal actor Kristy McNichol identifies as a lesbian? And because it's pretty camp? Is a queer streaming series from the United Kingdom, like *Heartstopper* (2022–), or from Sweden like *Young Royals* (2021–4) an Australian queer text because it is watched, debated and has fan fiction written about it by Australians, and may be more identifiable to a contemporary Australian queer audience than, say, *Head On* (1998)? We may ask if text should have easily recognizable Australian settings to be properly Australian queer screen media, even though we may need to ask how much of the outback in *Priscilla* would be known to the average Australian audience member, or if the Warrandyte setting of *Downriver* (2015) has ever been visited by audiences who live in inner Melbourne only 30 kilometres away?

In other words, just as the term queer had multiple origins and retains multiple uses, the inability to pin down exactly what queer is (Jagose 1996) reminds us that it is not particularly easy to work out what exactly 'counts' as an Australian queer screen media text. And, indeed, we may not wish to know.

Certainly, there have been many attempts to make lists of every Australian queer screen text, episode and film, including by the authors of this book. And whether lists of queer media are even attractive today is debatable: lists imply a limitation, a relative scarcity in contrast to other representations. For a list to be useful to anyone, it cannot be unmanageably large. In today's media culture, the presence of queer, trans and other stories, folk and readings are common enough that creating lists so long tells us very little except about historical shifts in number and frequency. And those, in themselves, are not the most important part of grasping and understanding Australian queer screen media. But keeping in mind also the desire and political need *not* to foreclose on particular identities or readings, it is likewise important not to make lists that will actively exclude screen media from being considered Australian queer screen texts in the future. Instead, in this book, we work across and around the various lists, recognized texts and ways of perceiving and interpreting them to come at broad, diverse and open ways of understanding what it might mean that a text speaks from and to queer representation.

Renaissances

With this diversity of textual meaning in mind, our book is one that also acknowledges there are key points or phases in queer screen production that can be determined if we identify texts in particular ways. This is to point to the fact that all shifts and trends in what is – and who are – represented *both* build on and diverge from the rich history of the past: no text is produced in isolation from the languages, concepts, frameworks and practices that precede it.

To make sense of renaissances is to begin by reasserting the myth of queer invisibility. This, as we say regularly throughout this book, is a myth so palpable that it produces a certain kind of relationship with memory in which to remember a childhood of queer screen spectatorship is to remember not merely an overtly cisgender and heteronormative screen media culture, but a wholesale absence or lack. This oft-repeated view became outdated subsequent to the mid-1990s renaissance in mainstream LGBTQ+ representation across television and mass-circulation film (Cover 2000, Padva 2004, Lipton 2008). What the mid-1990s revealed was that questions about *how much* representation were no longer contemporary and instead there was a need for producers, audiences and scholars to ask about the conditions that make gender and sexuality diversity possible, interpretable and palatable to screen audiences, and how these texts are used in ways which speak to social pedagogies, well-being, acceptance, inclusivity and screen diversity.

Contra invisibility, the reality is that even the oldest among us was preceded by early film representations of gender diversity and same-sex attraction, as we demonstrate in Chapter 2 where we work through the early filmic histories of queer screen presence. Chapter 3 does the same for television, both tracing genealogies that can be recognized in today's significantly more regular representation.

If we are to think about Australian queer screen cultures in terms of various shifts and renaissances, then we might consider them in terms of three phases, none of which are mutually exclusive and none of which foreclose on the continuities of key elements of the earlier ones, but which speak to the mutuality of thinking about both frequency and style of representation.

An early phase represents both the coded and subtextual readings – no matter how sometimes obvious – of early film, and the growing production of underground, festival, arthouse and alternative texts deliberately produced for minority and radical audiences, most of it occurring prior to the early 1990s. For example, Lawrence Johnston's 50-minute film *Night Out* (1990) is an Australian queer drama that ultimately was screened at the 1990 Cannes Film Festival. It was not widely circulated in major cinemas in Australia and remains relatively hidden among the history of Australian queer cinema today. At the same time, this first phase incorporates radically different but nevertheless equally limited representation on television: early gay and lesbian characters who provided spectacle for soap audiences, issues-based episodes of Australian television dramas (usually medical dramas) such as *A Country Practice* (1981–93) and *G.P.* (1989–96) in which queer characters gave fleeting examples of vulnerability, difficulty and struggle before the next episodes returned the status quo to the main cast. There are, of course, outliers in this phase, and we might include here the first iteration of *Prisoner* (1979–86).

A 1990–2010 renaissance can be discerned, building on the richness of the first phase, but operating somewhat differently in terms of tone, focus, circulation and frequency. Here, Australian film and television experienced a more explicit focus on LGBTQ+ themes and narratives, often operating for both queer community audiences and a wider mainstream, and available for masscirculation and prime-time broadcast: *The Sum of Us*, *Priscilla*, *Head On*, *Love and Other Catastrophes* (1996); increasing use of longer-term supporting characters in television series like *Sweat* (1996), *Neighbours* (1985–) and *The Secret Life of Us*, among many others. Here, a limited form of liberal-tolerant diversity enables queer representation on a grander scale, albeit one arguably limited to foregrounding difference and distinctiveness, to treating queer lives with a kind of anthropological lens, and often a lack of depth and complexity in characterization – although, of course, the extent to which these criticisms may be felt by all audiences is variable.

The third and perhaps most current phase is one in which LGBTQ+ characterization, narrative and extensiveness of representation expands beyond the limitations of the first two phases. Here, from about 2010 onwards, Australian media production catches up somewhat with what Jimmie Reeves and colleagues (1996) identified as the vast diversification of North American film and television production owing to the proliferation of cable networks over the limited cinema distributors and broadcast networks allowing for a diversity of stories, characters and themes that did not have to appeal to a perceived normative majority. DVD, too, plays a role in making available that which would otherwise not receive significant programming. That is, in contrast to the 1980s/1990s demand for mass-circulation film to maximize returns and the limited air-time of a small number of networks, options for creating work that straddled the small-circulation of art house and the public appeal of quality text enables both film and series with even more marginal, increasingly intersectional characters and stories: films like *Downriver, Drown* (2015), and series such as *Please Like Me* (2013–16), *Barracuda* (2016), *Heartbreak High* (2022–5) and *Wentworth* (2013–21) are able to appeal to niche-marketing audiences and smaller-share viewership without failing to be profitable to funders. In many respects, this phase has begun to see a move away from queerness as topical, spectacle or as an 'issue' to one in which non-cisgender and non-heteronormativity is increasingly a (small) part of the everyday landscape of Australian life – at least life as it is represented on-screen. These are not the only ways in which to periodize Australian queer screen culture, but represent one particular way of framing at the most simple level – a simplicity we ourselves critique throughout the remainder of this book.

Another way in which Australian queer screen texts can be understood, coded and framed is through the extent to which they appeal and are made available to international audiences – a factor that has many variables but arguably provides a way to think not just about what is included in Australian queer screen media, but what that media *does* beyond Australian audiences.

From the early Australian Westerns, like *Rangle River* (1936), to international co-productions, such as *The Power of the Dog* (2021), Australian films have always been internationally engaged. Sometimes this is a matter of the attention garnered by Australian queer films on both mainstream and queer film festival circuits. Such titles include *52 Tuesdays* (2013), *Cut Snake* (2014), *Holding the Man* (2015), *Downriver, Sequin in a Blue Room* (2019) and *My First Summer* (2020). These films found audiences across the film festival spectrum while also receiving limited theatrical releases and, eventually, streaming releases.

Of particular note is the 2021 Australian co-production *The Power of the Dog*, which received critical and commercial success. Since its worldwide 2023 release on Netflix, well over 4.8 million hours of the film have been watched (Netflix 2023). The film also landed on numerous high-profile 'best of the year' lists and received considerable attention after Jane Campion received the Academy Award for Best Director, and the film received eleven other nominations. In other words, while Australian queer screen media has always had an international audience of some kind, we can trace its history through the various measures of international success as well.

Queer screen scholarship

This is among the first books of Australian queer screen scholarship, which is somewhat surprising given not only the richness of Australian queer screen presence but also the fact that queer media scholarship has been an area of study for over three decades, and grew substantially in North America and Europe nearly a quarter of a century ago in the very early 2000s. A diverse array of journal articles and chapters, a dedicated journal *Queer Studies in Media & Popular Culture* and a number of monographs and anthologies relate the significance of queer screen research elsewhere. Among the anthologies are several texts released between 2000 and 2015 about various *national* cinemas and television, such as Robin Griffiths' *British Queer Cinema* (2006), Allison MacLeod's *Irish Queer Cinema* (2018) and Jamie Zhao's *Queer TV China* (2023).

Much of this work builds on a genealogy of scholarship going back to early writing on the interpretation of non-heteronormativity in cinematic and television texts, particularly the work of Vito Russo (1981), Larry Gross (e.g. 1991), Richard Dyer (e.g. 1993) and Keith Howes (1993). These early canonical works, simultaneously scholarly and activist, focused on instances of representation of gay men and lesbians within a media framework that persisted at times in stereotyping and self-censorship. This early work also foregrounded the idea that 'positive' representation was to be understood as an important goals necessary for the well-being of gender- and sexuality-diverse persons, particularly to overcome the perceived isolation and loneliness of growing up non-normative. Arguably, this early textual representation scholarship has provided a scaffolding that influenced later and recent work on the topic, particularly resulting in the dominance of textual analysis as methodology and approaches focused on valuing positive representation or promoting what were sometimes thought of as negative stereotypes (but often actual reflections of queer community life) of recreational drug use and casual sexual expression.

Among the key concepts that have dominated queer film and television studies is the presumption of the benefits of 'visibility'. Russo (1981), for example, made a profound argument for the ways in which LGBTQ+ characters, themes and stories had long been embedded in film representation in ways that required active reading to recognize them. Other early texts, such as Howes' (1993) encyclopaedic collation of LGBTQ representations in international films and television series, *Broadcasting It*, seek to make apparent the sheer extant visibility of gay men, lesbians and trans persons on international screens. Certainly, this early work countered public claims to a relative invisibility *per se* of non-cisgender and non-heteronormative lives on screen.

However, other scholars had reiterated the claim of relative invisibility of LGBTQ+ personages on entertainment screens. For example, Gross (1991) argued there was a relative absence of LGBTQ+ subjects in mainstream media, calling on scholars to press upon the media their claims for 'equitable and respectful treatment' (45). In a genealogy of queer screen scholarship, the claim of relative invisibility has had bearing for much subsequent scholarship, particularly in the 1990s and 2000s. The emphasis on visibility is arguably the result of gay and lesbian screen studies emerging from the same roots as the 1970s and 1980s gay rights movement, and that the movement for gay rights based its claims at least partly on liberationist articulations of coming out, visibility and inclusion through recognition of presence in everyday settings. The framing of queer visibility as the core social concern of LGBTQ screen media has subsequently remained central to much scholarship that either celebrates LGBTQ+ representation or is interested in unpacking the meaning of the depiction.

Amy Villarejo's pivotal text *Ethereal Queer: Television, Historicity, Desire* (2014) pointed to the conflicting public perceptions of queer visibility on television screens, with common claims of an explosion in representation and a simultaneous claim of relative invisibility. Villarejo's point was to move beyond simplistic scholarly understandings of visibility to consider what might constitute visibility in more critical ways. Similarly, Patricia White's *Uninvited: Classical Hollywood Cinema and Lesbian Representability* (1999) focused on representability rather than representation in American cinema, arguing that censorship of the Motion Picture Production Code produced ways of signifying queerness without necessarily portraying LGBTQ+ identities. These imperatives have been taken up in recent years in queer screen studies with a greater focus on critical engagement with *what* and *who* is representation rather than an uncritical celebration of all queer depictions. This approach added a stronger, more nuanced set of approaches to queer screen studies following some of the longer-standing developments in other areas of media studies, including audience research.

One strand of queer media scholarship has explored, analysed and contested the use of stereotypes in LGBTQ+ screen representations. Stereotypes are a form of communication that links an identity with a set of attributes including visual or bodily norms, behaviours or attitudes. They operate through broad social agreement based on their repetition across culture and over long periods of time. Because stereotypes are a means of communicating information about an identity group very quickly and efficiently, they have been regularly used in film and television representation of LGBTQ+ characters. For example, the well-known 1970s British sitcom *Are You Being Served?* (1972–85) never once asserted directly that one of its key characters, Mr Humphries (John Inman), was gay, but through visuals, comportment, speech and the representation of taste and aesthetics, made clear to any culturally-aware audience member that he was a gay man. Despite their efficiency in visual media, stereotypes are considered problematic because they reduce an identity group to a set of expectations, such that younger LGBTQ+ persons are lonely, melancholic and potentially suicidal (Dyer 1993). Over the past half-century, film and television production teams have responded to calls from activists – including the Gay and Lesbian Alliance Against Defamation (GLAAD) – to produce more complex, diverse characters and stories about LGBTQ+ persons, and in recent years there is a discernible attention to representing intersectionality and more complex characterizations rather than gestural inclusiveness.

Queer studies methods of analysis and engagement with queer film and television texts have focused on textual representation; there is a gap in research in terms of using other methods such as audience studies, although there has been some scholarship and a more insistent move in recent years towards considering the role of the audience as active interpreters and participants in queer screen media. Among the more significant empirical audience studies is Evan Cooper's (2003) 'Decoding *Will and Grace*' which is often cited by subsequent writers when considering questions of the role of diverse representation in producing social change among broad mainstream audiences. It is notable that queer studies' audience research has more recently begun to deploy a range of methods for understanding audiences as makers of meanings, including surveys, interviews and focus groups, and ethnographic accounts (e.g. McKinnon 2016), something we endeavour to foreground in this book in the last section.

About this book

This book brings together research undertaken by five Australian scholars of queer screen cultures, including drawing on, sharing and mutually critiquing the work across a range of different projects and individual trajectories of research. This team of co-authors does not, of course, include everyone working on Australian queer screen media, and we acknowledge the significance of scholars who have been researching in and around this topic for longer such as Deb Verhoeven (e.g. 1997) who has been pivotal in drawing international attention to some of the key historical instances in Australian queer production, as well emerging key scholars such as Damien O'Meara (e.g. O'Meara and Monaghan 2024), and the many PhDs completed on Australian queer cinema in-between (e.g. Peach 2005).

Several different projects contribute to the research in this book. One of them is the *AusQueerScreen* study ('Representation of Gender and Sexual Diversity in Australian Film and Television, 1990–2010'), which was funded by the Australian Research Council Discovery Programme led by Rob and on which Tinonee also researched. The study provided one of the first comprehensive accounts of the full cycle of Australian queer media from production to text to audience, and its contribution to Australian gender and sexual minority representation. Completed in 2023, its goal was to understand how queer media processes and content are implicated in healthy identities, acceptance of minorities among mainstream audiences and communities, and the implications for screen entertainment's role among young people in the context of digital media. The project undertook literature reviews, archival analysis, and gathered new data from in-depth interviews with twenty film and television stakeholders (actors, producers, directors and funders), and forty audience members (aged 18–55) from across most regions of Australia, including both urban and rural/regional settings, and from a broad range of reported gender and sexual identities. All of our interviewees agreed to speak after ethics clearance granted by The University of Western Australia; we don't identify them in this book. Some of the key insights of the study were that there is an over-representation in Australian queer screen media of youth vulnerability and youth suicidality in contrast to English-language screen media from the United Kingdom and the United States (Cover 2021); that there is widespread interest in gender diversity across several generations of Australian screen texts including particularly intersections between trans subjectivity and drag performance which may or may not be productive (Cover, Prosser and Dau 2022); and that younger audience members tend to be more critical of the quality and depth of queer characters while older audience members tend to celebrate most representation, indicating a substantial growth of critical engagement among Australian LGBTQ+ audiences.

Another project that contributed to this book was a fellowship undertaken by Whitney in 2019 at the Australian Film Institute Research Collection, located at RMIT University. This project, 'Queer Television in Australia: Lesbians, Gays and Bisexuals on the Small Screen from 1970 to 2000', charted the inclusion of lesbian, gay and bisexual characters on Australian entertainment television from 1970 to 2000. One of the key findings of this project was a gradual shift from one-off storylines towards greater inclusion of lesbian, gay and bisexual characters. This project formed the basis of later research into queer themes and trends in contemporary Australian television (O'Meara and Monaghan 2024) as well as Whitney's recent research into the politics of inclusion in the streaming era (Monaghan 2024). And, of course, the ongoing work of each of the authors – both individually and collectively – contributes to the broad conclusions of this book: that Australia not only has a very rich culture of queer screen media, but that this media is important and meaningful to many audiences both at home and internationally, and both those with lived experience of gender and sexuality diversity and those who comfortably inhabit the genders and sexualities in the mainstream.

This book has been arranged in four sections. The first section of the book provides an account of the historical, contextual and intertextual formation of LGBTQ+ representation in Australian screen entertainment media (film and television). It presents analyses of the role of early subtextual representations of 'queerness' and how they operate as antecedents for later texts, on the formation over time of Australian LGBTQ+ character representation in television, and the role of activism and community participation in fostering a cultural environment of production and reception.

Chapter 2 investigates the genealogy of early queer film representation leading to today's queer cinema environment. Well before landmark films like *The Set* (1970) or *Priscilla*, ostensible queer representation in Australian cinema was largely taboo, or represented as shameful or to be mocked, much as Russo found in North American and British film of the same period. And like international experiences, Australia's early instances of queerness were subtextual. Several examples of characters cross-dressing in early Australian cinema and same-sex affection were often opportunities for humour rather than meaningful engagement with non-normativity and diverse lives. The chapter explores some of the key early examples such as *Dad and Dave Come to Town* (1938), *Lovers and Luggers* (1937) and *Rangle River*, running through to more recent texts such as *Priscilla*, and the ways in which the production and funding arrangements played a substantial role in the shifts in cinematic depictions of queer subjectivity. These texts are more than just historical curiosities of Australia's screen past, but condition the sayable and unsayable, the ways in which later producers respond to changing norms of belonging and representation, and how audiences make meanings around the wider corpus of queer representation.

Chapter 3 challenges the perceived invisibility of queer identities on Australian screens, revealing the rich queerness of Australian television culture. In the 1970s, Australia was a world leader in televising queer identities, broadcasting the first so-called 'positive' representation of a gay protagonist on a soap opera, one of the first kisses between two women, and one of the first transgender characters portrayed by a trans actress. Exploring the queer history of Australian television, this chapter charts the inclusion of queer characters, themes and narratives from the 1970s onwards. Procedural dramas of the 1970s such as *Cop Shop* (1977–84) and *Homicide* (1964–77) were likewise significant for the inclusion of one-off queer characters and episodes presenting queer themes and narratives alongside ongoing queer representation in groundbreaking series such as *Number 96* (1972–7), *The Box* (1974–7) and *Prisoner*. While the 1980s saw fewer representations, queer characters, themes and narratives were present within a number of popular soap operas and dramas such as *A Country Practice*, *Carson's Law* (1983–4), *Flying Doctors* (1986–92), and *Sons and Daughters* (1982–7). In the 1990s, queer characters and themes were more regularly represented through longer and ongoing storylines in series such as *G.P*, *Heartbreak High* (1994–9), *Pacific Drive* (1996–7) and *Water Rats* (1996–2001). The chapter traces these shifts over time as setting the scene for the more substantial representation depicted in today's television programming in Australia, and making possible the much wider representation we see on Australian broadcast and streaming screens in the 2020s.

The fourth chapter examines the role of cinema in the emergence of Australian LGBTQ+ activism. For many 1970s activists, whether as audience members, filmmakers or exhibitors, the movies were inherently political. Activists analysed the films they viewed, seeking out and advocating for 'positive' representations of lesbian and gay life while condemning films seen as damaging to homosexual people and their place in society. A new generation of local queer filmmakers, dissatisfied with the way mainstream cinema depicted queer lives, created their own documentary and short films, exploring questions of identity through the lens of feminist and liberationist politics. In Australia's larger cities, activists created opportunities to watch films with queer audiences, in the process forming new publics and transforming the experience of film viewing. The chapter points to the enduring legacy of this screen-based activism on Australian queer cultures, showing that one of the ways in which audiences, producers and communities respond to on-screen representation is through a political lens of anti-invisibility.

The second section of the book considers Australian queer screen media from a production angle. The chapters in this section draw on a range of studies and research projects to present an account of the key issues faced in the production of LGBTQ+ themed film and television texts. Chapter 5 reports findings from interviews with key Australian stakeholders involved in Australian films with gender- and sexuality-diverse characters, themes and narratives. The study found that directors, creative producers, screenwriters and actors involved as stakeholders of Australian LGBTQ+ film expressed a desire to make an impact on their audiences in ways that emphasize the value of entertainment texts for minority representation, pedagogy and social change beyond pure storytelling. This chapter presents three key frameworks through which film stakeholders expressed their understanding of, and motivation towards, impact beyond storytelling: (a) as filling a gap in LGBTQ+ representation in contrast to what was otherwise perceived as relative invisibility; (b) their perception as stakeholders dealing with LGBTQ+ content as having a special role as 'educators' for the benefit of vulnerable youth; and (c) an understanding of their texts as contributing to social change in Australia, including wider acceptance of LGBTQ+ persons, family members and communities. A significant finding discussed in this chapter is that screen media about LGBTQ+ topics continues to be perceived as playing a role *connected with but exceeding* entertainment in contrast to the wider entertainment media field.

Chapter 6 considers one of the realms of production distribution: film festivals. The queer film festival has always been an integral player in the development and promotion of queer screen media, as a primary purpose of festivals is to showcase films and short series that would otherwise struggle to secure mainstream circulation in cinemas and through broadcast television. The development of queer cinema from a radical impulse to a niche market was propelled by the increased professionalism of the queer film festival. These festivals simultaneously serve the queer community and promote social empowerment while responding nevertheless to financial viability demands. This arduous journey from being an informal event to a professional organization continues to challenge many arts organizations given the precarious nature of funding in Australia's creative industries. This chapter explores how contemporary queer film festivals continue to challenge heteronormativity and homonormativity.

The third section of the book shifts from production and distribution concerns to some of the ways in which meaning is made, understood and analysed in Australian queer texts. We do not present here a survey and reading of every Australian queer text – an impossible task for a single book and, in today's queer media climate, probably an unnecessary one. Rather, our two chapters here look at two key contexts for understanding queer content in the context of contemporary queer political and scholarly issues: the role of criticism and the changing framework of gender diversity in Australian queer screen content.

Chapter 7 explores a very important cognate area of screen cultural content and how it is understood, recognized and appreciated: queer screen criticism. We identify here how queer criticism first emerged among activist communities in the 1970s, and extended through LGBTQ+ print media's self-conscious role in documenting and shaping queer media criticism in Australia. Most LGBTQ+ media publications contributed to the negotiation of the politics of visibility and stereotyping, and to the ways in which queer meanings were made in the context of a vast array of media representations over the decades. This chapter relies on the key example of Sydney-based lesbian magazine *Lesbians on the Loose* (*LOTL*), first published in 1990, as a case study for understanding the role of print publications in both enabling screen engagement and critiquing film and television texts. It demonstrates how community-based writers and critics grappled with shifting societal attitudes towards LGBTQ+ issues and increasing visibility of LGBTQ+ stories on screen. Analysing film and television coverage within this publication, this chapter shows how community publications themselves are arbiters of content, storytelling and meaning-making.

Chapter 8 focuses on the complex field of trans and gender-diverse representation in Australian queer screen texts. Outlining a brief genealogy of gender diversity on Australian screens from early cinema and across some key examples of twentieth-century film and television, we are primarily interested here in some key breakthrough moments in which the representation of gender diversity is transformed. Focusing on the recently rebooted *Heartbreak High* (2022–5), the miniseries *First Day* (2020–2), the representation of a trans character in *Neighbours* (1985–), and the film *52 Tuesdays* (2014), the chapter investigates how gender diversity shifts from being understood as outsiderness, humorous transgression and exotic spectacle to one grounded very much in everydayness and the ordinariness of the Australian cultural landscape. Alongside these developments in theme, depiction and content is, of course, the role of changing distribution frameworks, including the introduction of streaming which has actively diversified audiences and tastes in ways that enable more diverse content, including the earliest depictions of non-binary and post-binary subjectivities in Australian screen content.

Chapter 9 investigates audience reception cultures by way of two controversies about the policing of gay spaces in 1980s Sydney: one sparked by a violent American movie and another by police raids on a local gay sex club. By 1980, although gay sex remained illegal in New South Wales and rates of anti-gay violence were high, the gay social scene on Oxford Street was thriving. In this context, the arrival of the Hollywood film *Cruising* (1980) prompted genuine concern. Many gay men feared this story of a New York cop hunting a murderer in gay S&M clubs would inspire homophobic attacks. Three years later, Sydney police caused outrage when they raided 'Club 80', an Oxford Street venue not unlike those seen on-screen in *Cruising*. Hundreds of the club's patrons were detained and five were arrested and charged. The chapter places these controversies in the context of campaigns to decriminalize homosexuality, demonstrating the ways in which divergent meaning-making of a single text within Australian screen culture became a key contributor to a community battle to define and police spaces of queer sexuality. Rejecting the primacy of *Cruising*'s heterosexual gaze, which defined gay sex clubs as perverse and criminal, Sydney's gay men responded by publicly celebrating these spaces as liberated and pleasurable. The chapter demonstrates how textuality and audience reception about a very high-profile international text are not only responded to by communities in Australian local contexts, but point to the intersection between community practices and screen representation.

The fourth and final section of the book takes us to our various analyses of Australian audiences in the context of queer screen media. It comprises three chapters that account for a range of ways in which wider cultural practices inform audience reception and foster particular kinds of 'utilizations' of Australian LGBTQ+ screen representation. Chapter 10 explores accounts of how LGBTQ+ people born in the 1970s and 1980s experienced queer characters, themes and narratives in Australian film and television while they were 'growing up'. Drawing on audience interviews, we examine the significance of physical spaces such as video shops, libraries, loungerooms and cinemas for accessing queer film (and queering 'straight' screen texts). Participants foregrounded the materiality of VHS cassettes and shared household TVs during this period in relation to discussions with, or commentary from, family and friends. Place and localness were central to these accounts; from growing up queer in regional Australia, to recognizing and 're-mapping' familiar city streets seen on-screen, to figuring ways in which the familial domestic space of shared television viewing and the public space of cinema spectatorship are implicated in the capacity to live a queer life. Again, these past practices condition the positive response to today's 'everydayness' of some forms of queer on-screen presence.

Chapter 11 discusses the cultural relationship between minority screen representation and mental health. Drawing again on audience interviews, this chapter argues that everyday Australians have nuanced responses to the value and form of minority on-screen visibility, positive representation and the role of peer and family discussion about queer screen content. We highlight how audiences frame what counts as a positive or negative representation, how it has an impact on well-being, and the audience practices of assessing character, theme and narrative quality in ways that are, today, positioned as relative to mental health and well-being.

The final chapter considers the role of queer screen content in producing social change. Approaches to mapping the relationship of LGBTQ+ screen representation to social change have often focused on 'making visible' rather than exploring the ways in which on-screen representation of gender and sexual diversity plays a role in shaping and reshaping attitudes among a wider, contemporary audience. This chapter draws on empirical research to describe firstly how queer audiences perceive the role of LGBTQ+ screen representation in terms of social change among their cisnormative and heteronormative peers, including shifts towards supporting marriage equality and gender-diverse inclusivity.

We end the book by thinking through what some of the 'screen affordances' of LGBTQ+ screen storytelling might tell us about queer screen futures in the turbulent culture wars of the 2020s and to consider some of the ways in which scholars, policymakers and community members can approach the importance of diversity in Australian screen entertainment.

Part One

Histories and Formations

2

The Politics of Film Representation

Introduction

Queerness has long been represented in Australian cinema. The first Australian feature length film to depict characters that were explicitly gay was *The Set* (1970). Before this, however, there was a long history of implicit queerness within our local film industry. Many of the early traces of queerness in Australian cinema were celebrated in 2004, when Australia's National Film and Sound Archive curators Barry MacKay and Marilyn Dooley (2004) gave a retrospective presentation at the Mardi Gras Film Festival titled: *Imagining Queer: Historical Views From Australian Film and Television in the National Screen and Sound Archive*. Here, they underscored the fact that queer people were not historically absent from Australian cinema screens:

> Camp, queer, drag, butch, femme, . . . sissy, tom-boy, lesbian and gay, 'gender benders' have always been represented in Australian moving images, not always, however, in ways that were perhaps obvious to everyone. Sometimes you had to look behind the images with a certain sensibility (Dooley and McKay 2004).

While instances of diverse genders and sexual orientations were not explicit in Australian film until much later, there were several character types and narrative tropes where queerness could be read by a knowing audience. As such, queerness existed in terms of connotative caricature.

The Australian Queer Archives have compiled a series of digitally accessible short videos of these early moments of queerness. One of the notable videos in this collection is a reel from 1913, which features theatre owner and entrepreneur, Sir Benjamin Fuller, interacting with several others at a fete in Poverty Point, NSW. One of the people with whom he engages with is a woman cross-dressing as a man, which makes this reel the first Australian woman filmed in drag. In another early film, *Silks and Saddles* (1921), a young woman,

Figure 2.1 One of Australia's first tomboys on screen in *Silks and Saddles* (1921). *Silks and Saddles* directed by Robert F. Hill © Universal Pictures 1929. All rights reserved.

Bobbie (Brownie Vernon), presents as a tomboy. Bobbie is a dungaree-wearing sportswoman who engages in larrikin behaviour with other men, such as playing two-up. In the film's conclusion, she draws on her physical prowess to ride a horse to victory. At one point, the film features Bobbie looking longingly at the film's villain, high society woman Myra Fane (Evelyn Johnson, see Figure 2.1). Bobbie in *Silks and Saddles* (1921) is a typical example of the gender play in early Australian cinema. Arguably, such gender play marks the Australianness of much Australian cinema, whether that is texts that are archived as LGBTQ+ or otherwise – aspects of play carry through many other popular Australian screen texts, whether that is the so-called 'Larrikin girl' stereotype of Australian screen women or the hyperactive homosocial mateship of Ned Kelly's gang in various screen iterations over the years (Freeman and Ross 2022). However, it also, we argue, provides a genealogical thread to more recent queer screen depictions of the kind discussed throughout this book.

The Tomboy and the Jillaroo

There were several instances of characters cross-dressing in early Australian cinema. These performances were mostly opportunities for laughter rather than any meaningful engagement with gender variance. Joanna McIntyre's (2011) overview of transgender representation in Australian film identifies several examples, such as *The Laugh on Dad* (1918), *The Breaking of the Drought* (1920), *Should a Girl Propose?* (1926), *The Squatter's Daughter* (1933) and *Bitter Springs* (1950). These performances are usually for comedic purposes as 'these transgender representations do little to destabilize traditional sex roles or reveal the ambiguities of gender' (Mcintyre 2011: 9). *Sunshine Sally* (1922) is such an example of this approach to gender in early Australian cinema.

Sunshine Sally follows the exploits of Sally (Yvonne Pavis) and her friend Tottie (Joy Revelle) in Woolloomooloo. She denies the advances of her larrikin friends Skinny (Dinks Patterson) and Spud (John Cosgrove). After being rescued in the surf by lifesaver Basil Stanton, she falls for him and his upper-class lifestyle resulting in the two getting married. While a heterosexual romance is at the centre of the film, Sally is represented as a tomboy who struggles to behave as a refined lady and wears masculine clothing in order to go to Sydney Stadium to see a boxing match. 'Sal' is a working-class larrikin like the other boys, Skinny and Spud.

Another example is *Jewelled Nights* (1925), based on the 1924 novel by Marie Bjelke Petersen, where Elaine Fleetwood leaves a man at the altar, disguises herself as a man and goes prospecting, where she ultimately falls in love with Larry Salarno (Gordon Collingridge). While the film has not survived in its entirety, archivists have managed to restore 20 minutes of the film from a mix of newly recently discovered footage and animation (Bryan 2012). There are several moments where Elaine's masculine disguise causes humour. For instance, the

Figure 2.2 *Sunshine Sally* directed by Lawson Harris © Austral Super Films 1922. All rights reserved.

character of Gus the Poet (Charles Brown) drunkenly sees the 'boy' as a girl and falls in love with 'him' resulting in similar comedic effects to other films of the time regarding gender appearance. Jeannette Delamoir (2012) argues that the film explores anxieties about women's fashion – whether or not women should wear boyish clothes or cut their hair short. Delamoir also notes how at the time, there were two popular male impersonators touring the Australian vaudeville circuit at the time – Ella Shields and Effie Fellows, the latter dubbed 'The one and only perfect boy . . . The only male impersonator who has dared to visit Scotland Yard . . . in male attire, and got away without being discovered' (1924, cited in Delamoir 2012). Many of these examples revolve around cultural panic surrounding changing gender norms.

Australian sissies

Much like early stereotypes in Hollywood, Australian cinema featured the sissy as a counterpoint to the male hero. A notable example of this queer coding is that of Cinesound productions *Dad and Dave Come to Town* (1938) and *Lovers and Luggers* (1937). These characters were coded as queer through their effeminate demeanour, akin to Vito Russo's (1981) work on the sissy in early Hollywood. As Wotherspoon (1991) notes, during the early years of film exhibition with sound, the majority of films screened in Australia were from Hollywood. As such, much of the industry imitated our American counterparts, including responses to censorship codes. In *The Celluloid Closet* (1981), Russo famously argued that the sissy figure – a harmless, effeminate man – existed *between* genders. The sissy, Vito wrote, exhibited characteristics 'that properly belonged to women' (Russo 1981: 17).

Building on this gender variance, McIntyre (2011) notes that the sissy is just as relevant to a discussion on transgender representation as it is with homosexuality. In *Lovers and Luggers*, Archie (Campbell Copelin) is an upper-class gentleman, fitting into an Australian perception of Englishmen being effeminate (McIntyre 2011). Similarly, the retail associate of Mr Entwistle (Alec Kellaway) in *Dad and Dave Come to Town* is coded as queer through his gender appearance, *not* his sexuality. Another character mocks him for his love of clothes saying that 'All he can think about is frocks – why, he can't even see the woman inside them.' While he's mostly played for laughs, he's also a brave, loyal friend to the titular Rudds in the film. This endearing character also returns in Ken G. Hall's later film *Dad Rudd MP* (1940). Mr Entwistle is depicted as the typical sissy character type here, remaining feminine and asexual while still being a supportive figure for the protagonists in the narrative. In *Dad Rudd MP*, Mr Entwistle supports Dad Rudd (Bert Bailey) in his political campaign against competitor and neighbour Henry Webster (Frank Harvey).

Similar coding appeared in *Rangle River* (1936), where the effeminate Englishman Reggie Mannister (Robert Coote) seeks the attention of Australian Dick Drake (Victor Jory). The film is a clear product of the early Australian film industry being influenced by global trends as, according to Deborah Tudor (2014), it is a generic hybrid of Hollywood Western and the English drawing room comedy. Adapted from a novel by American author Zane Grey written after a visit to Australia, the film presents Marion Hastings (Margaret Dare) returning home to her father's cattle station in Queensland after several years living in Europe. The dual narrative structure sees Marion resolving her romantic tension with Dick, her father's foreman, in order to team up with him and Reggie to figure out why the river on her father's property is running dry. With the help of Reggie, Marion and Dick discover that her father's neighbour is damming the river to put them out of business. After the dam breaks, Dick saves Marion from the flood and the farm is saved. The heterosexual romance at the centre of the film adheres to the classic 'enemies to lovers' trope, as Dick initially resents Marion's worldly, affluent tastes but is soon won over by her charms. There is also, however, a budding friendship between Dick and Reggie, who initially fell for Marion at the airport and tricked her into inviting him to stay at the ranch. While a dominant reading of this friendship would be of Australian 'mateship', there is the potential for queer subtext.

Like many representations in Australian film and literature at the time, Englishmen were depicted as more feminine and worldly than the Australian, who was often rugged and 'of the land'. This difference has long been seen in Australian storytelling. In *Inventing Australia*, for instance, Richard White (1981) notes the popularity of colonial themes in boys' stories, where there was the persistent characterization of effete Englishman in contrast to the masculine colonial figure. White notes, for instance, that these 'boy annuals' featured 'The Coming Man' narrative, which were 'chock-full of gripping tales of virile men fighting the wilds in Australia, Canada, New Zealand, India and Africa' (83). White argues that it is no surprise that an emergent nation beginning to grow its own identity would appropriate popular values from elsewhere to represent them as its own.

This dichotomy is seen in the difference between Reggie and Dick. While Dick functions as a continuation of this heroic conqueror of the land akin to the many preceding colonial narratives, Reggie is an upper-class Englishman as defined by his accent and his 'sporting' attitude. In comparing the two men, Deborah Tudor (2014) identifies Reggie's sporting approach to the landscape by putting his hand up in giving things a go, such as helping with the stock drive. He is, however, a comic figure, in contrast to Dick's masculinity that is more attuned to the harsh Australian bush. While Reggie struggles to manage a horse, Dick is more capable of driving the cattle. Typical to his Englishness, he is more adept when it comes to his intelligence at recognizing the coincidence of Marion's father's beef contract occurring while the river is drying up. He is also more socially competent, for example, in conversing with Marian's Aunt Abbie (Rita Pauncefort) in the scenes that adhere to the drawing-room comedy genre, in which she is unable to recognize the humour in his playful language. Finally, the subtle queerness is evident beyond Reggie's adherence to the effete Englishman trope. In one scene, Reggie visits Dick in the bunkhouse following the fight. As Reggie expresses his regard for Dick, he also tends to Dick's injuries. In what could be viewed as a scene of bonding, affection and tenderness, the two men express their fondness for the other. While a dominant reading of this scene is of the formation of homosocial mateship that will be important for subsequent challenges, it is available to be read in more 'romantic' terms through the codes of mutual and affective care between two vulnerable bodies. Following this scene, Reggie no longer functions as a romantic rival for Marian but rather a companion to Dick and the Hastings' household. Similarly, this contrast is seen in 1946 British–Australian Western *The Overlanders*, where Chips Rafferty's heroic Dan McAlpine is contrasted against Peter Pagan's Sinbad, with the latter's affected speech depicting the Queen's English compared to McAlpine's more rugged tone.

Sexploitation and *The Set*

Being the first Australian film to explicitly depict gay subject matter as its central theme, Frank Brittain's *The Set* (1970) is a landmark title in queer film history and arguably Australia's first sexploitation film. The script was written by Roger Ward, best known today as the writer of popular Australian film *Mad Max* (1979). It was based on his unpublished sociological novel of Australian life in the 1960s. The film was released just prior to the 1972 Gough Whitlam Labor government's injection of substantial new funding into the Australian film industry. Billed as a local sexploitative version of *La Dolce Vita* (1960), the film was reviewed as being technically incompetent regardless of its crew's experience. Lead character Paul (Sean McEuan) is a sexually confused, youthful, floppy-haired dilettante whose arty aspirations and British accent place him at odds with his beer-swilling 'ocker' dad. After his high school sweetheart Cara (Amber Rodgers) leaves him for Europe and he moves to Sydney, he meets and begins a rocky relationship with the wealthy Tony (Rod Mullinar) while working as a theatrical set decorator, where he builds the titular set, a mock-up that sits on their kitchen table. The title also refers to the film's exploration of the sexual habits, both gay and straight, of Sydney's arty Eastern Suburbs' 'set'. The film's final act features Paul and Tony breaking up, Paul attempting suicide and his final reunion with his old girlfriend Cara. After initial viewing, this film can be read as depicting the gay relationship as a fall from grace, a downward spiral that stands at odds with Paul's pursuit of happiness, and an obstacle to be overcome through restoration of heteronormative romance.

The Set, however, is too easily dismissed as a homophobic relic of the past given that a more critical reading leaves it less clear if the film positions same-sex attraction as something that must be overcome or if it is a camp eccentricity that is exciting to temporarily explore. With the gay content being deemed scandalous at the time, the film provides a 1970s window to changing societal attitudes to homosexuality. It is the first Australian-produced film to include sex scenes and graphic nudity. The film also gestures to the local queer community of the time by featuring drag performer Ken 'Kandy' Johnson, an icon in Sydney's drag scene. A notable scene in the film features Kandy crooning 'don't be subtle, wake me, rouse me' at a Sydney cocktail party. In an interview with *Metro* magazine, scriptwriter, Roger Ward, commented that the film caused a lot of buzz when it was first released and that it opened to sensationalist headlines (Pfeiffer 2016). Indeed, alongside the representation of homosexuality was the fact that Hazel Phillips appeared nude in the film – Phillips was a popular actress and daytime television host. To argue that the film is homophobic is too simplistic, as the aesthetics of the film align with sexploitation cinema of the day. Further, the 'Britishness' of Paul as a softly spoken young man aligns with the historical trope of queerness being depicted as 'other' to the rugged Australian male, exemplified by Tony.

In reading the film for its juxtaposition of ruggedness versus sensitivity, we are able to recognize the depiction of non-heteronormativity in multiple ways. Through his own masculine performances, Tony serves as a reminiscent representation of Paul's father. In an early scene, Paul is having dinner with his parents. Wearing a white workers' singlet, Paul's father is hunched over his food and drinking a beer from the can. As he yells at Paul he spits food out of his mouth: 'Why don't you get a proper girlfriend instead of knocking around with those Italian girls?' This juxtaposition of different expressions of masculinity is paralleled later in the film with Tony becoming the angry man of the house and Paul dutifully catering to him. Tony, who is described by Paul's cousin as 'a big and brown man that smelt all salty and masculine', is an angry and sad young man who behaves as if he can do what he wants with the women around him – with one exception: in the modern and sophisticated setting of Sydney, the women are not won over by his charm. One wealthy young woman calls him an ignorant know-nothing slob. Subsequent to sleeping with him, she argues that she is so frustrated she could kill him. After Peggy seduces him, he lies back in post-coital glory, stating that the sex was great, only for her to reply:

> **Peggy:** Great? You're joking! I've heard about being left in mid-air but this is ridiculous. [*Peggy laughs*] Oh I just can't win. A husband who's lost all interest and a boy who wouldn't know how.

The union between Tony and Paul is, then, a violent and anachronistic modelling of the masculine character dominating the feminine. After Paul consoles him following another rejection from a woman, Tony wakes up to Paul holding his hand. Tony hits Paul:

> **Tony:** You dirty little . . .
> **Paul:** Tony, don't you understand? I love you.

What follows is a montage of Tony behaving in an angry manner only to return, assessing and angrily staring at Paul.

> **Paul:** Not like this [*fade to black*].

Soon afterwards, the film depicts Paul waiting on Tony, fetching him beers from the fridge and handing him his cheques, having adopted a feminine position in their unstable relationship. After Paul attempts suicide following Tony's departure, Tony returns only to sit by Paul's unconscious and dying body, drinking beer and mocking his unconscious lover: 'a woman's way, right to the end . . . I would be doing you a favour if I walked out of here; or is it just a gesture . . . a big flamboyant gesture that misfired?' An awkward jazz soundtrack accompanies this pivotal scene non-diegetically.

A return to conventionality operates in the film's conclusion, whereby Paul reunites with Cara after both having moved on from same-sex dalliances. Peggy returns to her husband after she learns that Bronoski is seeing other women, being a sexual liberalization too far. For all characters the experimentation with liberal sexuality and homosexuality is over. Tony brings two gay men to the party as a way to shame and punish Paul among the other sophisticates, but all are pushed in a pool in a moment of exuberance.

While seemingly at odds with the darkness of the gay-themed representation, the film is a camp sexploitation. This expose of alternate sexualities is part of the exploitation and scandal. As Ward notes in several interviews, Brittain requested that he take all the homosexual-themed content from the book and make it into a screenplay. The scandalous nature of gay representation was the drawcard. As Hoberman and Rosenbaum (1991) and Grant (1991) write, gender-play and non-normative sexualities have long been a feature of exploitation and cult cinema, and this distinction permits the representation of fluid sexualities, experimentation and non-heteronormative representation in this key work of Australian cinema.

And yet there are further elements of the sexploitation that can be unpacked and which arguably lay the groundwork for much of the genre in the later 1970s. The early scene featuring Cara and Paul having sex on the beach focuses on the nature of pleasure and youth. Cara reveals that she is moving to Italy and that she has been having relationships with other women: 'It happens Paul; mature girls herded together year after year in boarding school.' Peggy's boredom with her life – she describes being married to her husband as having to live with a Franciscan monk – is up-ended when she travels to Sydney with her daughter and begins sleeping with other men. As discussed, actress Phillips was very recognizable to Australian audiences, having served on *The Mavis Bramston Show* (1964–8) and *Beauty and the Beast* (1964–73). As such, her topless appearance and representation as a woman sleeping with multiple men is a key feature of the sexploitative nature of the film. When she commenced the affair with artist Bronoski, she was chased around his studio, both in their underwear, in a camp, comedic representation of a matador bullfight.

The early foray into the Sydney artistic and sophisticated set is primarily represented as fun and silly, including when dealing with a character's death.

After the death of Paul's early design mentor, he is taken to a cocktail party where characters dismiss the significance of his bereavement: 'so Marie's dead; That's life.'

Finally, the film's poor formal quality remains not a stumbling block but a key part of the film's continuing appeal. The camera struggles to focus on performers, actors stumble between lines resulting in awkward pauses in dialogue, cuts between scenes are jarring, with no establishing shots often creating further confusion. There are also long montages to the jazz soundtrack that make very little sense, such as Tony playing cricket in the street with random children. This is part of the pleasure. Exploitation cinema offers a mix of ineptitude and unintentional amusement, where their cheap look is a core part of the aesthetic. In addition to low budgets, the speed of production and paucity of skilled actors and filmmakers led to a recurrence of 'stiff acting, bad lighting, and continuity errors' (Schaefer 1999: 47–8). It is important to be wary in how we connect *The Set* to American cult and exploitative cinema, such as *Performance* (1970), *Beyond the Valley of the Dolls* (1970), *Trash* (1970) and even *Flaming Creatures* (1963) and *Scorpio Rising* (1963) and other texts outlined in scholarship of the genre (e.g. Staiger 2000). Rather, the film needs to be understood not as formed by the antecedents of North American sexploitation but as the genealogical product of a range of socio-cultural and media performances operating in an exclusive Australian context in which humour, campness and problematic film values were utilized as critical commentary on socio-political changes of the time. Writing on the sexploitative Australian film *Alvin Purple* (1973), for example, Alexandra Heller-Nicholas (2017) notes that rather than dismissing the text as fun and silly, the film must be viewed as commentary on changing sexual and gender mores. *The Set* is arguably part of this very same tradition and therefore provides significant insight as a creative text rather than an anomaly of Australian screen culture. Catharine Lumby (2008: 25) likewise defends *Alvin Purple*, claiming that although base humour filled with problematic stereotypes, the film 'shouldn't have to live or die in Australian film history on the grounds of how well it translates for contemporary viewers'.

More recent criticism has pointed to the creative and interpretative possibilities of *The Set*. For example, in a retrospective review of the film, Wilson (2007) suggests that *The Set* represents homosexuality as an immature phase, a stumbling block to be overcome on the way to mature identity and belonging, but does gesture to the possibility of reading non-heteronormative sexualities as eccentricities that can be celebrated by the sophisticated set. That is, whether read for the narrative return of heteronormativity among the core characters or the significance of a dalliance with non-heteronormative sex and romance without losing status within the community, the film is arguably a key example of cinematic progress in queer representation in Australia. This is depicted clearly in the closing scenes: several openly gay characters are present at the party and welcomed by the larger group as a part of the sophisticated Sydney set, evidencing on-screen the reality of urbane flexibility and acceptance.

The Australian New Wave

A popular focus on the landmark film *The Adventures of Priscilla, Queen of the Desert* has tended to give a false impression that LGBTQ+ screen culture began in Australia in the 1990s. Leading up to 1994, queerness was predominantly seen as a scandalous subject when depicted in Australian film, as evident in a number of films of the 1970s and 1980s, including some of those described above. Beyond this, queerness was evident during the boom of Australian cinema in the 1970s, as noted by Sophia Gluyas' (2013) analysis of *Picnic at Hanging Rock* (1975), *The Getting of Wisdom* (1977) among others. Gluyas implores readers to counteract the authorial disavowal of early texts and claim these as decidedly queer.

Several films of the 1970s and 1980s tackled the controversial subject matter of homosexuality, such as the mockumentary *The Naked Bunyip* (John B. Murray 1970) and *The Everlasting Secret Family* (1988). *The Naked Bunyip* tells the story of Graeme Blundell as a shy, everyday man exploring the sexual mores of contemporary Australia. Alongside his adventures were interviews with pop singers, academics, homosexuals, strippers and the Moonee Ponds housewife, Edna Everage. After the Australian censors requested a total of five minutes of footage removed, Murray provokingly superimposed sketches of a bunyip instead (Murray 2006).

The Everlasting Secret Family, billed as a 'down under' *Dorian Gray*, depicts a secret society of men across the lifecycle, commencing at an elite all-boys school and moving through political, professional and legal circles where authority figures are members of a ritualistic homosexual, fetishistic and sado-masochistic secret society (Stein 1989). Arguably, this presents a negative and homophobic representation of non-heterosexual subjects, riffing off long-standing stereotypes of men engaged in alternative sexualities acting secretively and in self-supportive ways in society (DiPiero and Gill 1997). The homophobia implicit in the film stems from screenwriter Moorehouse's (1988) own views on the topic, where as a young man he was forced into homosexual promiscuity in what he perceived as a cultish organization and community. Commenting on homosexuality after the advent of HIV, Moorehouse notes in the film's press kit that he felt he made a fortunate escape from such organized communality. Many reviews of the film (e.g. Maslin 1989) link principle actor Mark Lee, who played the young man drawn into the queer secret society, to his earlier role in *Gallipoli* (Peter Weir 1981), in which he portrayed a presumed heteronormative and broadly masculine, albeit sensitive, Australian hero. Surprisingly, given the film's latent homophobia, the film played at a number of international queer film festivals (Thomas 1988), suggesting the significance of any queer screen representation as appealing, even when problematic (Cover 2023a). Ultimately, this critique of the film as homophobic stems from the lack of clarity over the film's narrative.

During the Australian new wave, queer subject matter was often aligned with scandal and pity. In *Wake in Fright* (1971), the mysterious figure of Doc (Donald Pleasance) is depicted as perverse after he drunkenly seeks physical intimacy with John. Doc's sexuality is predatorial and aligns male queerness with loneliness and madness, as well as an outsider status aligned with the remote and non-urban setting of the Australian outback town. For Kotcheff, the outback culture he was depicting was not intended to be perceived as a gay setting but as one in which the absence of women lends itself to the slippage from homosocial masculinity to perverse crossing-the-line, that is, as men who wanted or needed some form of physical intimacy (Caputo 2009). Some reviewers described the film itself as a form of homosexual assault, reading the molestation of John as 'ambiguous in its violation of John's free will . . . The act is represented with no erotic impulse and its intent is to horrify either than titillate' (Savage 2012: 36), and therefore aligning non-heterosexual intimacy with shame and despair.

The suicide of the potentially lesbian Sara (Margaret Nelson) in *Picnic at Hanging Rock* (1975) – undoubtedly caused by the heartbreak over Miranda's (Anne-Louise Lambert) presumed death and the subjective incompatibility of her sense of romantic loss – compounds the association of shame and homosexuality at the time. Further films of the Australian New Wave in which queerness was positioned as inherently problematic, shameful, evil or insidious include *Mad Max 2* (1981) and *High Rolling* (1977).

The Set also paved the way for more successful sexploitation films in the 1970s and established a public perception of Australian cinema as an object of interest, value and investment. Notable sexploitation and lowbrow comedies that followed were Tim Burstall's *Stork* (1971), which starred Jacki Weaver in her debut and Graham Blundell. Several ocker comedies followed, including Bruce Beresford's *The Adventures of Barry McKenzie* (1972) and *Barry McKenzie Holds His Own* (1974). Burstall also released the drama *Petersen* (1974), starring Jack Thompson. Unsuccessful films included *Scobie Malone* (Terry Ohlsson, 1975) and Tim Burstall's *Eliza Fraser* (1976). While this wave of ocker sexploitative cinema revelled in the highly sexualized subject matter, they often were full of homophobic jokes aimed at 'bloody poofters'. Thus, while the New Wave saw a substantial increase in the representation of non-heteronormative characters, themes and stories, much of this reinforced an Australian alignment of masculinity and homophobia, whether through depictions of queer characters as problematic and non-heroic subjects or through the use of abusive and marginalizing language.

Film co-operatives

Crucial to the emergence of a queer screen culture in Australia were the film collectives that gave rise to independent, avant-garde and experimental film in Australia. These provided an alternative to the productions with substantial major funding and marked a somewhat different approach to how queer subjectivity, narratives and themes were represented on Australian screens. Australia's film co-ops were the product of a financial, political and creative response by independent filmmakers who struggled to bring to audiences their experimental and avant-garde work, and films with more radical themes, that were broadly less welcome in public television broadcasting and commercial cinema distribution (Hughes 2015).

The Sydney Film Co-operative began as the more informal Ubu Films. Many members of both Ubu and the Sydney Film Co-op produced work that featured queer themes. Although Ubu may not have been totally queer, this provided a foundation for experimental and independent film, which makes it an important part of queer cinematic history in Australia. These filmmakers produced same-sex-themed films, such as Gillian Armstrong's *Satdee Night* (1973), Jan Chapman's *Showtime* (1978), Jeni Thornley's *Maidens* (1978) and Peter Wells' *Foolish Things* (1981). The Gay Film Fund was established by members of the Film Collective to support queer projects and filmmakers between 1976 and

1980 (Peach 2005). Digby Duncan, director of *Witches and Faggots, Dykes and Poofters* (1980) has explained that the lack of success in the mid-1970s bringing a script to celluloid due to funding rejections resulted in community members encouraging the exploration of alternative funding alternatives. This produced a gay film fund launched in 1976 using profits drawn from community screenings (Peach 2005). The Gay Film Fund ran dances in 1977 and 1978 to raise funds for film production and to provide a space for the community to socialize. These dances were held at Balmain and Petersham Town Halls and included bands such as Wasted Daze, Wendy Saddington, The Faye Lewis Band and Stiletto. Films to benefit from the Gay Film Fund included Duncan's *Witches and Faggots, Dykes and Poofters* (1980).

Figure 2.3 A poster for a screening of *Witches and Faggots, Dykes and Poofters* (1980).

Such collectives and co-ops often held queer screenings and fundraising events. In 1975, for instance, the Melbourne Film Collective ran a season of three queer films comprised of *Point of Departure* (1975), *Homosexuality: A Film for Discussion* (1975) and *Turkish Baths* (1975). Such events are often recalled as critical, financial successes and triumphs in engaging the wider public in social change and acceptance. Creed's film, for instance, was subsequently distributed in secondary schools (Creed 2014).

Documentaries were significant during this era as they give a snapshot of queer lives during this period, including Creed's *Homosexuality*, Duncan's *Witches, Faggots, Dykes and Poofters* (1980) and Fiona Cunningham Reid's *Feed Them to the Cannibals* (1993). Writing on this era, Ricardo Peach (2005) noted that the support of co-operatives in producing such documentaries offered the wider public and the growing LGBTQ+ communities in Australia an important counterbalance to the negative and sometimes homophobic or transphobic portrayal of queer characters in both mainstream Australian and international film. Serving as an intervention, the screenings often engaged publics through forums in the presence of the filmmakers that enhanced the self-representation and critique of the films themselves (Peach 2005). Significantly, the films sponsored by Co-operative frameworks operated alongside the growing and well-subsidized Australian film industry of the time, creating a separate space for activists, intellectuals and those seeking to bring experimental or alternative themes and stories to Australian screens (Hughes 2015).

Post-Priscilla

The Adventures of Priscilla, Queen of the Desert (1994) was a pivotal moment in Australian queer cinema. Receiving significant critical and commercial success, the film was part of what is now referred to as the Glitter Cycle alongside two other films released in the same two-year period: *Strictly Ballroom* (1992) and *Muriel's Wedding* (1994). These three films presented a camp departure from the earlier Australian Film Commission's production of a high-culture, European-aligned screen identity (Rustin 2001). Phillip Brophy (2008: 39) has argued that they offered a brash pastiche of Australian identity by 'overloading its archetypes and icons with implosive characteristics'. That is, they provided a 1990s alternative to the authorized and funded screen representation of Australian national identity as white, male, heterosexual and rural (Sanders 2008), enabling an expansion of Australian subjectivity that included both LGBTQ+ lives and a queer and alternative perspective on the lives of those otherwise marginalized from the heteromasculine mainstream on Australian screens.

At the same time, and contrasting the drag queens in *Priscilla* and the camp celebration of alternative belonging in the two other films, was *The Sum of Us*. Based on David Steven's play of the same name, the film was produced by Hal McElroy who was well-regarded in Australian production as the producer of *The Cars That Ate Paris* (1974), *The Last Wave* (1977) and *Picnic at Hanging Rock* (1975). *The Sum of Us* gained immediate attention from recognizable actors such as Russell Crowe and Jack Thompson, the latter of whom was known for playing the larrikin in many Australian films, and gained further attention when screened at the 1994 Cannes Film Festival. Although sentimental, the film aimed to veer away from a lot of the darker portrayals of queer lives in previous mainstream production (Free 2018) and contrasts with the glitter films by placing queer lives very much in the Australian domestic scene.

The Sum of Us and *Priscilla* were significant developments in the history of Australian queer cinema as they were explicitly queer films made available to wide audiences. Nevertheless, it should be noted that the initial positive critiques of both films engaged with them only in terms of their 'queerness' rather than reviewing them *as* films (Richards 2019). Subsequent critiques and public discourse on both films have had a more nuanced response, often criticizing the wider overall narratives of the films and, in the case of *Priscilla,* the use of problematic racial stereotypes (Riggs 2006) and humour at the expense of First Nations characters.

Later in the 1990s, however, feature films *Love and Other Catastrophes* (1996), *The Well* (1997) and *Head On* (1998) were films with queer themes, characters and stories that received widespread critical acclaim for their productions as films. Much like the New Queer Cinema wave in the United States of America, these films were considered innovative, well-produced and coherent. *The Well* tells the story of two isolated women living alone in a cottage, whose lives are turned upside down when they hit a man while driving. The film is a Gothic drama that deals with the sexual repression of the two women. *Love and Other Catastrophes* is a screwball campus comedy set at the University of Melbourne that follows a collection of students across twenty-four hours. *Head On* follows Ari (Alex Dimitriades) across a day and night as he clashes with his conservative Greek parents, parties with his drag queen friend Tula (Paul Capsis) as the night descends into sex, drugs and dancing. The punk aesthetics to the film positioned Kokkinos as an art house director of considerable acclaim on the international film festival circuit.

Conclusion

Queerness has always been represented on Australian cinema screens, either at the ostensibly textual level and in marketing to target audiences or at a subtextual level made available for queer reading. No film industry, genre or topic is created without reference to the genealogical antecedents, and this is no less the case with Australian queer screen media today. Sexuality- and gender-diverse characters have long been juxtaposed to the myth of Australian identity as founded on narrow normative gender representations, and the origins in early Australian sissy men and tomboy women carry through into later screen depictions, albeit in increasingly nuanced ways, and in forms that are more often contested by audiences and communities today.

Sexploitation films opened the possibility of more ostensible depiction of non-heteronormativity but tended, of course, to rely on titillation, surface characterizations and narrative restoration in ways that can be understood as ultimately reinforcing norms. Australia's New Wave included films that reduced the possibilities of alternative genders and sexualities, only depicting those even more so in ways that juxtaposed them with normative Australian identities, primarily as a result of the funding regimes.

This difficulty found its response in the development of film co-ops which utilized an alternative funding framework to make available representations that were otherwise impossible. It is, however, when we get to the 1990s that the silos of these two funding regimes are overcome, allowing for more positive, albeit often problematic, representation of queer characters and stories in films such as *Priscilla*. Narrative attempts to present more critical depth to characters emerged only in the late 1990s with more experimental works, including particularly films such as *Love and Other Catastrophes* and *Head On*. And it is these that make possible the kinds of representations that we discuss in several other chapters.

3

Australian Queer Television

Introduction

In the late 1980s, television critic and historian Keith Howes (1988) was told by a contact at an unnamed Australian gay newspaper that 'gay people weren't interested in TV: most don't watch it' (44). Underlying this was the assumption that Australian television rarely included queer characters, themes and narratives. That is, television was apparently not interesting to the gay community because gay audiences were unlikely to see their lives represented. In this chapter, we challenge this pervasive claim about Australian television, charting the rich history of queerness on the small screen. As we illustrate here, queer characters, themes and narratives have been ever-present on Australian screens. We explore the queer subtext of the 1960s, the world-leading representations of queer identities in the 1970s, the social interest storylines of the 1980s and 1990s and more recent shifts in the politics of queer representation.

The 'invisibility' claims in Australian TV

Visibility is the focus of a popular strand of queer screen scholarship centred on the politics of representation on television. Carrying the ethos of 1970s gay liberation, this scholarship emphasizes the relationship between media representation and social change. For instance, in 1991, American communications scholar Larry Gross argued there was a relative absence of LGBTQ+ subjects in mainstream media, calling on scholars to press upon the media their claims for 'equitable and respectful treatment' (Gross 1991: 45). A driving force behind the cultivation theory of media, Gross had previously developed the concept of 'symbolic annihilation' with communications theorist George Gerbner, arguing that 'representation in the fictional world signifies social existence; absence means symbolic annihilation' (Gerbner and Gross 1976: 182). While not uncritically celebrating the visibility of LGBTQ+ identities on television, Gross considered television to have significant power to shape norms about gender and sexuality. In *Up from Invisibility: Lesbians, Gay Men, and the Media in America* (2001), he traced developments in representation, rehearsing a narrative of progress: from exclusion, invisibility and silence to greater inclusion, visibility and power. This perspective is echoed in later work on American television by Stephen Tropiano (2002), and the ongoing efforts of media advocacy organization GLAAD, which has published an annual report on the state of queer representation in America since 1996.

The visibility framework has since become a central focus for both queer screen studies and the film and television industry. In an Australian context, one of the more pervasive myths about our local screen industry is that LGBTQ+ people are actively or unwittingly invisibilized and that it is rare to find instances of queer representation. Writing in the early 2000s, for instance, Howes complained, 'What is glaringly obvious in the Australian television landscape of today is the complete lack of any regular and open discussion of lesbian and gay issues and lives' (Howes 2002). This claim is echoed through media and industry reports that emphasize historical and contemporary invisibility (or under-representation) of gender and sexual diversity on Australian screens.

With a focus on the screen industry, in 2016, Screen Australia's *Seeing Ourselves: Reflections on Diversity in TV Drama* (2016) report put the issue of representation on the public agenda. With regard to gender and sexual diversity, Screen Australia identified that lesbian, gay, bisexual, trans, queer/questioning and intersex people were significantly under-represented on the small screen, when compared to population data. Though the Australian Department of Health and Ageing had estimated 11 per cent of Australians were LGBTQ+, television did not seem to be representing this community accurately (or at all). Examining TV dramas from 2011 to 2015, Screen Australia found only eighty-eight main characters that were identifiably LGBTQ+, which was about 4.5 per cent of the characters in the study. Breaking this down further, Screen Australia's data showed that sixty-two of the LGBTQ+ characters on Australian TV were men and twenty-six were women, which included two transgender characters. The study found that there were no intersex characters and did not explore non-binary representation. While some of the programmes examined by Screen Australia had multiple LGBTQ+ main characters, 73 per cent had none.

In 2023, the much-anticipated follow-up report further emphasized the visibility (or lack thereof) of queer characters and stories. Examining TV drama during the period 2016–21, *Seeing Ourselves 2: Diversity, Equity and Inclusion in Australian TV Drama* (2023) expanded its definition of 'TV Drama' to reflect the changing screen landscape. This report considered traditional broadcast television, streaming services such as Netflix, Stan, Paramount and Amazon Prime, and online content on YouTube, Facebook, Instagram, TikTok, Vimeo and Hyvio that had been commissioned by Screen Australia, state and territory funding agencies, local broadcasters, and streaming video services. Updating language around gender- and sexual-diversity to 'gender and sexual orientation' and the acronym LGBTQ+, *Seeing Ourselves 2* highlighted that some progress had been made. Firstly, the overall rate of LGBTQ+ representation had increased to 7.4 per cent of characters. The 228 LGBTQ+ characters found in the study included more LGBTQ+ women as well as more transgender and non-binary characters, though notably an absence of asexual or intersex representation. Screen Australia also found fewer titles without any LGBTQ representation (69 per cent had no identifiably LGBTQ+ characters) and considered some issues of intersectionality – such as age, social status, disability status, ethnicity and location. In the report, Screen Australia noted that this data reflects 'a positive improvement in seeing LGBTQ+ main characters on our screens but remains under the population benchmark' (Screen Australia 2023: 69).

The story presented here is that LGBTQ+ characters are on a steady trajectory from exclusion to inclusion. Though once marginalized in society and absent from our small screens, the LGBTQ+ community are gradually becoming an accepted and expected part of television in Australia. However, for many queer screen scholars, this story could not be further from the truth. Another strand of queer screen scholarship, which also emphasizes visibility (albeit in a different way), maintains the fact that LGBTQ+ characters and queerness have always been a part of television history, in Australia and beyond. Challenging the steady narrative of progress, this alternate perspective argues that media 'has always been *queer. . .* [but] it has only recently been or become recognizably *gay*' (Villarejo 2014: 3). In the United States, Vito Russo's *The Celluloid Closet* (1981) famously maps out an alternative gay history of Hollywood cinema. More recently, Quinlan Miller's (2019) *Camp TV* and Isabel Cristina Pinedo and Wyatt D. Phillips' (2023) edited collection *Camp*

TV of the 1960s: Reassessing the Vast Wasteland argue that queer gender was a constitutive element of many pre-1970s American television sitcoms. Howes' *Broadcasting It: An Encyclopaedia of Homosexuality in Film, Radio and TV in the UK, 1923–1993* (1993) takes up similar ideas in the UK context. Bringing this back to Australian television, though Howes (1998) lamented the absence of gay and lesbian stories on Australian television in 2000s, in other writing, he described 'a gay sensibility' that 'has been everywhere on Australian TV' from its very first broadcast in 1956 (42).

Camp TV in the 1960s

Australian culture is known for celebrating hegemonic masculinity through figures of the 'bloke' and 'ocker', yet like the early cinema we discussed in Chapter 2, early Australian television often transgressed gender norms. However, in contrast to the cultural panic associated with early cinematic queerness, television joyfully played with gender. This was a result of its lineage from vaudeville and variety theatre. For instance, on Melbourne's first night of television on 4 November 1956, audiences enjoyed a 45-minute telecast of *Olympic Follies*, a live variety show held at the Tivoli Theatre in Melbourne, which reportedly included one of Barry Humphries' first performances of the character Dame Edna Everage (Groves 2012: 78). From these origins, popular Australian comedy series of the 1960s often featured flamboyant, queer-coded characters. In a notable sketch broadcast on *The Mavis Bramston Show* (1964–8) in 1965, actor Gordon Chater portrayed the character Fred Jackson, a showgirl drag queen with a rough, gravelly voice who worked 'professionally under the name Jock Strip'. When asked about gender, Fred forthrightly remarked, 'It's hard to believe that under this veneer of beauty and radiance I am a mere male.' Later, *The Bulletin* described 'Mavis Bramston' as 'an expert commentator on the queer side of life' (Roberts 1966: 45).

Early Australian television also celebrated the irreverent and often playfully camp antics of TV figures such as Graham Kennedy, whose variety show *In Melbourne Tonight* ran from 1957 to 1970, and John-Michael Howson, who played a clown on the children's series *Adventure Island* (1967–72), a programme described as the 'first unabashedly, unrestrainedly camp children's show' (Howes 1998: 41). Later, drag would be an important component of the absurdist comedy series *The Aunty Jack Show* (1972–3).

From sensationalized non-conformists to world-leading LGBTQ+ characters

While queerness flourished beneath the surface of early Australian television programmes, it wasn't until the late 1960s and early 1970s that LGBTQ+ identities were represented on screen for the first time. As Beirne describes, 'although Australian television began broadcasting relatively late, in 1956, by the 1970s it was well advanced in terms of queer representation' (Beirne 2009: 25).

LGBTQ+ people first appeared in a series of current affairs programmes and television documentaries that explored unconventional lifestyles. As a critic for *The Bulletin* wrote in 1966, 'Television programs about people with non-conformist habits are arousing a great deal of interest' (Campbell 1966: 29). These included a *7 Days* episode 'Love is Love' in 1966, *Encounter* in 1967 and *The Bailey Report* and *This Day Tonight* in 1970. Though described as 'heavily biased' by *The Bulletin* (Roberts 1966: 45), Sydney's *The Sun-Herald* described 'Love is Love' as 'an honest and intensely moving look at a little known facet of society' (Marshall 1966: 82). Later, *The Bulletin*'s Ross Campbell claimed that:

> Lesbians and male homosexuals are very pleased with the sympathetic treatment of their problems on TV. They feel the public is coming to realise that the average male homosexual is a decent sort of fellow, and the lesbian is not so very different from the girl next door–indeed, she may be the girl next door (Campbell 1966: 29)

However, for the most part, these early documentaries focused on LGBTQ+ identity as a social problem. They often focused on perspectives from psychiatrists that framed queerness as a mental illness and, when interviewing LGBTQ+ people, emphasized negative experiences such as familial rejection, secrecy, unhappiness, discrimination and violence.

On 17 October 1972, the ABC broadcast a groundbreaking episode of *Chequerboard* titled 'This just happens to be a part of me.' The episode featured a lengthy interview with Peter 'Bon' Bonsall-Boone and Peter De Waal, activists from the group Campaign Against Moral Persecution (CAMP), described as 'a happy couple living in a nice house.' At the beginning of the episode, they shared a quick kiss hello. This was the first gay kiss on Australian television. Their interview focused on aspects of their lives as homosexual men in Sydney. They responded to myths about gay relationships and challenged stereotypes, openly discussing domestic life, work, religion, family, stigma, violence, identity, the criminalization of homosexuality, stereotypes and their activism. The episode also featured interviews with lesbian couple, Sue Wills and Gaby Antolovich, who reflected on their relationship and the issues faced by lesbians in Australia.

Contemplating this in *The Bulletin*, Don Anderson highlighted the significance of the documentary as one of the first to give voice to the queer community, writing: 'Homosexuals have received a very bad deal on television. They have been discussed by "experts" who may know a lot about statistics and nothing about the personal situation, they have been ignored, misunderstood and maltreated' (Anderson 1972: 39). Anderson described the episode as a welcome opportunity for the wider public to view homosexuals discussing their own lives rather than being assessed by experts. However, following its broadcast, Peter Bonsall-Boone was dismissed from his job as a secretary for St Clements Anglican Church in Sydney's North Shore (Reynolds 2002: 44).

As we will explore, later fictional programmes such as *Number 96* (1972–7), *The Box* (1974–7) and *Prisoner* (1979–86) featured a number of beloved queer characters, paving the way for television around the world. However, it was police procedurals such as *Division 4* (1969–76), *Homicide* and *Cop Shop* where gay and lesbian characters were first represented in Australian television drama.

Division 4 (1969–76) was a police drama set in a fictional inner-Melbourne suburb, which featured gay characters in a number of one-off storylines. The most notable of these was episode 84, 'Point of View', which was broadcast in 1970. The episode followed the police officers on two seemingly unrelated investigations. The first: a series of burglaries where expensive antique furniture had been stolen. The second: two men living together were accused of being homosexuals. Throughout the episode, the police officers were represented as tolerant and accepting, but reluctantly investigated the men alongside their pursuit of the furniture thieves. In the episode's final minutes, it was revealed that the gay men had been stealing the antique furniture to make their apartment more fashionable. While this was not an outright condemnation of the gay characters for their sexuality, they were ultimately represented as deviant criminals. Later, *Division 4* again represented gay male characters in episodes about a gay male sex offender (episode 215, broadcast in 1973) and a council member that is suspected of being gay (episode 229, broadcast in 1975).

Similar queer victim and villain tropes were represented on *Homicide* (1964–77), which was broadcast at 7.30 pm on Tuesday nights, with daytime repeats throughout the 1970s and 1980s. For example, episode 411, 'A Crime Against Nature', which was broadcast in 1974, followed the homicide detectives investigating the assault and murder of a gay man in an area known for 'poofter bashing'. The episode was broadcast at a later time (9.00 pm) as the subject matter was considered unsuitable for children. Later, in episode 440, 'The Animal that Had to be Fed', a police officer stumbles upon a torture chamber where manipulative lesbians, Wanda and Susan, had been murdering men. The Broadcasting Control Board ruled that this episode should not be screened before 8.30 pm. Later, *Silent Number* (1974), *The Last of the Australians* (1975) and *Shannon's Mob* (1975–6) included short storylines framed around a character's suspected homosexuality.

As the 1980s approached, *Cop Shop* (1977–83) debuted with a two-part gay-bashing storyline. The series later featured a storyline about a relationship between a schoolboy and his male teacher. In 1978, *Cop Shop* introduced Ronnie (Ron Challinor), a gay character who appeared sporadically across several episodes and was described in script notes as 'warm and humorous and a loyal confidante' for one of the female characters. Meanwhile, *Hotel Story* (1977) featured a manipulative lesbian character and *Skyways* (1979–81) introduced a lesbian airhostess named Robyn. In character profiles for *Skyways*, Robyn is highlighted as a character 'we believe will be passing through for just a few weeks but maybe longer depending on how that character is received both by you and others' (Monaghan 2020: 53). She appeared for only ten episodes and her storyline ended in a gruesome murder.

Alongside these single-episode and limited storylines, a number of world-leading LGBTQ+ characters were introduced in primetime soap operas *Number 96* and *The Box*. *Number 96*'s Don Finlayson (Joe Hasham) is regularly credited as the first 'positive' representation of a gay man in a soap opera, depicted as 'normal and loved' (Huber, cited in Giles 2017: 58), which was a significant contrast to earlier representations. As Andrew Mercado (2004) has noted:

> he was a well-adjusted, upstanding lawyer and the first regular gay character in a TV series anywhere in the world…Don wasn't a limp-wristed, mincing caricature but a hero who would help out every other character on the show (49–50).

However, the series wasn't as kind to its lesbian characters. As Beirne highlights, 'One of *Number 96*'s queer characters was fiendish lesbian witch Karen Winters (Toni Lamond), whose defining moment was stripping her flatmate Bev Houghton (Abigail) for a sacrificial Black Mass' (2009: 26). Also notable on *Number 96* was the casting of transgender woman, Carol 'Carlotta' Byron as the trans character Robyn Ross, which in 1973 was a world-first. Robyn was a transgender showgirl who came out to her unsuspecting boyfriend. As McIntyre highlights, her storyline 'grappled with the perceived "threat" that male-to-female transgender poses to heterosexual masculinity when functioning outside of staged performance' (McIntyre 2015: 4).

Later, in the pilot episode of *The Box* (1974–7), Australian television broadcast another world first: a brief encounter between two women. At the end of the pilot episode, the character Vicki Stafford (Judy Nunn) kissed Felicity Baker (Helen Hemingway). The episode aired two weeks before the UK's first televised lesbian kiss in the BBC drama *Girl*. *The Box* also featured flamboyant and lovable Lee Whiteman (Paul Karo), who 'had an amplitude of zingy one-liners, an easy-going air and could be said to have embodied, within an older theatrical tradition, a newer, less apologetic, gay mood' (Howes 1998: 41–2).

After *Number 96* and *The Box* had finished airing on television, Australian audiences were introduced to a rowdy group of queer characters on *Prisoner* (1979–86), which later became an international cult hit spawning a popular Australian remake, *Wentworth* (2013–21) and international versions including *Dangerous Women* (1991) in the United States and *Hinter Gittern – Der Frauenknast* (1997–2007) in Germany. The series featured a wide range of lesbian characters that broke with prior norms of casting attractive and feminine actors as lesbian women (Beirne 2009: 26). These characters included the short-haired, overall-wearing Franky Doyle (Carol Burns), Judy Bryant (Betty Bobbit), a victimized character who manipulated situations to enter prison in order solely to be with her girlfriend, and Joan Ferguson (Maggie Kirkpatrick), the sadistic lesbian prison guard. Though overwhelmingly focusing on women's experiences, the series featured a gay male cook in 1984.

The return to the 'social problem': Queer themes in the 1980s

The 1980s saw fewer representations of LGBTQ+ characters on Australian television. Although *Prisoner* continued into the 1980s, there were very few other lesbians on-screen until the mid-1990s (Beirne 2009: 27). Likewise, gay men were substantially absent from television during the period, a result of what Howes (2002) has described as the pressure of financial constraints and overseas marketing curtailing the radicalism of the 1970s (Howes 2002). Yet queer characters, themes and narratives were present within a number of soap operas and procedural dramas and the occasional current affairs programme. In 1982, the ABC's *Four Corners* broadcast 'Sydney: The Golden City of the Gays', in which reporter Jack Pizzey encouraged audiences to 'switch off now if you don't think it an appropriate subject' and described Sydney's vibrant LGBTQ+ community as 'brazenly gay and yet illegal'. Much like the television documentaries of the 1960s and 1970s, critics responded positively to the report, describing it as 'refreshing and heartening' (Schmith 1982: 2), 'sympathetic' and 'controversial, yes. But . . . neither shocking nor offensive' (Hooks 1982: 7).

Within fictional television, gay and lesbian characters were present in short-lived series. For example, the series *Arcade* (1980), which followed the lives of shop owners in an arcade, included a gay character in the effeminate gym owner. Around the same time, an Australian remake of *Are You Being Served?* (1980–1) was produced. In this series, John Inman reprised his role as Mr Humphries from the original British series. *Daily at Dawn* (1981) featured an effeminate journalist named Leslie (Terry Bader) and period law drama *Carson's Law* (1983–4) included a short storyline in 1983 about a lawyer who was convicted for his homosexuality.

As Howes describes, through this period, when television series did include queer characters, 'their intention was missionary and awareness-raising' (Howes 2002). In 1986, *The Flying Doctors* (1986–92) featured the first HIV/ AIDS storyline on Australian television. The storyline focused on a war hero with AIDS who was rejected by his community when he returned from overseas service. *A Country Practice* (1981–94), a series known for its attempt to deal with social issues (McKee 2001), also represented gay characters through HIV/ AIDS and gay bashing storylines. Finally, *Sons and Daughters* (1982–7) had a gay character appear for forty-three episodes in 1985.

These examples challenge the claims of invisibility about queerness on Australian television while also reflecting a return to the once-off character and short issue-based storylines of the early 1970s. Throughout the 1980s, queerness was again relegated to the realm of 'social problem' television. While queer characters were no longer villains, deviants or morally corrupt, their storylines through the 1980s largely focused on queerness as a social and health issue through which LGBTQ+ characters were portrayed as sympathetic but ultimately powerless figures.

The queer character arc in the 1990s

Within published histories of queer representation on Australian television, the 1990s are often characterized as a period of increased representation after the absence of queerness on screen in the preceding decade (Beirne 2009). The driving force behind this re-emergence was the commencement of the annual telecast of Sydney's Gay and Lesbian Mardi Gras. In 1994, the ABC aired an edited highlights reel of the parade in the primetime slot, which Howes described as a 'a cannonball' (2002) for Australian viewers. Highly controversial, the first broadcast led to a public debate about the visibility of queerness on Australian television and its perceived threat to Australian family values (Harris 1995). At the time, the ABC was caught in a complex bind as Searle explains:

> a climate of increasing economic rationalism has diminished national broadcasters' abilities to provide programs that complement rather than duplicate mainstream fare, at the same time that complementarity is demanded through the organisations' charters (Searle 1995: 13).

Alongside this discourse about the inclusion of queer themes on Australian television, fictional series continued to depict LGBTQ+ characters through the social interest storylines that had been popularized in the 1980s. Across this period, there was a marked gendering of queer narratives with story arcs about men largely focusing on characters dealing with homophobia, violence and HIV/AIDS, while women's storylines emphasized romance and family. For example, police drama *Blue Heelers* (1994–2006) featured once-off episodes on homophobic violence; long-running soap *Neighbours* (1985–present) included a brief storyline about a teacher being fired for being gay; *A Country Practice* (1981–94) had a number of HIV/AIDS and gay-bashing storylines and *G.P.* (1989–96) featured HIV/AIDS-related storylines and a short-lived romance between characters Lucy (Louise Crawford) and Kelly (Gabrielle Maselli). Later, firefighter drama *Fire* (1995–6) included a side plot about lesbian characters seeking a sperm donor. These short-lived storylines often focused on minor or temporary characters or as Howes (1998) describes, 'another dead or dying queen, usually unrelated to any of the regulars – here today, gone tomorrow' (40).

However, more developed storylines were emerging as the industry began shifting towards greater emphasis on diversity and the inclusion of queer characters. In 1994, *Neighbours* introduced its first gay character, a builder named Macka. Later, the teen drama *Sweat* (1996) featured a storyline about a teenage cyclist named Snowy (Heath Ledger) who grappled with his sexuality and came out. *SeaChange* (1998–2000) also included the stereotypically camp Barry Boston (Robert Grubb), who appeared in five episodes. In 1997, *Home and Away* (1988–present) gestured at queerness when Shannon Reed (Isla

Fisher) had something of a relationship with lesbian character Mandy Thomas (Rachel Blake). When Fisher left the series, her character Shannon was said to have moved overseas to be with Mandy. Reflecting on the soap opera as genre that both includes and disavows queerness, Beirne notes, 'With the constant thirst for storylines and romantic complication inherent in soap operas, soaps have often been willing to include lesbian desires and trysts, although somewhat more hesitant at truly including lesbian characters and their relationships as an integral part of their story arcs' (Beirne 2009: 27).

Around the same time, *G.P.* (1989–96) featured a gay main character, Dr Martin Dempsey (Damien Rice); *Heartbreak High* (1994–9) included an ongoing storyline about gay teacher, Graham Brown (Hugh Baldwin); and police drama *Water Rats* (1996–2001) included a lesbian main character, Helen Blakemore (Toni Scanlan). In these examples, queer characters were central to the series and their sexuality was a part of their identity, but not the only storyline they were featured within. For example, on *Heartbreak High*, Graham was depicted as an openly gay teacher. He was popular with students and had close friendships with other teachers at the school. However, his sexuality was only occasionally the primary focus of his storylines. In episode 14, for example, his sexuality was the centre of the narrative as he was falsely accused of touching students inappropriately, harassed by students, and attacked by a homophobic parent. However, in other episodes, Graham's sexuality was less of a focal point. Similarly, Helen Blakemore in *Water Rats*, appeared throughout the series, but her sexuality was not a major focus. While she did have some relationships with women, her storylines more regularly related to the police procedural elements of the series.

Later series *Pacific Drive* (1996–7) and *Raw FM* (1997–8) are significant examples that reflect the beginning of a shift towards further centralization of queer characters and themes, though both were short-lived series. On *Pacific Drive*, the main character Zoe Marshall (Libby Tanner) had multiple relationships with women. As Mercado (2004) highlights, Zoe was a new kind of queer character on Australian television:

> Zoe Marshall wasn't a witch, a predator or a criminal – she was just a new, guilt-free dyke who, the Sydney Star Observer noted, didn't have to go through 'some kind of angst ridden crisis of conscience and confidence' in coming out (333).

Similarly, *Raw FM* was about a group of young people running a radio station and featured several queer characters in its ensemble cast. However, the series was critiqued for its representations of queer women (Beirne 2009) and villainous LGBTQ+ characters (McNeil 1998).

Queering the 2000 and 2010s

The 2000s and 2010s saw a significant increase in the number of LGBTQ characters on Australian television. As O'Meara and Monaghan (2024) found, this comprised over seventy regular and recurring LGBTQ+ characters and the establishment of new trends in queer representation. For men, this included 'an abundance of narratives about "coming out" which contrasted with series featuring "already out" gay and bisexual characters, the emergence of a "gayngst" trope that internalizes homophobia of the preceding decades, and the growing representation of sex between men' (5). Some of the more prominent examples included: *Above the Law* (2000–1), *The Secret Life of Us* (2001–5), *Always Greener* (2001–3), *Dance Academy* (2010–13), *Home and Away* (1988–), *Neighbours*, *Winners & Losers* (2011–16), *A Place to Call Home* (2013–18), *Please Like Me* (2013–16) and *The Family Law* (2016–19).

For women, storylines tended to focus on characters who were either assured of their sexuality or those who were depicted as temporarily exploring same-sex romantic or sexual attraction without necessarily claiming an LGBTQ+ identity (O'Meara and Monaghan 2024: 8). For example, *The Secret Life of Us* introduced an out lesbian character in 2003 who began a romance with series regular Miranda (Abi Tucker), a character who was previously coded through on-screen relationships as heterosexual and who did not identify as LGBTQ+.

One of the more significant shifts of the 2000s was the introduction and rapid popularization of reality television. This had significance for LGBTQ+ on-screen representation in Australia with a substantial inclusion of openly LGBTQ+ participants, performers and contestants. Programmes such as *Australian Idol* (2003–24) and *Big Brother Australia* (2001–23), among many others, featured a range of transgender and gender-diverse contestants, delivering audiences representations of non-heteronormative and non-cisgender subjectivity (McIntyre 2017). The first season of *Australian Idol*, for instance, featured drag performer Courtney Act in her television debut. As McIntyre suggests, Australian reality TV was not, in itself, a utopic fruition of affirmative action but nevertheless 'revealed itself to be uniquely suited to repositioning transgender in relation to gender norms on- and off-screen' (88).

Big Brother Australia featured a wide array of queer housemates over the years. In its first season in 2001, John Cass was notable as being one of the few openly gay men on television at the time. During his stint in the house, he received the nickname 'Johnnie Rotten' from the media and fans after the show edited the highlight reels so it seemed he would hug everyone he nominated before they were evicted. The phrase 'Johnnie's love is dangerous' became increasingly popular, and, thus, one of Australia's first reality television villains was born. Writing on the experience of watching Johnnie, Gary Dowsett (2003) argues that it was no coincidence that audiences were so readily able to position Johnnie as the season's villain. Indeed, as entertainment journalist Stephen Dow (2001) put it: 'Cinema, of course, has a long tradition of portraying homosexuals as evil. If Hitchcock were directing *Big Brother*, he'd have had Johnnie strangling one of the housemates and stuffing them in a trunk under the dining table.'

There was, however, a noticeable backlash in queer media publications due to this 'villain edit.' After his elimination, it was clear, however, that he had had an impact on the housemates and the public, with popular housemate Blair McDonaugh talking of 'admiring, respecting, even loving Johnnie, and what a role model the older gay man had been' (Miller 2001, cited Dowsett 2003). This respectability emerges through the witnessing, as Dowsett (2003) notes, of the mundanity of personal interactions that include a non-threatening queer figure depicted as non-sexual.

Australian Big Brother, much like other reality television formats, saw a cultural localization of an international format. For Doris Baltruschat (2010), format localization is based on a media ecology, which involves lengthy collaborative processes between the owners of the programme, licensee and contracted production crew, who adapt the programme for local audiences under the supervision of the original producers. Local versions of global reality television formats point to the ways in which glocalization brings together local and virtual communities through adaptation of international genres for local audiences. This, for Baltruschat, is achieved through the 'insertion of local stories as well as skilfully embedding it into local communities through media events [and] tapping into the symbolic matrix of national and cultural familiarities' (111). For *Australian Survivor*, for instance, this saw early seasons of the reboot have a focus on the good heterosexual Aussie bloke and the conflicts of voting out a mate (Richards 2018). For the first season of *Australian Big Brother*, this saw audiences and the straight housemates become familiar with an ordinary Australian gay man.

Later seasons featured other queer contestants who would share their lives in the mundane setting of the *Big Brother* house. Season two featured Sahra Kearney, who finished third in the season, and Nathan Morris, who went onto a successful radio career. In season 6, David Graham, affectionately dubbed 'farmer Dave', came out to his fellow housemates and ended up being one of the most popular contestants on the show. When he came out, he said he referred to himself as simultaneously a 'token' farmer and a 'token' gay guy, which displayed an awareness of how queer contestants would always be in the minority in much popular reality television. In season 8, Ben Norris won the season and proposed to his partner during the live finale, which was a significant statement for marriage equality at the time. Several other reality television shows featured LGBTQ+ contestants. The first season of *The Block* featured Gavin and Warren, dubbed 'Gav and Waz', which, while the butt of several jokes in the media at the time, still featured a gay couple squabbling along with the other renovating couples. *Australia's Next Top Model* (2004–16) has also featured a handful of queer contestants, including Jane Williamson (cycle 2), dubbed the 'gay rock chick' of her season, Lola Van Vorst (cycle 5), Kelsey Martinovich (cycle 6) and Taylah Roberts (cycle 8).

While unscripted television wasn't new by the time shows such as *Big Brother* arrived – *Sylvania Waters*, for instance, was broadcast in 1992 – the inclusion of queer Australians into the genre saw an expanded picture of everyday Australians. The rise of reality television in Australia also coincided with major shifts in the medium, which, according to Matt Hills (2007), saw a shift away from 'discourses of the symbolically bounded and discrete text' towards series such as *Big Brother*, that spill 'beyond textual boundaries' (46). This era of television also coincides with what Derek Johnson (2007) refers to as TVIII, which saw 'contemporary "multi-platforming" strategies deploy television content to be consumed serially across a range of media (both digital and analogue)' (62). As such, this dispersal of reality television also saw the dispersal of who was considered an everyday Australian to wider audiences.

Reality television of the early 2000s contrasts considerably with scripted television of the same era, which only represented one transgender character in the 2000s: Chantal Wilkinson (Kate Fitzpatrick) in a short, two-episode storyline in *Always Greener* (2001–3) focused primarily on cisgender characters recognizing and making fun of Chantal's trans identity. While *Packed to the Rafters* depicted a similar storyline in 2010, later 2010s series included more compassionate representations and shifted to a focus on authenticity, which coincided with our transgender and non-binary actors portraying these roles. For instance, in 2018, audiences were introduced to the character of Chloe (Liv Hewson) in *Homecoming Queens* (2018), the first out non-binary character on Australian television. The following year, Georgie Stone portrayed the character McKenzie Hargreaves, the first transgender character on *Neighbours*.

Perhaps the most important shift in LGBTQ+ representation across the 2000s and 2010s is the move towards the foregrounding of diverse queer communities, what can be referred to as 'queer story worlds' (O'Meara and Monaghan 2024: 13). In essence, this is a shift away from the single-episode storylines and once-off inclusions of LGBTQ+ characters of previous decades, such as the police procedurals *Division 4*, *Homicide*, and *Cop Shop* of the 1960s and 1970s, towards the depiction of multiple LGBTQ+ characters at the centre of a series' overarching narrative. For instance, the ABC series *Outland* (2012) was the first Australian series to feature an entire cast of gay and lesbian characters. Similarly, though not having an entirely queer ensemble, *Wentworth* (2013–21) featured eighteen lesbian and bisexual women characters and three trans characters (two transgender women and one transgender man) over eight seasons.

The emergence of web series

Alongside these shifts in representation across the 2000s and 2010s were increasing opportunities for LGBTQ+ creators to tell their own stories and connect with audiences via digital video sharing platforms such as YouTube that hosted user-generated content. After launching internationally in 2005, YouTube was considered 'a more or less "empty" platform to be filled by the YouTube community with originally produced content of various kinds' (Snickars and Vonderau 2009: 10). This environment encouraged experimentation with new forms of digital storytelling through a range of formats, including web series.

Sometimes described as web television, web series is a form of episodic digital storytelling distributed via the internet. Unlike the digital series made popular through streaming services such as Netflix, web series are typically short-form, low-budget and independently produced. For this reason, web series is regarded as a form of independent digital storytelling that promotes diversity and bypasses traditional media gatekeepers (Leder 2021). As web series are often self-financed or crowd-funded, they are thought to offer greater creative freedom with fewer ties to broadcasters or funding bodies (Keltie 2017). This enables web series creators to focus on stories that may have struggled to find a home in more conservative broadcast settings (Monaghan 2017). This was the case for notable Australian LGBTQ+ web series *The Horizon* and *Starting From Now,* which both found substantial audiences on YouTube.

Launching in 2009, *The Horizon* quickly became one of the most popular queer web series in the world. Focusing on a group of gay men in Sydney, *The Horizon* ran for eight seasons from 2009 to 2017 (sixty-four episodes). The series was created by Adam Jones and Boaz Stark, a former scriptwriter on Neighbours, and was initially funded via ACON, the AIDS Council of New South Wales, and attracted further funding from health organizations and fashion brands. As a result of this funding, *The Horizon*'s storylines embedded health and social themes. While its episodes were only 4 to 11 minutes long, the series featured discussions of post-exposure prophylaxis (PEP), pre-exposure prophylaxis (PrEP), and condoms, as well as emphasising support for characters who were HIV positive. *The Horizon* exceeded 80 million views and maintained a global online fan base on YouTube that continues to the present day as audiences rediscover this landmark Australian series.

Similarly, lesbian-oriented web series *Starting From Now* was first shared via YouTube in 2014 and grew a considerable global audience (at the time of writing, its episodes have more than 140 million views). Initially self-funded, the series consisted of five seasons (thirty episodes between 6 and 13 minutes in duration), following a group of young queer women living in Sydney's Inner-West: Steph (Sarah de Possesse), Kristen (Lauren Orrell), Darcy (Rosie Lourde) and Emily (Bianca Bradley). Self-described as a 'lesbian love quadrangle drama', *Starting From Now* explored the group's complex friendship and relationship dynamics, told via short narrative snippets through the web series format. Episodes focused on new romances, difficult feelings about ex-partners, supporting friends through addiction, and the character's seemingly endless search for happiness and community.

As *Starting From Now* grew in popularity, it moved beyond its original digital home on YouTube into more traditional broadcast settings, which led some to claim it was reflective of a revolution in Australian television as the first Australian-produced lesbian television series. Later seasons were also funded through Australia's national screen agency, Screen Australia. However, though Seasons 4 and 5 were broadcast on SBS 2 in 2016, coinciding with their coverage of the Sydney Gay and Lesbian Mardi Gras, it remained a digital series that was primarily hosted on YouTube. With this in mind, we might consider whether the inclusion of LGBTQ+ identities and stories in the web series format might speak more to emergent forms of production and distribution or experimentation with new opportunities afforded by technological change, than to Australia's screen industries attempting to be inclusive of a wider range of sexualities and gender diversities. However, we also recognise shifts in funding web productions through Screen Australia and digital-oriented initiatives such as SBS's Digital Originals, which have spawned engaging short-form queer series such as *Homecoming Queens* and *Triple Oh!* (2024). We see these as examples of both the professionalization and institutionalization of the web series format, which differentiates it from other forms of digital content creation such as TikTok and Instagram. In Chapter 8, we explore this professionalised web storytelling further in relation to gender diversities and post-binary identities and the introduction of streaming platforms into Australia's screen landscape.

Conclusion

Our exploration of Australian television history from the early days to the 2010s reveals that LGBTQ+ characters, queer themes and narratives have been ever-present, and the popular claims to 'invisibility' are inaccurate and mythical. As we discussed, the television of 1960s frequently subverted social norms, celebrating and joyfully playing with gender. This gave way to the world-leading documentaries and scripted television representations of the 1970s, which were largely received positively by their audiences. Though the 1980s and 1990s are often viewed as a wasteland of LGBTQ+ representation, we highlighted the emergence of social interest storylines, through which queerness was framed as a social and health problem. As the 2000s gave way to the 2010s, queerness was no longer a sensationalized issue to be dealt with and later forgotten, but a valued part of the Australian television landscape. Challenging the long-held assumption that Australian audiences rarely see LGBTQ+ characters on television, we have highlighted the rich queerness of Australian television over six decades.

4

Framing Politics

Filmgoing and Activism

One aspect of queer politics has been a long-standing activist thread, and in a media-saturated world that includes an attentiveness to media representation that governs the ways in which communities respond to, think about, produce and interpret the depiction of queer stories and lives. Since the beginnings of queer activist movements in Australia, film and television have been positioned as targets of significant protest, as well as tools through which activists hoped to reach their goals (McKinnon 2013, 2016). Activists through the 1970s embraced a politics of visibility, urging queer people to come out and live proudly in their homosexual, bisexual or transsexual identities (Wotherspoon 1991, Willett 2000). Positive representation of queer characters on film and television was seen as critical to the community's coming out process. Activists directed their anger first at film censorship regimes, which were blamed for keeping queer characters from the screen, and second at filmmakers, who frequently depicted lesbians and gay men in harmful, stereotypical fashion. Film and television were seen as either a hindrance, disempowering LGBTQ+ people through negative imagery, or a help, allowing queer lives to become visible and, in the process, to shift public opinion.

This chapter focuses on the relationship between screen media cultures and the first ten years of Australian lesbian and gay activism in Sydney. The earliest Australian LGBTQ+ activist organizations led by openly homosexual people were both formed in 1969. The first was an Australian arm of the American lesbian rights group Daughters of Bilitis, which was founded in Melbourne. It was followed by the Campaign Against Moral Persecution (CAMP), founded in Sydney by Christabel Poll, a lesbian, and her gay neighbours John Ware and Michael Cass. CAMP would go on to have national influence, with local CAMP groups founded in several capital cities and on university campuses. As the decade progressed, the new movement split between the relatively conservative, reformist aims of CAMP and a range of radical and revolutionary gay liberation groups.

Given the diverse political viewpoints of these organizations, it is unsurprising that perspectives on and uses of film and television varied significantly across them. Commercial media was a primary target of reformist groups, who believed that positive imagery would increase tolerance of queer people among the broader population while also helping closeted homosexuals to develop positive self-image. Often disdainful of the commercial mainstream, gay liberationists embraced the radical possibilities of global art, underground and alternative cinema, much of which was newly accessible in Australia thanks to reforms to censorship laws in 1972 and which screened in inner-city spaces with political intent. Queer forms of expression, developed through experimental filmmaking, deliberately pushed at the boundaries of Australia's notoriously staid and conservative gender and sexual cultures.

Through the work of activist groups, the 1970s saw the creation of new lesbian and gay identities, which were specifically defined by the claim, not only to be seen, but to be understood in ways defined by queer people. Believing themselves to have been long censored from the screen or only ever depicted in ways sensitive to the views of the heterosexual mainstream, lesbian and gay activists demanded a place in movies and television, through which they could come to be understood as equal citizens and valid humans. Political identities were formed and expressed in part through engagements with the screen. The terms with which 1970s activists responded to film and television had long-term ramifications for queer film cultures.

LGBTQ+ activism in Sydney

According to historian Robert Reynolds (2002), CAMP activists through the 1970s rapidly redefined homosexual identities in Australia, including through the promotion of the idea that, 'homosexuality could be a political identity and that homosexuals might act coherently as a distinct political constituency' (34). In the period subsequent to the Second World War, homosexuality had been defined as either a sin requiring repentance or a crime warranting punishment. This framing was partially reshaped in the 1960s by members of the medical establishment, who argued that homosexuality was a symptom of mental illness that could be cured through treatment, including electric shock treatments and, in some cases, lobotomization. CAMP activists specifically rejected each of these religious, criminal and medical framings by mocking the politically powerful Catholic Church, by demanding reform of laws criminalizing male homosexual sex, and by protesting against psychologists whose so-called treatments were causing extraordinary harm. Behind each of these actions was a belief that, in the words of Reynolds (2002: 35), 'It was no longer the homosexual who, by definition, was pathological, but rather the society in which he or she was embedded and objectified.'

In fighting for changes to criminal law and increased mainstream acceptance of homosexual lives, CAMP activists were invested in notions of equality and tolerance, seeking reforms to Australian political, social and cultural life in ways that would benefit lesbian and gay people. In the first edition of the organization's magazine, *CAMP Ink*, Poll and Ware (1970) argued that the overall aims of CAMP were, 'to bring about a situation where homosexuals can enjoy good jobs and security in those jobs, equal treatment under the law, and the right to serve our country without fear of exposure or contempt' (2). The edition included an article by Ware condemning the impact of psychological treatment on homosexuals and a classifieds section encouraging CAMP members to meet, especially those living in isolated areas.

The idea of homosexual equality was, of course, perceived as substantially radical to many Australians; yet to many queer people immersed in 1970s counterculture, the goals of reform, tolerance and job security were considered inherently conservative. On university campuses and in bohemian spaces of the inner city, utopic visions of sexual revolution were emerging. Sydney's first gay liberation groups were founded in the early 1970s, with the goal of fostering radical social change. At the heart of their arguments was a belief, not only in the liberation of homosexual people from mainstream homophobia, but the liberation of all people from fixed sex roles and sexual identities.

Whether reformist or liberationist in their outlook, activists often placed *visibility* not only as a politically valuable strategy through which to shape public opinion, but also as the direct responsibility or obligation of all queer people. Although Sydney's lesbian and gay social scene was rapidly evolving from a disparate collection of bars and clubs into a vibrant city neighbourhood, many participants in that scene remained closeted in their work and family lives. From the viewpoint of activists, lesbians and gay men who refused to come out publicly needed to take some of the blame for their own continued oppression.

According to the editors of *CAMP Ink*, the closeted homosexual's 'acceptance of his relegation to a shadowy existence allows the politician to placate his conscience by ignoring the issues. It is time for us to come out of the shadows and loudly demand our rights as human beings' (Camp Ink 1970: 2).

Putting their views into practical action, activists took to the streets, loudly demanding specific changes such as an end to police violence, the decriminalization of homosexual sex, and reforms to anti-discrimination laws. They also insisted on being witnessed within public spaces on their own terms. Gay liberationists, for example, deployed a tactic known as 'zaps', in which groups of activists would occupy public spaces in ways designed to draw attention to their presence as openly homosexual people. Riding up and down an escalator in a busy department store while chanting 'Ho! Ho! Homosexual!' was one way of joyfully throwing off the shackles of oppression and ensuring the visibility of proud lesbian and gay people.

As Jesse Matheson (2019) has argued, the focus of the movement on visibility framed on-screen representation as a central cause of political action (16). While there was no doubt among activists that positive imagery of homosexual lives would be of benefit to the community, what became apparent over time was that an on-screen image considered positive by some queer people may well be read as retrograde or politically suspect by others. In the pages of Australian activist newsletters and the commercial gay press, debates raged over which films were helpful and which were harmful to closeted queer people, to the movement or both (McKinnon 2016). Among the points of general agreement were that state censorship had long kept queer characters from the screen, that more positive lesbian and gay imagery was needed in order to advance the aims of the movement, and that films made by and for homosexuals would reverse the negative impacts of much mainstream cinema.

Fighting the censors

Australia's paternalistic and highly conservative censorship system had its basis in colonial-era restrictions on theatre and the views of religious leaders of the time (Cettl 2014). The nation's film censorship regimes were developed in a somewhat haphazard fashion over time, cobbling together a confusing array of national and state-based legislation and government bodies. The first federal system was enacted in 1917, although several Australian states maintained their own censorship bodies until the 1956 introduction of the Commonwealth Film Censorship Board. Censorship continued to be envisaged by governments and Christian church leaders as a means through which to protect the morals of the nation from corrupting influences. The figure of the innocent and corruptible Australian child (typically understood as white, sexless and heterosexual) was often deployed as a core justification for strict film censorship laws (Cettl 2014, McKinnon 2020).

Through the 1960s, the Australian censorship system came under heavy attack from a number of groups, including liberals, the progressive left and members of the emerging counterculture. Indeed, counter-culturalist groups took issue with paternalistic decision-making and censorship and raised it as a key political activity (Willett 2000). The output of the Australian film industry of the 1950s and 1960s was limited, meaning the vast majority of films were imported. While the French New Wave, Italian neo-realist and American underground cinema movements were revolutionizing global cinema cultures, Australian censors were suspicious of this foreign content. The fact that much of what was considered the best of world cinema was either refused entry to Australia or only arrived on local screens in heavily edited form was condemned by large sections of the media, film festival organizers and cultural leaders (McKinnon 2020).

Lesbian and gay activists added their voices to demands for censorship reform, framing the work of censors as one means through which the state ensured homosexuals remained closeted and broadly hidden (McKinnon 2012, Matheson 2019). Liberationists embraced the idea that social transformation was possible through the representation of topics previously condemned as obscene. Although homosexuality was never specifically banned in Australian censorship legislation, censors nonetheless understood that legislated restrictions on indecency and obscenity encompassed representation of non-heterosexual desires.

In a 1960–1 report, for example, the Film Censorship Board bemoaned the fact that a growing number of films were focused on 'sordid' themes, including 'rape, nymphomania, homosexuality' (Film Censorship Board 1961: 2). The Board claimed that it was willing to take a liberal stance on such themes, but only when 'they are presented in a manner which is not obscene or likely to encourage imitation of the practices portrayed'. As a result, some films that included openly gay characters were screened in Australia through that decade, including *Victim* (1961), *Advise and Consent* (1962) and *The Killing of Sister George* (1968). Any scenes of same-sex intimacy, however, were declared obscene and had to be cut before distribution would be allowed. The Board insisted, for example, that *The Killing of Sister George* would only be suitable for Australian audiences if a lesbian sex scene was heavily cut (McKinnon 2020).

Films like *Victim*, in which a homosexual man commits to a sexless marriage with his wife, and *Advise and Consent*, in which a homosexual man dies by suicide, were unlikely to encourage any 'imitation of the practices portrayed'. Banned altogether by Australian censors, however, were a range of films far more likely to be deemed obscene because the gay sex was more ostensible. These included all of Andy Warhol and Paul Morrissey's films, such as *Lonesome Cowboys* (1968), *Flesh* (1968) and *Trash* (1970), along with James Bidgood's *Pink Narcissus* (1971) (McKinnon 2012). In assessing on-screen queer representation in the context of Australian LGBTQ+ histories, it is important, therefore, to acknowledge that many films now viewed as classics of global queer film cultures were either screened in Australia in heavily edited form or were not screened at all until years after their production.

In 1972, demands for changes to censorship laws finally found fruition. Liberal Party MP Don Chipp, in his role as Minister for Customs and Excise, introduced reforms that revolutionized the kinds of films Australians were permitted to view. By creating a new model of film classification, which included an 'R' rating for films only accessible to audiences over the age of eighteen, the government allowed that not all films needed to be suitable for children.

CAMP activists celebrated these reforms in the October 1972 issue of *CAMP Ink*, which featured a cover image of noted sex symbol and star of several of Warhol's previously banned films, Joe Dallesandro. In the issue, activist Garry Dennison reported on some of the gay films newly viewable to Australian audiences. While Dennison (1972) celebrated the possibility of a more mature Australian film culture, he was ultimately disappointed with most of the new films with queer themes, characters and narratives that had become available, including *The Gay Deceivers* (1969), *The Boys in the Band* (1970) and *Fortune and Men's Eyes* (1971). He argued: 'Judging from the camp films that have been released since the "R" certificate came in, homosexuals are still a sorry lot of tired queens in dire need of a transfusion . . .' (4).

Positive images only please

If once viewed as sly and even pleasurable rebellion against censorship regimes by filmmakers, pre-liberation queer film characters were redefined by

1970s activists as harmful biproducts of homophobic state-based oppression. Characters that had only ever been understood by audiences as homosexual through implication were relabelled as either not queer at all or as inherently negative under a form of visibility politics that considered any opacity or tentativeness in representation as anathema to the movement. Thus activist and scholar Dennis Altman (1971) argued, 'To the best of my knowledge no film depicting homosexuals as anything but pitiful and scarred or at least pathetic and ridiculous has come out of Hollywood, and where necessary the movies falsify history to preserve accepted notions of morality' (59–60).

Through the 1970s, activists critically analysed both old and new films seeking out 'positive' images of homosexuality. Although placing an extraordinary burden of representation on queer film characters, this process was an important means through which lesbians and gay men contemplated their newly public place in society. If being seen was a core goal of homosexual activists, then the question that quickly arose was, 'how do we want to be seen and by whom?' The intended audience of a film was important to this analysis. A sexually explicit movie might be arousing, liberating and joyful to queer audiences, but would it be too confronting to heterosexual people? Similarly, a romantic drama focused on a same-sex couple might be reassuring to people still coming to terms with their sexually, but would it re-enforce heteronormative ideas of relationship formation that liberationists were trying to disrupt?

Analysing older films was also configured by activists as an important means through which to understand mechanisms of oppression. To dismantle the systems that marginalized or subjugated non-heteronormative sexualities, it was first necessary to understand how those systems had been made hegemonic, including through popular culture. Among other Australian activists of the 1970s, Altman (1978) advocated for, and assisted in the programming of, gay film festivals that included older movies now considered harmful. The aim was to assess these films as a group and from the point of view of politicized queer identities and a queer cinema-going public that hadn't existed when the films were first released.

When any new film focused on homosexual characters was released, activists responded quickly with assessments and critiques. In October 1972, for example, a group of gay liberationists attended a screening of the American film *Some of My Best Friends Are . . .* (1971) at a cinema in Mosman, a white, middle-class neighbourhood far from the Darlinghurst gay ghetto (Lee 1972). The film charts a Christmas Eve party at a gay bar in New York's Greenwich Village.

Today most notable for performances by author Fannie Flagg, Warhol superstar Candy Darling and a pre-*Golden Girls* Rue McLanahan, the film adheres to the model set by *The Boys in the Band* the year before, in which a seemingly happy gathering of gays ultimately descends into mordant self-loathing. As with *The Boys in the Band*, it isn't entirely clear whether the film sees the depression and neuroses of lesbians and gay men as a product of an oppressive society or as somehow inherent to homosexual people.

Activist John Lee (1972) reported on a gay liberation trip to Mosman in the group's newsletter, decrying *Some of My Best Friends Are . . .* as 'yet another effort in cashing in on the popular interest in viewing homosexuality as funny/pathetic' and as 'a sort of cheap, souped-up version of *The Boys in the Band . . .* in which all the imaginable popular homosexual stereotypes appear as characters' (3). In the same issue, fellow liberationist Paul Foss (1972) accepted that the depiction of a contemporary American gay bar was realistic, but criticized the film's 'onesidedness . . . and the creation of an attitude that misleads and eventually corrupts' (9). Foss argued that homosexuals needed to be telling their own stories by referencing the Peter Weiss play *Marat/Sade* in which, according to Foss, 'the inmates create their own play that enforces their sense of sanity and potency and which eventually spills out of their confines and engulfs the mocking audience. There is a lesson to be learnt from that' (11).

Notably, John Lee (1972) was less concerned by the messages that might be conveyed to heterosexual viewers in *Some of My Best Friends Are*, and instead worried about the impact the film might have on gay men in the audience. According to Lee, about '90% of the audience' was gay. He wrote, 'This in itself was the most depressing thing about the film's showing for it was yet another example of homosexuals seeking information about their own existence, only of course to have this invalidated' (3). Lee expressed concern that the 'furtive behaviour' of those entering the cinema indicated their uncertain relationship to their sexual identity. In response, Lee and his fellow activists had prepared a leaflet countering the film's negative imagery with information about gay liberation. The leaflets were distributed to audiences at subsequent screenings.

This example suggests the degree to which activist identities shaped public, queer and audience engagement with queer films. As a liberated, politically active gay man, Lee saw himself as better equipped to endure the film's negative imagery without negatively affecting his sense of self-worth. Through participation in the movement, he had developed the necessary skills through which to identify, interpret and dismantle the oppressive mechanisms sustained through negative depictions of gay men and lesbians in film. Participation in the movement as a liberated subject also carried with it an obligation to support and inform unliberated gay people who may be affected by the negative representation. Far from passive consumption, watching a film was perceived in that time as an inherently political act. Over the course of the decade, other activists began to take this active engagement with film a step further, creating opportunities to develop, film and screen content by and for queer people.

Recording and watching our own stories

As discussed in Chapter 3, the emergence of an openly lesbian and gay community in Sydney was of occasional interest to Australian television and current affairs programmes throughout the 1970s. If often relatively even-handed in their approach, programmes like *Chequerboard* and others like it were nonetheless produced by heterosexual journalists, with heterosexual viewers in mind. From the point of view of lesbian and gay activists, there was value to be had in this form of representation, if it was done correctly. Desperately needed and exceedingly rare, however, were stories of homosexual lives made by homosexual people for homosexual audiences. The act of witnessing lives like one's own on-screen was seen as a self-evident good, while the lack of such films was both evidence and mechanism of continued oppression.

In this context, activists enthusiastically pursued opportunities to produce and screen documentaries by and about lesbians and gay men. The importation of the American documentary *Word Is Out: Stories of Some of Our Lives* in 1978 provided critical evidence to local activists of the positive impacts of such films. Emerging from an idea by independent filmmaker Peter Adair, *Word Is Out* was created through a collaboration of six lesbians and gay men with varying degrees of film experience, who collectively named themselves the Mariposa Film Group. The film interweaves interviews with twenty-six homosexual people of varying ages and races, mostly filmed in the interviewee's homes, discussing their lives as lesbians and gay men in 1970s America. Simplistic in its form and structure, *Word Is Out* nonetheless offered a radical departure from the heterosexual gaze deployed in previous on-screen investigations into queer lives to that date.

Intriguingly, *Word Is Out* provided opportunities for its interviewees to describe the powerful, and often negative, impact of cinema on their lives. One interviewee, a young Chinese-American man named Dennis Chiu, described the isolating experience of racial and gendered difference from the masculine social norms created by Hollywood. He stated, 'When you're a kid you have John Wayne and you have Steve McQueen and if you're a slant-eyed Chinese kid and you happen to be slightly effeminate, it really drives knives into your stomach.' It is interesting to consider how this description resonated with queer moviegoers watching *Word Is Out* in theatres filled with other lesbian and gay people. The film was likely creating feelings of connection and community through shared memories of isolation and difference, aiding in the development of a queer political constituency and viewing public.

The first Sydney screening of *Word Is Out* was at the Images of Gays film festival, held at the Paris Theatre in March 1978. Formerly part of the Hoyts cinema chain, by 1978 the 600-seat Paris, located on the edge of the city's gay district, was being run as an alternative film, music and theatre space by Johnny Allen, a gay man deeply immersed in 1970s counterculture. Allen programmed the Images of Gays festival with Dennis Altman and selected *Word Is Out* as the opening night film, where it played to a capacity crowd. Allen later recalled: 'A film like *Word Is Out* would not have been possible ten or even five years earlier, just conceptually wouldn't have been possible. . . . With a film like *Word Is Out*, we we're trying to say, going forward, this is a radical change' (Allen 2013).

Sydney gay critic Peter Page (1978) similarly noted the film's landmark status, describing it as 'the first feature-length film to present gay people talking about their gayness, (which) as such fills a serious gap in the spectrum of filmic images of homosexuals' (23). To Page, *Word Is Out* revealed the activist value of homosexual people telling their own stories on film. He argued, 'Since gayness is often and easily hidden, most straights and many isolated gays have had little choice but to believe the lies about gays which abound in movies.' *Word Is Out* provided an opportunity to counter negative representations by placing authentic lesbian and gay experiences on screen.

Not everyone was impressed, however, by the film's efforts to normalize homosexual lives and relationships. Having attended the Images of Gays screening, Lesbian Feminist Organisation member Chris Burke stated, 'From a feminist perspective, I was a bit disappointed with *Word Is Out*' (cited in Cee 1978: 20). To Burke, the film offered a limited vision of homosexual relationships that were mostly modelled on 'heterosexual stereotypes'. The goal of radical activism was not to obtain acceptance or tolerance by claiming equivalence between gay and straight lives, but rather to celebrate queer lives for their potential to reshape social norms.

For others in the audience, however, watching *Word Is Out* surrounded by hundreds of other lesbian and gay people was profound. Activist Lee Franklyn (1978) described the event in rapturous tones: 'It was an amazing human experience: a theatre chock-a-block full of gay and non-gay women and men hooting, laughing, cheering and crying. It was a communal wave of human emotion: anger, joy, compassion and sorrow. More than anything, it was a mass sensation of pride' (3). Notable in Franklyn's description of the screening's emotional impact was the value of the *shared* experience. Eight years into the activist movement's history, opportunities to participate in a mostly queer crowd of that size remained rare.

Franklyn (1978) also marvelled at the honesty of the American participants in the film and wondered if Australian gays and lesbians yet had the same ability to communicate their experiences as articulately. Highlighting the relative youth of the Australian gay liberation movement, he argued, 'A *Word Is Out* documentary on gay Australians? Yes, we'll give it a go. But first let's give ourselves a go. We've only begun to be, but word is out that we're determined to get there' (3). Unaccounted for by Franklyn, however, were the range of efforts already underway by lesbian and gay activists to produce gay and lesbian documentaries – if not Australian versions of *Word Is Out*, certainly documentaries that would place the lives of queer Australians on screen.

Highly significant among these efforts was a short documentary film directed by Digby Duncan and the lesbian collective One-in-Seven titled *Witches, Faggots, Dykes and Poofters* (1979). Duncan and her collaborators intended the film as an exploration of the history, legal status and contemporary experience of homosexuality in Australia. The film begins with an animated history lesson, reaching back to homosexual oppression in Medieval Europe and charting changes over time, before providing examples of the impacts of homophobia in the present. These early scenes provided the grounding for the film's demands for change. As recalled by editor, Melanie Rodriga, 'We were trying to change the world, but in order to do that, you had to know what the world was like' (Queer Screen 2018).

Witches, Faggots, Dykes and Poofters charts the events of the 1978 Gay Mardi Gras, a pivotal moment in the nation's queer activist history. By 1978, many activists were becoming frustrated by the slow progress of their movement, which had begun vibrantly at the start of the decade, but which eight years later seemed not to be achieving its aims. A key frustration was the seeming resistance of the gay social scene to participation in the activist movement. One

CAMP activist, Ron Austin, having been inspired by images of an American pride parade while watching *Word Is Out* at the Paris, decided that a similarly celebratory event had the potential to draw Sydney bargoers onto the streets in a visible act of pride and rebellion. Fellow activist Marg McMann dubbed Austin's idea 'a Mardi Gras' and the event was added to the programme of an International Day of Gay Solidarity being held on 24 June, the anniversary of the New York Stonewall Riots.

Arriving at the event, Duncan was unaware that she and her collaborators were about to record a pivotal piece of history: 'We thought we should go to the Mardi Gras when it was on because we might like to get some colourful footage to brighten up what we thought was an increasingly dull programme.... What we ended up with was not very colourful, but very, very aggressive and sad and violent footage' (Queer Screen 2018). Although organizers, including gay liberation activist Lance Gowland, had ensured the event had necessary permits, police shut the Mardi Gras down and instructed participants to disperse. Police then violently arrested more than fifty people, dragging them back to the Darlinghurst Police Station, where several arrestees were bashed in the cells.

Having captured images of the riot, Duncan followed up by filming activist meetings and events over the next several days, where responses to police actions were debated and planned. With editor Rodriga, Duncan combined the footage into a documentary that now stands as an extraordinary record of critical moments in the city's queer activist history. Film critic Gabrielle O'Brien (2019) later noted that the act of 'recording the marches, arrests and meetings is also an act of defiant refusal – a refusal to be ignored, a refusal to be stereotyped – but, most of all, it is a material commitment to the preservation of visibility'. In *Witches, Faggots, Dykes and Poofters*, a lesbian activist collective utilized the camera as a mechanism of liberation.

Reviewing the film in *Campaign*, Dave P. Sargent (1980) highlighted the capacity of queer-made films to counter the harmful portrayals of homosexuality created by heterosexual people. Sargent criticized the mainstream media for portraying Mardi Gras as 'roving packs of "lezzos and poofters", dancing in the streets with a terminal case of Saturday night fever' (30). In contrast, he argued, the One-in-Seven Collective's film 'finally captures in filmic form the homosexual point of view, and exposes the significant issues which made lesbians and male homosexuals "angry" and vocal'. Similarly, gay liberationist and Mardi Gras co-organizer Ken Davis (1980) celebrated the activist potential of films such as this, declaring it, 'One of the best endeavours yet by the Australian lesbian/gay liberation movement . . . a valuable addition to our arsenal, a very worthwhile contribution to the fight' (34).

Conclusion

The engagement with cinema by lesbian and gay activists in the 1970s largely set the terms by which LGBTQ+ people have continued to analyse and debate their representation on screen, framing how Australian audiences respond both to queer themes and characters in information and entertainment. It provided the framework that has governed many subsequent political responses to screen media in the longue durée: that queer on-screen representation and visibility are perceived as necessary and vital to the well-being of the queer community, to political and social change and to individual members. More significantly, perhaps, it provided the groundwork for the alternative emphasis in response, being that positive and realistic are even more important than visibility per se. Film after film has sparked often angry debates over whether its representation of homosexual lives should be seen as positive or negative.

Importantly, however, many of the criteria for assessment of a film's worth have changed markedly over time. Calls for greater racial diversity in queer films, for example, have become increasingly prominent. Although the 1970s gay liberation movement saw itself as anti-racist, the dominant whiteness of much queer cinema was rarely if ever criticized. Similarly, contemporary LGBTQ+ critiques of cinema are far more likely to demand diversity in terms of bodily ability, neurodiversity, and non-binary gender identity today than in previous decades. In essence, while 1970s activists sought increased representation for lesbian and gay people in reaction to homophobic oppression, over time the need to address marginalization and discrimination within LGBTQ+ communities has become a key focus in the relationship between activism and screen representation among newer queer generations.

Part Two

Australian Queer Film Production

Motivation and Impact among LGBTQ+ Screen Stakeholders

Introduction

To understand the field of Australian queer screen requires going beyond analysing what we actually see on the screens to include understanding the context of production. This is to place queer screen studies as a further component in the (simplified) communication cycle of production-text-audience. One aspect of this is to make sense of how those involved in the creation of Australian queer screen texts – from directors and screenwriters to producers and actors – understand and value their impact on audiences, what motivates them to produce works with queer themes, stories and characters, and what inspires engaging in a struggle for funding and support in periods in which it has been difficult to obtain for queer texts.

Much existing scholarship exploring how filmmakers perceive their own desire and motivation to have an impact on audiences and society is focused on documentary television and filmmaking related to bringing social issues to light (e.g. Aguayo 2019, van der Naald 2015). Creative artists in general are, arguably, just as much motivated by a sense of impact, social change or desire to help others, although this is often not an aspect discussed in either scholarship or public discourse about screen creativity, with the exception perhaps of some work relevant to marginalized or minority communities (Couldry and Dreher 2007). Indeed, it is more typical that public sphere discourse investigates the motivation of a creative producer when their work generates debate or controversy (Nestingen 2011).

Conversely, entertainment films made for LGBTQ+, queer and intersectional community audiences are somewhat more often represented in public discourse as having been at least partly motivated by a utility beyond pure entertainment or storytelling. Such interest acknowledges that queer storytelling may be motivated for the purposes of encouraging social change and inclusivity for minorities (Richards 2019, Papanikolaou 2008). While it is the case that no text can predict social impact and all texts are available to be 'read' diversely for their propensity for social change or their unintended uses (Radway 1984), there is value in actually asking what creative producers think about their text, how much of their stories, art form or creativity is deliberately motivated for impact, and what kind of impact they are thinking about.

Understanding the motivation of producers, directors, writers, funding personnel and screen actors (which we refer to in this book as screen 'stakeholders') who create works for or about LGBTQ+ people is important, since such texts have now long been recognized as having an important role in the lives of minorities, either producing dignity through enabling the reflection of the self or by providing resources, guidance and a sense of belonging for those who are otherwise isolated from face-to-face engagement with similar others (Cover 2000). Creative texts about queer people bind audiences as cultural communities (McKinnon 2016), and they are perceived as enabling social change among mainstream audiences by resourcing practices of tolerance and acceptance of minorities (Snider 2016, Hart 2016). Although entertainment cinema and television have, of course, an intrinsic value grounded in gratifying taste and pleasure in entertainment, as well as sometimes artistic or aesthetic value (McKee 2016), we need to understand better the *tendency* described in public discourse for screen stakeholders to assert their motivations for creating queer content.

This chapter draws on work undertaken in the *AusQueerScreen* study we described in the introduction. Among its activities, the study interviewed Australian queer screen stakeholders to ask what motivated their interest in creating their texts, and to consider some of the ways in which obstacles may have created a struggle to fulfil those motivations. All of the screen stakeholders interviewed in the project spoke openly of their wishes to make an impact on audiences, often emphasizing a pedagogical component for young queer audiences and a contribution to greater tolerance or acceptance among mainstream audiences. Here, we present an analysis of three of the core ways in which screen stakeholders expressed their sense and understanding of impact beyond 'only' telling stories: (a) as filling a representation gap often with a sense that without these texts queer people were relatively invisible on Australian screen; (b) through a perception that their role in creating films and television with LGBTQ+ content was a form of 'education' aimed at benefiting minority young people; and (c) in terms of understanding their texts as contributing to social change in Australia, including promoting wider acceptance of LGBTQ+ communities and individuals. A key finding from the study was that screen media with queer themes, characters and stories was most often perceived as playing a role *connected with but exceeding* entertainment itself.

Thinking the production side

Queer screen scholarship has not often addressed or studied the views among producers, directors, actors or other members of film and television creative teams. There are a few reasons for this – including the reduced ease with which minority screen studies research is funded to the level necessary to conduct that kind of empirical work – although we might also say that at the heart of it is the genealogy of queer scholarship. Much of the earlier work in queer screen scholarship was highly focused on representation and textual analysis, particularly that of Vito Russo (1981), Larry Gross (1991, 2001), Richard Dyer (1993) and Keith Howes (1993). The focus of much of these early works was both scholarly and activist: pointing to readings of representation of queer peoples within a media framework that, at the time, still often marginalized and censored alternative genders and sexualities, and that in highlighting representation and visibility it was possible to drive further inclusion.

Resulting from that genealogy, the bulk of literature on gender- and sexuality-diverse subjects, characters, and narratives in film and television has focused primarily on the work of reading particular screen texts and, at times, the socio-legal circumstances through which visibility and representation are able to be read, particularly within senses of invisibility and censorship. That has been somewhat detrimental to queer screen studies because the absence of research interrogating creative processes and practices leaves the field narrowed into interpretative analyses. Although there is a little more study of audiences and reception, this too is only very nascent in scholarship, as we discuss in the later chapters dealing with Australian queer screen audiences.

One way in which to make sense of creative practices, as the *AusQueerScreen* study endeavoured to do, is to ask screen stakeholders what motivates their work and practice. Motivation, in a psychoanalytic perspective, is actively produced by the *absence* of that which is desired (Fuss 1995), which may include the absence of a social arrangement that is sought, such as tolerance or acceptance of minorities, or an absence of effectiveness of a politics seeking to end hate speech and other forms of violence. Motivation is, however, actively conditioned by the cultural vocabularies made available to us (Hall 1988). In the context of screen stakeholders, we might say that motivation is produced by a desire for some kind of change or to provide support for young minorities when that support has been perceived as unavailable – perhaps through the stakeholder's own personal experience – but is also formed in the context of the ways in which screen personnel are permitted to speak about their creativity and work in the various genres of public speech and interviews. To try to unpack some of the ways in which screen stakeholders think about their motivation, the *AusQueerScreen* study asked a range of questions that sought to put production at the heart of the study of queer texts and thereby enabling ways of reading those texts *differently* in the context of new information about their creators' motivations. Here, we unpack three of those commonly described by the stakeholders interviewed.

We can say that it is broadly felt that screen media created and marketed as entertainment finds its primary value in taste and pleasure in contrast to informational or educational value; that is, the perception that viewing the text provides knowledge for living well. Entertainment is also typically positioned in contrast to texts with an arts-aesthetic value, such as that viewing the text is good for one's soul, subjectivity or being. As Alan McKee (2016) has noted, the perceived value of a screen entertainment text emerges in the capacity to produce pleasure, enjoyment and fun aligned with various taste practices (33). Value itself, however, is discursively produced through linguistic, cultural and conceptual practices that govern how we speak about what is valued (Griffin 2016). This, then, suggests that there is always a potential for a text to be valued otherwise, at the margins of the norm and the intelligible. This is to *queer* the idea of valuing texts according to their genres, forms and marketing. And that, then, opens the need to incorporate a production perspective: asking after the impressions, understandings, and ways of talking about motivations and desired impact among creative producers in order to *expand* the ways in which a text is valued.

Representation and visibility

One of the ways in which the film stakeholders interviewed for this study outlined their sense of value of their film texts was in filling what they saw as a gap in *representation* or *visibility* of LGBTQ+ Australian stories in the cinema. As one filmmaker whose work was prominent from the late 1990s put it in relation to stories about LGBTQ+ peoples and communities: '*Any* representation is, you know, really very important.' Another noted that visibility and representation were significant for those who have not to date seen role models on screen:

> visibility onscreen is important for self-esteem, and I think that because so much of our lives these days are spent looking at screens, I think that then becomes important for everyone. I certainly know the lack of visibility has a corrosive effect on self-esteem.

In this perspective, visible, on-screen representation of characters identifiable as LGBTQ+ is perceived as an important remedy to what has circulated culturally as the harms of LGBTQ+ under-representation. A long-standing discourse in community health has suggested there is value in visibility where it serves as role models for under-represented minorities or helps overcome a sense of isolation (Searle 1997). Among the filmmakers and key stakeholders interviewed in the *AusQueerScreen* study, those who were involved in earlier Australian texts (1990s and early 2000s) to understand increased visibility over time as having social utility in itself, often regardless of the extent to which those representations might be deemed negative, stereotypical or gestural. Such a perspective is, as Griffin (2016) has argued, to equate the political benefits of representation with on-screen accumulation, and the absence of even negative depictions with deprivation (76). The valuation of visibility *per se* was represented among about one-third of the stakeholders interviewed, primarily those who pioneered earlier Australian queer cinema.

Most of the stakeholders noted that the value of visibility and representation was not limited to their own perception, motivation, and goals of their work, but measured often by the extent to which audience members, even years later, had expressed gratitude for making visible minority sexualities and genders with which they identified. This is an important consideration, as it permits the audience members – albeit in a non-measurable way – voice in what constitutes a useful or valuable representation, rather than one assessed by scholarly expertise. As one director put it:

> If I base my response on the number of times people have told me it profoundly affected them and opened up conversations about sexual and cultural identity in a meaningful way.

Visibility was a key lens, then, by which stakeholders understood their own motivation towards creating texts and stories that they intended to have an impact on audiences by contributing to an increase in representation of LGBTQ+ stories, themes or characters. Visibility was thereby a key mechanism by which to value their texts as more than pure entertainment but as that which has social utility.

The critique of visibility-in-itself, alongside the assumption of a profound invisibility of queer screen characters or stories in the past, is something we have discussed and return to regularly in this book. The idea of 'making visible' queer lives on screen is part of a long-sustained discourse that perceives visibility as a political outcome. The origins of the visibility fixation emerge in the earliest of queer screen studies, particularly in Vito Russo's *Celluloid Closet* (1981), where he argued that '[i[nvisibility is the great enemy. It has prevented the truth form being heard]' (244). For Russo, this critique of visibility and social concern about invisibilization led to his valuable research on the subjugation of queer visibilities across much of the twentieth century, based primarily on both censorship and self-censorship regimes in the motion picture industry (121–2). The sustained focus on visibility is arguably the result of gay and lesbian screen studies emerging from the same roots as the 1970s and 1980s gay rights movement, and that the movement for gay rights based its claims at least partly on liberationist articulations of coming out, visibility, and inclusion through recognition of presence. The framing of queer visibility as a core goal of LGBTQ+ screen media discussed by activists and community commentators has remained central to much of the scholarly and public sensibility of the significance of LGBTQ+ representation and was clearly a powerful framework by which the earlier creative stakeholders perceived and discussed their sense of their texts' value.

Among the screen stakeholders whose first works were released during the decade after 2010, there was a considerable contrast in how visibility per se was appreciated. This group was likely to express a somewhat more nuanced view on the significance of visibility, tending to note that visibility mattered most when it was related to the *quality of storytelling*, to positive representations, or to avoiding or combatting problematic older stereotypes. One film director expressed it this way:

> I think it's important for minority audiences to be able to see themselves
> represented and to feel, like, that they're worthy of having a screen story told

about them or a novel written about their experience, for minority audiences to see the shades of diversity within their own minority community.

Much of the later stakeholder discussion of visibility was, therefore, not to posit LGBTQ+ visibility as a utility in itself, but instead to open discourse about more complex questions of diversity, intersectionality and the extent to which different kinds of representation might be important for young queer well-being and others who may identify with such characters (Capsuto 2000). Some international queer screen scholarship has, indeed, begun to articulate an understanding of visibility that has shifted away from claims of an *a priori* value, or that instances of visibility can be meaningfully rated as positive or negative, and opened deeper questions about whether visibility is able to counteract stereotypes that, while positive, do not necessarily eliminate heteronormativity or cisgender norms (Peele 2007). In this respect, the screen stakeholders who were involved in more recent film and television were more likely to reflect the wider cultural shifts in how visibility is valued through complexified understandings of gender and sexuality (Cover 2019).

Entertainment as educational resource

The *AusQueerScreen* interviewees presented a second framework outlining the value of their screen work and the motivation for this work: that it served as a form of cultural education for audiences. To suggest this involved re-positioning the work as not only entertainment or creative storytelling, but as an educational resource particularly for younger audiences. Different from the earlier theme of visibility, the use of a pedagogical discourse framed the value of the stories and characters through their capacity to fill another perceived void – the presence of sexuality and gender diversity in formal educational curriculum. Indeed, many of the film and television production staff interviewed would refer to the absence of quality school curriculum for non-heteronormative and non-cisgender students that has been a matter of controversial debate at times over the past decade in Australia (Cover et al. 2017). The interviews didn't actually ask if any of the screen stakeholders had explored contemporary sexuality education (in any jurisdiction) or if they engaged with educators in the production or distribution of their work. Rather, a combination of their own educational experiences from a generation (or two) earlier alongside the force of public opinion giving rise to assumptions about the need for better gender and sexuality education helped, rightly, frame an altruistic motivation that screen entertainment may fulfil that pedagogical role. None of the screen stakeholders were young enough to have experienced the introduction of Safe Schools curriculum in Australia in the mid-2010s, although some were exposed not only to the debates but also to family members who spoke highly of the expanded curriculum albeit in ways that called for further representation and resourcing in media.

The concept of a cultural pedagogy acknowledges that experiences and opportunities for 'education' are dispersed across institutional and non-institutional settings, through everyday engagement with the environment, via nonauthorized and noninformational sources and through practices of engagement and spectatorship of screen media, including film and television entertainment and digital interactive content. For theorist Henry Giroux (2004), 'Pedagogy, at its best, implies that learning takes place across a spectrum of social practices and settings' (61). The kind of pedagogy that Giroux articulates is conceptualized at the margins of the more formal and familiar frameworks of institutional education, including particularly those that have been transformed negatively by the growth of transactional approaches to education in an era of neoliberalism (Giroux 2010, Duggan 2003). Recognizing, then, that pedagogical practices that operate alongside formal educational settings involves acknowledging the significance of entertainment media as always in itself available to serve pedagogical utilities, and thereby can be perceived as calling on creative artists and other screen production personnel to exercise particular kinds of care when producing works because they may unwittingly be educational. This, of course, is often a framework used by conservative politics to demean screen texts depicting anti-social behaviour, drug use or violence, or – more problematically – by wedge ideologies that complain about the presence of non-traditional or alternative ways of living and being (Fiske 1996). In that sense, the claim to film and televisions' pedagogical nature is often made by those who precede from an anti-queer perspective.

One producer's comments are representative of the views held by the screen media stakeholders interviewed, including those who were active in the 1980s, 1990s and 2000s and currently:

> So many young people tell me that seeing [film name redacted] changed their life because they found some kind of validation in it about their own lives. I'm regularly approached by people who saw it at the start and for whom it was quite

life changing, as well as young people discovering [it] now. . . . It was educational but that was not always in a positive sense, because I was criticized for not always showing lesbians and gay men in only a flattering light but as well-rounded, complex characters. That teaches all the audience something about humanity and the complex lives.

What this statement indicates is a recognition by creative producers and scriptwriters that audiences were active in *utilizing* queer texts in ways which provided guidance on identity formation, decision-making, practices of minority culture and ways of dealing with hostility and adversity in everyday life. Ultimately, to be a producer, director, actor or screenwriter working with gender- and sexuality-diverse content was broadly regarded as having a special kind of responsibility – different from those working with more normativized content – towards LGBTQ+ young audiences.

Significantly, the idea of being a creative producer, scriptwriter, actor or director of Australian screen entertainment media with queer characters involved situating oneself deliberately in an educational role as a result of the topic or content of the work produced. This was expressed on several occasions across the interviews by the repeated use of similar phrases such as 'making a difference in young people's lives'. We can draw on theoretical insights to help us unpack what 'difference' might mean. Since gender- and sexuality-diverse subjects often come to recognize their identities not through familial or institutional relations but through discursive frameworks encountered elsewhere (Butler 1993), the 'matrix' of educational discourses that includes screen and entertainment media is recognized as a core component in the formation of sexual knowledges (Gill 2012) and the formation of stable and healthy minority youth identities (Cover 2019). Catherine Ashcraft (2003) has pointed out that popular culture is a site of struggle in which adolescent sexual identities can either be *reinforced* or *transformed*. In this context, film representation of minority sexualities and genders may, indeed, be more significant than other more formal resources such as sex education in schools (Rasmussen et al. 2016) or peer education in online settings (Clarke, Cover and Aggleton 2018).

In this respect, Australian screen stakeholders saw their role as entailing a cultural pedagogical activity in providing resources to young minorities in ways that implied an educational responsibility:

We don't know if this is the first time some kid has ever seen a trans person, or if they have ever even thought about the possibility that you can transition gender. For someone whose future might be transitioning gender, how we show – positive, sensitive, accuracy [*sic*] – might be one of the most important encounters in their life. But no, there is *no chance* this might cause them to become trans, but encountering it here might means the difference between a life of despair and a life that's relatively okay.

Given the capacity of entertainment media *both* to reinforce social stereotypes of minorities *and* to provide the resources for a critical engagement with those stereotypes (Giroux 2003) for the broader population of their peers, it is notable that what this stakeholder recognized about the act of engaging with their text as an audience member was the significance of what might be an initial 'encounter' with non-normative discourses of gender and sexuality. By understanding queer entertainment texts as performing a pedagogic role, such stakeholders recognized general audiences as having diverse needs but *specific minority audiences* as having particular educational needs from such texts *if* they have few alternative resources for engaging with those texts.

Where screen media has often been recognized as the site of 'inauguration' into alternative and diverse sexual and gender knowledges excluded from other educational, institutional or family settings, our screen stakeholders remarked also on their sense of responsibility towards the health and mental health of their minority viewers whom they considered to be at risk from an extant pedagogical deficit. The idea of a lack of quality often referred back to the persistence of stereotypes. As one Australian actor put it in his interview, it was important both to himself and to the script that the character he was playing did not fall into the cliché of 'struggling' with his sexuality, but was a fully formed, nuanced subject 'who knows he's gay'. The struggle for the actor, he argued, was to avoid what he described as the 'pitfalls' of drawing on 'the cliches and the stereotypes of what that character could have been like'. In that sense, the sense of responsibility involved avoiding an over-representation of the *formation* of a gay male character, whose primary story was not about a struggle with sexuality. It also involved avoiding any implication – whether it was in the script or its rendering on screen – that the character should be seen as endemically vulnerable, depressed or suicidal. To do so would be to reiterate a 'damaging' stereotype that has been sustained in some media since the 1970s, the idea of the gay youth as a vulnerable, suicidal 'sad young man' (Dyer 1993). If the film, acting or characterization was seen to further sustain or circulate that stereotype, the film would be seen to be falling short of the responsibility of a quality cultural pedagogy that must present well-adjusted, non-stereotypical, complex but strong queer characterizations.

In resisting a normative distinction between pure entertainment (screen fiction) and education (pedagogical and well-being resources), Australian queer screen stakeholders thereby recognized the role of film and television to convey not story for its own sake, but stories that are implicated in the constitution and production of healthy identities for young audiences. This is not, of course, to suggest that queer representation has some kind of automatic 'media effect' on its audiences by producing their identities exclusively in the act of encountering them. Rather, such screen pedagogies operate as a cultural formation available to be engaged with by audiences in the context of discourses that make alternative possibilities and practices meaningful. Significant, then, is the way in which the stakeholders interviewed expressed a 'knowingness' of a pedagogical role that is not ordinarily part of the discourse of creative practices (outside documentary) that perceive motivation in storytelling, entertainment or aesthetic frameworks. In some cases, these reflected the known gender and sexual identities of the stakeholders and their own experiences; in other cases, they clearly drew on and incorporated contemporary knowledge frameworks about young people's gender and sexual diversity.

Exposing audiences to stories for social change

The final way in which the screen stakeholders interviewed by the *AusQueerScreen* project described their motivation and sense of impact was framed by wider social impact towards minority tolerance and acceptance. This was articulated through an understanding that the screen texts on which they worked had the capacity to have a positive impact on mainstream (cisgender and straight) audiences (Barber 2010). As Ahmet Atay (2019) has noted, visual storytellers across film and television have been responsible for 'telling straight people the stories about queer people, thereby teaching straight people about human sexuality' (234). These sentiments were often reflected in the description of what motivated screen stakeholders. As with the first motivation, visibility and representation were part of how they perceived impact, but in this case a 'making visible' through storytelling that would be viewed not only by and for the benefit of minority young people but a pedagogy's wider audience of their straight and cisgender peers, families, political leaders and others with social influence. Here, the motivation can be read as one of wishing to open possibilities to contribute to political, social and cultural change by telling stories and providing depictions of LGBTQ+ characters' personal plights, their normativity or evidence of their acceptance by other characters.

In several cases, interviewees indicated that making gender- and sexuality-diverse characters and stories was important not to provide role models or other on-screen representation for minority youth (because, in their view, these groups already had access to LGBTQ+ stories through personal experience, health information, community resources and independent film). Rather, they were interested in making a wider impact through the inclusion of LGBTQ+ characters, themes and narratives in mass-circulation film in ways that increased a mainstream audience's exposure to alternative genders and sexualities. The assumption was typically that increased exposure would lead to greater tolerance and acceptance of gender- and sexuality-diverse people. The concept of exposure was key to how most of the stakeholders argued the case for increasing the representation of LGBTQ+ themes, characters and narratives as a mechanism to reduce anti-tolerant perspectives, a view that has circulated in relation to North American television in particular (Tresca 2016). As one actor who had played an LGBTQ+ character in an Australian film put it:

> the more visibility in whatever way, the better, because people's prejudices are so entrenched until they get a story that takes them past those prejudices. . . . So, we're trying to get to them. They're our target market, they're my target market. I want them to watch because all the stories I want to tell are not popular stories, but if I can get to that market, then there's a chance of actually having an impact in a positive way.

Such a claim understands the link between representation, audience exposure and social change through a lens that relies on the argument, sometimes mythical but noted in literature, that sustained encounters with LGBTQ+ minorities through family, peer networks and workplaces are likely to reduce homophobia and transphobic attitudes (de Boise 2015, Bridges 2014, Oswald et al. 2018). This is to see wide-release film as 'standing in' for those personal relationships that foster a more positive or accepting attitude to gender and sexual minorities.

The idea that tolerance, acceptance or changed views is built upon exposure is, of course, more than simply *seeing* gender and sexual minority characters on-screen (Snider 2016). Rather, it depends on two factors: the way in which they are framed on-screen and the relationship that an audience member can forge that stands 'in place' of a face-to-face knowingness or a peer relationship (Cover 2000). In the context of the specific framing of representation, this took several forms, and stakeholders raised three different approaches to ensuring their characters had positive social impact. The first is related to the distinction between positive and negative representation. As described above, it was primarily the stakeholders who were active before 2010 who expressed a more binary positive/negative representation. Others, however, were more cautious about the extent to which 'inclusion' was enough, and outlined the care necessary to do this well to avoid a backlash for a 'lip-service gesture' or rejection by audiences angered by the presence of minorities. As one high-profile filmmaker put it:

> What I do is try, through storytelling, to impact on an audience, try to affect an audience, try to engage, stimulate, provoke people who are, you know, who choose to watch the work. And so, of course, to do that you have to have touchpoints, and you have to have the skill to then make those touchpoints work as *drama*, you know, work dramatically.

This indicated the need for impactful storytelling to go beyond assumptions that LGBTQ+ characters could be represented either positively or negatively. That is, earlier screenwriters and directors were able to differentiate between what was sometimes described as a 'sympathetic' portrayal versus a 'stereotype', or incorrectly assumed that even a camp stereotype that may be offensive necessarily sustains intolerance (McKinnon 2016: 89), which is to perceive audiences as unable to engage critically. Whereas, later stakeholders were better able to recognize that social impact came not from *inclusion* but *incorporation* into storylines, thereby overcoming the difficulty of the asexual gay character with little relevance to plot (Cover 2000).

The second related to ensuring the nuance and universality of characters by ensuring that they had, as one director described it, 'a lot of layers' and 'as much depth and conviction to them as anybody else'. One screenwriter noted that this was not always acceptable to a wider industry in Australia, which sometimes rejected more nuanced LGBTQ+ characters in favour of a more simplified or stereotyped assessment of diversity:

> people in positions of power who can greenlight or kill a film have their own concept of what diversity is, and they come to that from their own oftentimes non-diverse backgrounds And so it can mean sometimes that you get a feeling – and I had this in some script discussion – you get a feeling that your representation of what gay is, is 'the wrong kind of gay.'

The argument here is that sometimes the experience of screenwriters, directors and filmmakers is at odds with the perception of diversity and thereby on the kind of social impact it might have, particularly where it has been assumed that audiences may not appreciate or accept a complex, diverse or nuanced character. The contrary viewpoint was put forward by one screenwriter who stated the following:

> I think visibility is important for people outside of that [LGBTQ+] community
> – to see the rich lives that people can lead, that are different, that touch upon
> things that are universal, irrespective of what community that you feel a part of.

The idea that a depth of character, a nuanced approach, and yet the universality of stories of struggle is understood here as the key to providing a depiction that *ought* to play an impactful role in social change among wider audiences. At the same time, intersectionality was perceived as an important aspect of providing depth and nuance to characters, including particularly LGBTQ+ characters and experiences that are not grounded in white, male, cisgender experiences but are the experiences of those from other minority cultural communities, including Asian-Australian and Greek-Australian communities.

Finally, the third way in which this approach to motivation-towards-impact was discussed by screen stakeholders related to the extent to which LGBTQ+ characters could be represented not as 'issue' (where gender or sexuality was their purpose in the narrative) but as 'backdrop' (being non-cisgender or non-heterosexual as an *ordinary* part of everydayness). We address this further in Chapter 12 when we consider the well-being value of LGBTQ+ characters presented not as 'special issue' but as part of the ordinary everyday. Here, however, it is significant to see some of the ways in which screen stakeholders perceive the shift in focus away from telling stories of LGBTQ+ individual struggle towards texts that place a queer character into the everyday fabric of Australian society. The value of a text for impact on its audience, then, was to include LGBTQ+ characters without suggesting that they were engaged in an identity struggle, experiencing vulnerability or aggression, marginalized by the communities of other characters, persistently having to fight for acceptance and belonging or only finding belonging in niche queer communities. Rather than depicting minority sexuality or gender as the 'obstacle' over which a character must struggle as the core of the plot, it is to present gender and sexual diversity as a normative framework of Australian contemporary society. This, again, allows the presentation of an ordinariness or resilience among LGBTQ+ characters, rather than as victims of vulnerability, poor mental health or assumptions of suicidality – the tendency in Australian film and television to include suicide as a core aspect of gay male experience notwithstanding (Cover 2021). One screenwriter framed his questions over how to ensure impactful queer characterizations this way:

> And then in the end I decided or started to think about a world where all the characters were gay and that the story did not hinge upon their sexuality but I wanted ways in which their sexuality coloured the story. And that for me felt really right and natural.

Although yet to be fleshed out in scholarly literature on queer screen media, a 'just because gay' has been identified as a mechanism for framing diverse representation in young adult literature (Bittner 2016). While arguably most representations of gender- and sexuality-diverse characters in Australian films places them in a setting in which identity is the key struggle, there is a recent shift to reflect the ordinariness of LGBTQ+ lives, and this was increasingly recognized by stakeholders as a key way in which to have a positive impact on mainstream Australian audiences.

Conclusion

Even when screen production interviewees describe their motivations for participating in the creation of queer texts in the context of desired impact, motivation itself is – like experience – broadly unknowable and indescribable. That is because the act of describing the motivation for a past action or experience is conditioned by the context, which in this case is research deliberately seeking to understand and asking questions about the relationship between motivation, impact and creativity in queer screen media. Nevertheless, what is clear in unpacking screen stakeholders' commentary is that queer production involves motivations that are beyond the widely perceived association of screen entertainment with commercial goals. While commercial success actually enabled the expansion of LGBTQ+ screen representation both international and in Australia from the late 1980s (Wolf and Kielwasser 1991), the act of being involved in a queer creative project is typically reflected upon as serving additional purposes for impact on audiences in ways that motivate the desire to see the creative outcome.

We have described in this chapter three of the dominant ways in which Australian screen stakeholders spoke about what motivated them through the lens of their stated intention for their texts to have some kind of impact on individuals, audiences and Australian society. Stakeholders who were involved in earlier texts focused on questions of representation and understood their work's significance in making visible minorities who they felt were otherwise broadly invisibilized on Australian screens, whereas other stakeholders discussed their motivation towards audience impact through a pedagogical lens in providing resources and narratives seen to benefit younger LGBTQ+ audience members as forms of education and information, as much as entertainment. Finally, most stakeholders discussed the way in which their texts were understood to have an impact on a wider, mainstream audience by exposing them to characters and stories that were ostensibly representative of gender and sexually diversity. In this last framework, stakeholders regularly expressed the need to be careful to avoid over-simplification, despite funders' understandings of audience desires, and stakeholders who became active more recently tended to opt for more intersectional characterizations and more depiction of characters whose minority status was immaterial to the plot.

What is notable about entertainment texts produced for or about LGBTQ+ communities in Australia, then, is the way in which those involved in their production actively value, perceive and encourage LGBTQ+ representation as having social impact, either on minority or wider audience communities in terms of representation, education and social change rather than individualized taste practices and entertainment for its own sake. This, again, is not to argue that there is an ethical imperative for any producer – whether of a generic film topic or an LGBTQ-themed work – to impute added 'value', since such a claim is merely to reproduce a now-outdated 'high art' versus 'popular culture' dichotomy (Storey 1993, McKee 2016) that tells us little about production processes and motivations in the twenty-first century. Rather, it is to point to the ways in which the 'orientation' of a text towards or about a minority community presents a context in which stakeholders value films differently and are encouraged to see their texts as having value beyond entertainment.

6

The Australian Queer Film Festival

Introduction

The queer film festival has always been an integral player in the development of queer art, culture and politics. The purpose of these festivals is twofold. First, they provide a form of exhibition for films that would otherwise struggle to secure a theatrical release. Second, they provide the space for LGBTQ+ audience members to watch these films in a safe place. The development of queer cinema from its underground, experimental roots to a major component in art house cinema has been propelled by the increased professionalism of the queer film festival. These festivals must serve the queer community and promote social empowerment while remaining financially viable (Richards 2016, Rich 2013). This arduous journey from being an informal event to a professional organization continues to be a challenging one for many arts organizations given the precarious nature of funding in Australia's creative industries. In providing this important exhibition space, the Australian queer film festival developed a powerful node by which to challenge the dominance of a heteronormative screen culture in Australia.

As a space of promotion, spectatorship and audience exchange, the film festival plays a significant and ongoing role in queer screen sociality and is a core part of the 'production' regime of queer screen culture in Australia, partly as a site for distribution and viewership of a broad range of queer representation, and partly as a setting for the promotion, discussion and appreciation of Australian queer screen texts. This chapter begins by outlining the cultural role of the film festival before describing the early queer film festivals in Australia. We then turn to the professionalization of the festival circuit – an alignment of queer community institutions with strategic management practices that occurred alongside a range of other community institutions in the early 2000s (Cover 2024a). We then turn to the histories of some of Australia's core film festivals and the ways in which they have become globally recognized as part of Australia's contribution to queer screen culture.

What is a film festival?

While there have been many queer film screenings throughout Australia's history, not all have operated in the recognizable context of being a film festival. Marijke De Valck (2007) defines a film festival as a temporary event of limited duration where films are exhibited in 'an atmosphere of heightened expectation and festivity' (27). This connection of film exhibition to heightened expectation and festivity draws upon the very origins of the term festival. Alessandro Falassi (1987) famously defined the contemporary usages of the term 'festival' as either a sacred time of celebration, the annual celebration of a famous person or the harvesting of a particular product, a cultural event featuring a defined array of works, and finally a fair or event of gaiety and conviviality amongst a community of people. In defining the parameters of the film festival, Marijke De Valck (2016) identifies several factors. First, the *size* of the event, in terms of films screened or audience members, is generally higher than outside of the festival time. This isn't to say that larger festivals are better, but that the congregation of a particular community in the audience and the types of films screened are considered greater than what occurs outside of the designated period. Second, festivals are often discussed in terms of *outreach*, where they are considered cosmopolitan events simultaneously local and global (Nichols 1994). Third, film festivals provide *access* to films that are otherwise unavailable at that moment in time. Some festivals premiere major films as well as screening films that would otherwise struggle to be exhibited. The film festival provides the exclusive space for the exhibition of films in a space of heightened appreciation for a community of audience members that are invested in the success of cinema.

Festivals magnify the sense of community in a moment in time. 'A festival does not build communities', writes Anna Reece (2020: 110) 'it is communities that build a festival'. That is, festivals do more than showcase film productions but actively cohere otherwise atomize audience members into in instance of cultural commonality and exchange (Rastegar 2012). Film festivals are notable for the ways in which attendance produces an embodied practice of mutual viewership, with several scholars noting how the space of viewership interpellates flow and engagement between bodies in a physical albeit temporary setting (Dickson 2015, Harbord 2009). For Harbord, this is a 'dance' between the past of the recorded film and the present screening of this film. Here, the audience can affect the subjectivity of the film and the festival at large. This communal component of the film festival, where the audience is heightened, is key to the corporeality of film festival attendance.

In connecting this corporeality to the queer film festival, these events are, at their very core, *festive*. They are a celebration of the queer community. Writing on the history of the European film festival, Thomas Elsaesser (2005) argues that the audience functions as a self-celebration of community and a utopian forum in which community members perform a certain kind of sovereignty over the space and the practice of spectatorship. For Elsaesser, festivals are thereby operational only in the context of a physical presence in a space, generating cultural practices beyond the spectatorial component, such as the parties, the consumption of alcohol, and what he suggests is a sometimes unruly spirit carnival.

In connecting this conceptualization of the film festival to the queer community, then, queer film festivals notably occur often during otherwise festive times of the year, such as pride months, and broader LGBTQ+ festivals typically include several parties that celebrate particular communities within the broader queer spectrum. In analysing this space of the queer film festival, Richards (2016) has argued that these events have the potential to create a queer counter-public, where they not only challenge a heteronormative and cisgender hegemony of space but also a homonormative one. Often, many films programmed at the queer film festival invite marginalized communities within the broader LGBTQ+ framework to congregate and find forms of empowerment in a culture of pride that too often privileges cisnormativity, whiteness and masculinity. As such, in analysing the history of Australian queer film festivals, it is imperative to acknowledge these queer politics as being at the centre of much of their development.

Early Australian queer film festivals

If we define a film festival as an event that covers a limited period of multiple screenings and that involves a heightened sense of community, then we can trace the queer film festival in Australia back to the events held by early gay liberation clubs on university campuses and the screenings held by the early film co-operatives in Melbourne and Sydney. For instance, the Melbourne Gay Liberation Film Society held film screenings in 1974 and 1975 at the Gay Liberation Film Centre. In 1974, several films on gay liberation, such as *Fortune and Men's Eyes* (1971), were screened. In September 1975, the films that were screened included *The Mad King of Bavaria* (1972) and Curtis Harrington shorts, such as *Picnic* (1948) and *Children of Hiroshima* (1952). University collectives also held smaller, one-off festivals. The Melbourne University Gay Society (GaySoc) held a Festival of Gay Films in 1977, which screened several queer films, including *Sunday, Bloody Sunday* (1971) and *Les Biches* (1968). As Richards (2016) has noted, these early screening events were directly associated with activist networks. Likewise, writing on the history of the Australian film co-operatives we discuss below, John Hughes (2015) has noted that 'these social upheavals and ideological ruptures also played out in the interpersonal politics of the co-ops, and the lives of the people involved' (5). This was common for many early queer film festivals of this era. In San Francisco, for instance, the early years of the San Francisco Frameline International LGBTQ Film Festival, many of the experimental filmmakers that put on the event also worked in Harvey Milk's camera store and circulated in his political community.

This connection between film culture and politics wasn't always the case; however, there was an initial divide within the leading gay and lesbian activist group across Australia in the 1970s, Campaign Against Moral Persecution Inc (CAMP Inc), the key members of which actively debated whether or not art and cinema were a legitimate means to fight homophobic cultures (Peach 2005). Writing in the publication *CAMP Ink* in 1974, Anton Veenstra and Rod Byatt (1974) advocate for culture and politics to not be seen as two separate entities, as there were thoughts that saw the fight for political freedom *above* the decadence of bourgeois art:

> Obviously Gay lib has made a determined effort . . . to class Art and Culture as 'anti-revolutionary' . . . Given that Gay liberation has at last achieved recognition by the Australian left, one wonders how quickly (if at all?) the organization will assimilate standard socialist and Marxist concepts in Arts and Culture. (19–20)

This push to consider gay liberation as a form of cultural liberation was instrumental in Mardi Gras utilizing film to change social mores in preference to promoting extant film culture per se. This mindset informed the work of Ubu and the later Sydney Filmmakers' Co-op, which championed the development of independent and experimental film in Australia. In his thesis, Peach (2005) interviewed Gayle Lake, director of the Sydney Film Festival from 1998 to 2004, who also worked for the Co-op in the early 1980s and recalled that much filmmaking drew upon the societal movements that were happening at the time, whereby independent filmmakers drew on Aboriginal land rights and women's rights movements in framing their alternative production practices.

The co-op would hold its screenings, which, while not film festivals in the traditional sense, required an active form of spectatorship, whereby they intended that audiences were challenged on both an emotional and intellectual level. In 1976, the Sydney Filmmakers Co-op screened what we might describe as the first 'proper' queer film festival in Australia, which was the Festival of Gay Films at the Filmmakers Cinema in Darlinghurst. Films included a variety of Australian texts, including *Adam* (1976) and *Satdee Night* (1973). International films included *Coming Out* (1972) and *Holding* (1970). Many of these networks of activists and filmmakers would go on to develop the queer film festival industry with which we are more familiar today.

The professionalization of the queer film festival circuit

Internationally, the number of queer film festivals was increasing throughout the 1980s and the 1990s. Ragan Rhyne (2007) identified four distinct economic periods of the queer film festival's development. First, from 1977 to 1990, we saw the transition from informal screenings to professionalized non-profit screenings. Following this, from 1991 to 1996, we see the increasing association with corporate sponsors, through which audiences were re-positioned as target demographics and markets, transforming the concept of the festival through the conceptual frameworks of neoliberalism and industry. Third, from 1997 to 2001, the queer film festival circuit expanded into newer territories globally; finally, from 2001 onwards, we witness the rise of alternative distribution networks, including streaming, that provided newer avenues for queer representation.

The growth of the circuit of queer film festivals coincides with Skadi Loist's (2013) model of global expansion. The first ongoing queer film festival was in 1977 with San Francisco's Frameline International LGBTQ Film Festival, then called 'Persistence of Vision'. Following this successful series of screenings, festivals occurred in New York City (1979), Chicago (1981), Los Angeles (1982),

Pittsburgh (1982) and Boston (1984). In these early years, Loist identifies several developments in Europe, such as Yugoslavia (now Slovenia) in 1984, then Western Europe with Berlin (1985), London (1986), Milan (1986), Amsterdam (1986), Copenhagen (1986), Turin (1986) and Brussels (1987). In light of Rhyne's second phase, where these events become increasingly commercialized, Loist (2013) identifies the increasing success of the aforementioned festivals, and more occurring in Europe, such as Paris (1989), Hamburg (1990), Oslo (1991), Dublin (1992), Glasgow (1993), Vienna (1994), Barcelona (1995), Madrid (1996) and Amsterdam (1996). This period also saw the birth of *standalone*, ongoing queer film festivals in Australia, with Melbourne in 1991 and Sydney in 1993. Rhyne's third phase also saw the proliferation of queer film festivals in East Asia. While Tokyo and Hong Kong both had festivals in the early 1990s, Seoul and Bangkok both began in 1998, followed by Osaka (2005), Tokyo (2007), Phnom Penh (2010), Delhi (2007), Bangalore (2009) and Mumbai (2010).

Some of these festivals had difficulties with local authorities and religious groups, such as the Q! Film Festival in Indonesia, beginning in 2002, which faced the hurdle of holding queer film events in certain regions where homosexuality was prosecuted under local Muslim sharia law. Nevertheless, Rhyne's final phase of global queer film festivals saw the further expansion of events in Eastern Europe, Russia and Latin America. Events such as those held in St Petersburg (2008) and Bosnia-Herzegovina (2008) faced violent opposition. Key to Loist's (2013) argument is that these global developments should not be read as a form of Americanization and homogenization of the queer film festival. Rather, although many festivals adopted Western notions of sexuality and gender identity, they embraced national forms of capitalism and identity but also explicitly local norms of gender and sexuality. As such, with this global development in mind, the queer film festivals that began in Australia, both Melbourne and Sydney, occurred within a global expansion of queer film events, where such festivals adopted the queer label comparatively earlier than their international counterparts due to the activist nature of the programme directors at the helm.

The festivals in Melbourne and Sydney both lead the way for queer film festival culture in Australia. The professionalization of these festivals is shaped by several factors. First, and more broadly, the funding of arts organizations throughout the 1990s and 2000s was shaped by a transition from a more traditional cultural policy of supportive grants to one that adopted a creative industries logic within neoliberal frameworks of investment, return and sustainability (Richards 2016).

The queer film festivals in Melbourne and Sydney began as primarily community-oriented events. In the original framework, community art was associated with self-expression rather than the production of an arts culture, that is separation everyday artistic creativity was understood as separate from the more authorized and legitimated high arts; community arts were seen as beneficial for community and individual well-being without necessarily abiding by a need to contribute economic growth (Hawkins 1993). This early framework of support sustained the development of Australia's queer film festivals, although eventually they were subject to the kind of policy change that sought to collapse the distinction between community and other artistic production and institutions. Where community art was once focused on social inclusion and the development of self-expression in contrast to traditional, conservative framing of art and culture, policy levers were used in ways that sought to breakdown this distinction such that all practitioners, supporters and facilitators were instead to be understood as cultural 'producers', contributing to all kinds of outputs that were considered to have a market value. As such, the more dominant queer film festivals were caught up in a socio-cultural and political shift that warranted a more professional, strategically managed framework that soon became the norm.

The most significant driver of the professionalization of the key festivals is government policy. Throughout the 1990s, the Australian approach to arts funding transformed as a result of government direction. In 1994, the Australian federal government released the country's first Australian cultural policy, *Creative Nation*. The aim of this policy was to support Australian arts and culture while also promoting its economic potential. As with other forms of neoliberal industrialization of aesthetic and cultural formations, the then government sought to avoid indulging altruism by redefining the meaning of art, first as culture and then as commodity (Bereson 2005). Although queer film festivals in Australia are not directly funded by Commonwealth government agencies, with public funding sourced from a mix of state and local government grant schemes, this push towards a neoliberal logic shaped the dominant film festivals alongside other parts of the arts and culture sector in Australia. By presenting a rationale for how arts and cultural organizations were to be perceived, the Creative Nation policy prompted an investment in the development of audiences as markets, strategic promotion, the generation of revenue and international marketing aligned with tourism in place of the more traditional fundraising mechanisms (Radbourne 1996) and setting the standard that has marked major queer film festivals' activities, orientation and governance since.

Nevertheless, the community-oriented approach that was submerged in form if not practice in the major cities persisted in some queer film events, particularly among the smaller festivals held outside the major capitals. In Adelaide, the Feast Festival began in 1997 and was founded by Helen Bock, Damien Carey, Luke Cutler and Margie Fischer. In several years, it featured a queer film festival within the broader cultural festival. In 2024, this tradition was brought back as the Adelaide Queer Film Festival, curated by Stuart Richards, Jess Pacella and Feast director Tish Naughton. In Western Australia, the Perth Queer Film Festival was founded in 2017 by Mark Reid and Annette Hasluck. Prior to this there was no dedicated queer film festival in Western Australia. There is also the PrideFest Western Australia, which has featured several queer film events over the years. Likewise, the TasPride Festival has had a few film events in their program, but such inclusions have not happened every year. In Queensland, there is the Brisbane Queer Film Festival, which moved to New Farm Cinemas and became the New Farm Queer Film Festival, operating alongside the Gold Coast Queer Film Festival. There are also a number of general pride festivals that include a small number of one-off screenings, such as the Brisbane Pride Festival, the Cairns Pride Festival and the Sunshine Coast Mardi Gras. Similarly, the Darwin Pride Festival includes film as part of their arts program. In 2024, for instance, it screened *Housekeeping for Beginners* (2023), *Strange World* (2022), *The Adventures of Priscilla, Queen of the Desert* (1994) and *Love Lies Bleeding* (2024). Such screenings do not tend to have the commitment to furthering the business of queer filmmaking but rather speak to the community-oriented nature of these events via the functions of social inclusion and empowerment.

Several local and regional festivals are held throughout Australia. Some have been short-lived, one-off events or the results of major urban festivals 'touring' in the region. One such festival is the Queer Fruits Film Festival, organized by Tropical Fruits, an LGBTQ+ community group in the Northern Rivers region in New South Wales. The festival was established in 2009 and, although no longer running, Tropical Fruits is still involved in supporting film events in the region. This festival is considered broadly regional in that it is not a subsidiary of an urban organization but produced solely by locals. According to founding festival director Akkadia Ford (2017), this distinction may be a subtle one but is nevertheless important because it speaks to the ways in which regional festivals cater to substantially different audience demographics in often lower socio-economic settings. The responsibility of a rural queer film festival, Ford (2014) elsewhere writes, is to bridge the LGBTQ+ and wider community beyond a 'metronormative' lens, a term she borrows from Jack Halberstam (2005) to describe a particular framing of LGBTQ+ consumerism and a perception of LGBTQ+ individuals' means. Likewise, the Bendigo Queer Film Festival (BQFF) and the Geelong Pride Film Festival (GPFF) are supported by the Victorian government to support the well-being of regional LGBTQ+ people. As Benson (2020: 353) has noted, such festivals are funded in order to support local communities and to develop further, creating capital, mentoring and support for emerging creative artists outside of the capitals. In that respect, while there has been a substantial professionalization of many of the main Australian queer film festivals through alignment with strategic management discourses and adoption of contemporary marketing practices, more radical, alternative and community-focused events persist, albeit in regional settings.

The Melbourne Queer Film Festival

The first Melbourne Queer Film Festival (MQFF) was held in 1991 as part of Midsumma and was funded through a mix of commercial sponsorship and state funding through Film Victoria's community engagement grants. The primary purpose of the queer film festival was to provide content that was otherwise unavailable. For instance, even in 1994, the festival was not programming popular films, such as *Philadelphia* (1994), but rather films that weren't receiving a wide theatrical release. This funding positioned the festival initially as a community arts event, perceived as playing a substantial role in a city's creative ecosystem (Mulligan and Smith 2011, Ho 2012, Gibson et al. 2012). Madeline Swain was appointed in 1993 on a part-time basis as the festival director, alongside the formation of an advisory board to give the kind of legitimacy to which other organizations were responding in the journey towards greater professionalization. However, the board composition also responded to the community orientation and origins by incorporating queer elders who enabled a continuation of some aspects of the more radical roots of the festival (Richards 2016). In this respect, it is notable that the festival was the first in the world to adopt the then-politicized label 'queer', replacing the limiting term 'gay and lesbian'.

This shift to a professionalized industry is marked by the broader adoption of creative industries logic, where cultural value is driven by an economic agenda (Galloway and Dunlop 2007). Such a cultural policy shift away from the traditional emphasis on social and cultural capital rather than economic value creates cultural regimes of value (Frow 1995). Here, discourses of value are ascribed to 'high culture' in ways that reinforce the distinction between aesthetic and economic discourses, establishing competing ways in which communities, audiences and funders mark value, status and achievement. In this context, what is witnessed is a framework in which the non-economic, aesthetic value of the queer film festival experience is transformed into the key marker of status, feeding back into the economically beneficial output for stakeholders (Richards 2016). Here, this shift sees queer film festivals become events that have an impact on the creative branding of their cities. This neoliberal approach to the arts economy, however, places greater responsibility on organizations to become financially sustainable and less reliant on public funding. For sponsors of these organizations, particularly throughout the rise of the concomitant the 'pink dollar economy' in the late-1990s, the objective was to replace social altruism with new innovative approaches to exposure and profit (Richards 2016).

MQFF and Queer Screen in Sydney developed in this environment that promoted this turn to industry. MQFF's board of 'queer elders', for instance, was replaced with board members from the corporate sector that would professionally steer the organization (Richards 2016). This also shaped the reciprocal nature of funding from local councils. For instance, for some time, MQFF's main source of funding was under the City of Melbourne local council Triennial Arts Grant, the aim of which was to contribute to the branding of Melbourne as a creative city. This was, according to one former city councillor, due to the lack of state government support with the city council stepping in to ensure the MQFF was funded for sustainable existence into the future (Richards 2016).

Following from this, MQFF now receives funding support from both VicScreen and the Victorian State Government. This shift to multi-year funding was significant because, according to Jane Crawley, former manager of the City of Melbourne's Arts and Culture portfolio, festivals in the small-medium sector were unable to be funded by the Victorian State Government in the late 1990s and early 2000s because, at the time, the Arts Victoria agencies did not see screen as falling under the banner of arts, while Film Victoria primarily funded the competing Melbourne International Film Festival and the St Kilda Film Festival (Richards 2016). The result of this form of support, where arts organizations are key to a city's creative identity, sees the rise of 'arts-as-industry'. In that respect, although MQFF remains a key community event, it is one firmly grounded in the neoliberal logic (Duggan 2003) of commodification of arts and culture in ways that even more actively eschews the radical and alternative origins of queer film screening. It thus serves an important need in making texts available, but does so within the limitations of professionalized strategic intent in ways that are not always palatable to the queerness of queer community.

Queer Screen, Sydney

As with the Melbourne Queer Film Festival's original association with the annual Midsumma community festival, Queer Screen began as a subsidiary of the Sydney Gay and Lesbian Mardi Gras. The first festival under the banner of the Mardi Gras was in 1980, where a programme called 'Sexuality in Film' featured films including the Australian film *Farewell to Charms* (1979) and the American *A Comedy in Six Unnatural Acts* (1979). Part of the separation of the two festivals occurred as a result of a significant re-orientation of Mardi Gras when it was moved from June to February to coincide with summer in a way which, arguably, invisibilized some of the historical activist roots of Mardi Gras in favour of its emergence as a festive party (Wotherspoon 1991). The film festival, at the time, however, remained in June which allowed it to retain those political links with the global gay liberation date-markers of Stonewall (Peach 2005). By 1981, however, the film festival had re-aligned with Mardi Gras and was programmed for February. The decriminalization of homosexuality in NSW in 1984 and governmental support via the Australian Film Institute legitimized the queer film festival further. This led to the first-post decriminalization festival in 1985, 'The Gay Festival', held at the Chauvel and opened by popular drag queen Doris Fish. Over the subsequent years, the 'Gay Film Week' as it came to be called, grew in popularity as it continued to be supported by both the Australian Film Institute and Mardi Gras. By the late 1980s, the AFI's funding during this period, as with the early framework of MQFF, served a social inclusion and altruistic cause, with value understood to be for the benefit LGBTQ+ audiences and not yet aligning with marketing towards a wider, urban cosmopolitan audience.

By 1992, the Gay and Lesbian Film Week changed its name to the National Gay and Lesbian Film Festival. The festival became an independent organization in 1993 with a localized focus on Sydney. Queer Screen was born out of a debate between the Mardi Gras and the Academy Twin Cinemas: Mardi Gras feared that the Academy's direction would overtly commercialize queer cinema, while others resented Mardi Gras for dictating what was and was not classified as gay and lesbian film texts. Queer Screen was run in September and functioned as an alternative film festival to the more commercial films screened as part of the Sydney Gay and Lesbian Film Festival. Speaking to *Filmnews* at the time, festival director Denise Robinson said that providing a critical context for these films was important, where audiences could gather to discuss the films within the contemporary context of an emerging queer theory. 'The whole area of Queer Theory and Queer Cinema is fairly hotly contested' (Luby 1993: 5).

From this point until 2001, Mardi Gras was the principal funding body of Queer Screen. With the dissolving of the Sydney Gay and Lesbian Mardi Gras and the formation of the new Mardi Gras in 2002, Queer Screen lost its existing funding arrangement and turned to sponsorship and corporate partners. The organization became a leading player in queer film in Australia, programming QueerDOC, which for several years was the only queer documentary festival in the world. The festival also hosts My Queer Career, a short film competition designed to assist with the funding of local production. Both QueerDOC and My Queer Career are now part of the ongoing Mardi Gras Film Festival.

Queer Screen has several further initiatives to support Australian filmmakers, such as the Queer Screen Completion Fund, which has raised $162,000 since 2016, and the Queer Screen Pitch Off, which has raised $60,000 since 2018. In 2023 and in 2024, Queer Screen was invited to participate in the prestigious Goes to Cannes program at the Marché du Film, which runs alongside the Cannes Film Festival each year. This makes Queer Screen the only Australian and queer film festival to participate in the program. The Goes to Cannes program offers festival to showcase a selection of five original works-in-progress that are looking for sales agents, distributors or festival selection.

Conclusion

The strength of the queer film festival scene in Australia, as well as the increase in queer films exhibited in generalized film festivals, has seen a wider audience available now for Australian queer films. For instance, there are several notable examples of films that were programmed at both queer and general international film festivals, such as *52 Tuesdays* (2014), *Downriver* (2015), *Ellie and Abbie (and Ellie's Dead Aunt)* (2020), *Sequin in a Blue Room* (2019), *Lonesome* (2022) and *Sunflower* (2023). The queer film festival circuit also provides an audience for queer films that would otherwise be unable to reach an audience, such as *Monster Pies* (2013) and *Submerge* (2012). These films benefit from the maturation of the queer film festival. Even films that traverse across both circuits, screenings at queer film festivals allow these films to resonate with queer audiences in queer ways.

As outlined in the above history, the proliferation of Australian queer film festivals in the 1990s and early 2000s coincided with the rise of gay and lesbian segmented marketing. Sender (2004) critiqued this media as superficial, arguing that it evoked the dominance of an all-white predominantly gay male community and the hyper-sexualization of racial minorities. Chasin (2000) likewise argued that a depiction of chaste gay visibility would come at the cost of progressive political interventions. Indeed, this criticism of the increasingly visible gay community is a not a pre-existing one, but something imagined in critiques of the professionalizsation of queer culture in which the representation of the gay man of the late 1990s – such as Will from *Will & Grace* (1998–2006) or the profusion of marketing material aimed at the LGBTQ+ community (Cover 1999), is a heavily desexualized one. Sender argues that when featured in advertisements that were intended to be shown to a wider audience outside of the LGBTQ+ community, gay and lesbian images are desexualized as class and sexual culture become fused. In other words, queer people lose authority and status in a heteronormative society when they are seen to be sexually active subjects. With the rise of this mediated homonormativity, this is a reconfiguration of the ideal neoliberal citizen, who is a 'self-regulating homosexual subject who chooses stable co-habiting relationships' (Richardson 2005: 522). This culture, then, encourages the sexualized others to adopt constraining disciplinarity that obscures the genuine diversity of LGBTQ+ lives to meet neoliberal normativities.

In the context of the queer film festival, this formation's growth coincided with the neoliberal commercialization of queer visibility, where certain types of queer images and stories were 'safer' than others. It also saw an increased production and exploitation of creativity to produce wealth and job creation in ways that utilized queer culture largely for the benefit of corporate cultures, shaping both the drive for increased queer on-screen depiction and events, and de-emphasizing the social activism of such events. For many queer film festivals, this is a shift from being a series of informal screenings to being major arts organization within the matrix of the creative industries in a neoliberal framework.

While acknowledging the reality of the force of neoliberal logics in shaping the present arrangement of film festivals, we argue that the history of queer film festivals in Australia points to the need to retain a focus on their social and cultural value beyond financial metrics. Although neoliberalism retains significant ideological force in Australian politics and everyday community engagement with commodified culture, it remains the case that arts and screen cultures may be the setting in which an increasingly anti-neoliberal perspective is emerging more strongly, whereby a greater appreciation of the social foundations of cultural institutions is growing (O'Connor 2024). That is, while the creative industries promised economic prosperity for those that sought to harness commodified creative outputs, the natural result for film festivals was a consolidation and monopolization of the field, ultimately removing the autonomy that enables more radical, experimental and formative styles of festival that undertook the enabled Australian queer screen media and audiencehood to engage in a setting of social and cultural inclusion and celebrate its radical and alternative origins.

Despite this important critique, Australian queer film festivals do, of course, continue to play an important role in the circulation and exhibition of independent films and screen texts that may not be supported by the hegemony of the dominant North American film industry and distributor networks. However, what is important to ensure is sustained in any future developments – whether they be a consolidation of the neoliberal logic of transactional spectatorship or a backlash in favour of more community- and grassroots-oriented approaches to inclusivity – is the primary function of serving an audience, including particularly those audience members who find an affirmation of identity, a pleasure in community and an entertainment practice in engagement with films and filmmakers.

Part Three

Reading the Australian Queer Text

7

Australian Queer Screen Criticism

Introduction

In this chapter, we consider Australian queer screen histories and cultures through the lens of LGBTQ+ community newsletters and magazines. From activist pamphlets, newsletters and DIY zines to gig guides, event listings and glossy commercial magazines, print media have long played an important role in LGBTQ+ political and cultural life. Though LGBTQ+ newsletters, newspapers and magazines have always been incredibly diverse in their focus, format and readership, many emphasize LGBTQ+ relevant news and gossip (community, local, state, national and international), as well as information about community groups and activities (these include groups and activities linked to activism, support networks and socializing). Scholars have reflected on the significance of the queer press as sites of activism, community and identity in Australia (Calder 2016a, 2016b, Cover 2002, Matheson 2019, McKinnon 2016). The aspect of LGBTQ+ print publications that particularly interests us is the way these publications emphasize and value cultural life, contributing to screen culture through promotion and publicity for film and television, reviews and commentary, coverage of special event screenings and festivals, LGBTQ+ films, television series and celebrities. We focus here on these publications as contributing to and developing Australian queer screen cultures. We argue that, as a form of audiencehood, the critical reception of films and television series offer insights into the cultural impact of screen media. To explore this, we analyse the practice and content of the discussion of film and television in newspapers and magazines created for and by LGBTQ+ communities in various parts of Australia. Our framework for understanding how community publications contribute to and develop Australian queer screen cultures locates these publications as an important source of knowledge about screen media and a site where communities have been active in negotiating media representation, mainstream recognition and the politics of visibility on screen.

The role of the queer critic

What is a critic? And how do *queer* critics contribute to screen culture? While we might initially think of screen critics as reviewers or evaluators that guide audiences towards (or away from) films and television shows, critics also play a significant role in shaping understandings of cultural texts. For screen critics, this includes unpacking themes and aesthetics, placing particular films or television series within their historical, national and cultural contexts, engaging in social and cultural analysis, and developing interpretive frameworks to illuminate certain aspects of screen texts. Within film studies, critics have also played a significant role in the development of new knowledge about screen media, including conceptualization of important theories, defining genres and identifying new movements. In the context of queer cinema, for instance, the movement known as 'New Queer Cinema' was coined by cultural critic B. Ruby Rich (1992) in the film magazine *Sight and Sound* as part of her reflection on a number of queer films that had screened at film festivals in the early 1990s.

But how can we make use of screen criticism? What does it tell us about the relation between film, television and social change? Richards (2019) suggests that we can study film criticism using an approach that seeks to gauge the *interpretation* of screen texts within a given context. Exploring coverage of Australian queer films in mainstream Australian newspapers (e.g. *Sydney Morning Herald*, *Courier Mail*, *The Age*, *Herald Sun*, *Adelaide Advertiser*, *West Australian* and *The Bulletin*), magazines such as *Metro* and *Film Ink* and international newspapers such as *The New York Times* and *The Washington Post*, his work reflects on shifting critical perspectives on the value of queer cinema in Australia. While reviews of 1990s queer films *Priscilla* and *The Sum of Us* focused solely on the queer subject matter, more recent decades found the focus of criticism shifted beyond emphasizing sexuality and gender. This illuminates the value of criticism as a potential source of knowledge about a film's meaning at a given time or place.

But what of the queer film critic? Do LGBTQ+ critical interpretations differ from heterosexual and cisgender perspectives? Do queer screen critics produce different knowledge about a film or television show's meaning? English film critic Robin Wood (1978) gives some insight into this in his influential article 'Responsibilities of a Gay Film Critic', which was first delivered as a lecture in 1971 and later published in *Film Comment* magazine in 1978. Recently out as a gay man, Wood considered his personal and professional identity as a gay film critic, placing equal emphasis on each term while considering them together. He began his essay with this reflection:

> Critic: one concerned in problems of the interpretation and evaluation of art and artifacts. Film critic: one who makes the central area of that concern the cinema. Gay – not just the word and the fact it points to, but the word and fact asserted publicly: one who is conscious of belonging to society's oppressed minority groups, and who is ready to confront the implications of that for both his theory and his practice. (12)

Writing in the 1970s with the Gay Liberation Movement at the forefront of his mind, Wood saw his identity, his interest in critical theory and his practice as a critic merge into a lens through which he could understand, interpret and evaluate screen texts. Similarly, Vito Russo, the US critic and activist who wrote *The Celluloid Closet*, brought queerness, politics and criticism together in his regular film column in long-running US queer magazine *The Advocate* (1967–) throughout the 1970s and contributed reviews and critical insights to both queer and mainstream press. These examples point to the significance of the role of the LGBTQ+ critic, underscoring the notion that queer critics bring a unique sensibility to screen culture within both mainstream and queer media contexts.

This chapter focuses on this sensibility in the coverage of film and television in community-oriented LGBTQ+ newsletters, newspapers and magazines, and it is worth noting that unlike figures like Russo and Wood, screen critics in LGBTQ+ publications are not always professional film and television writers. Many are community members with an interest in film and television. Even those that do have a background in film and television often contribute to the LGBTQ+ press as a passion project. Keith Howes (1988), author of the television column in the *Sydney Star Observer* throughout the 1980s recalls its origins: 'Asking only for free photocopying . . . in lieu of payment, I began the "Small Screen" column in the *Sydney Star Observer*' (44). Rather than focusing on the issue of LGBTQ+ representation on television, Howes' queer sensibility focused on how television privileged heterosexuality:

the 'Small Screen' column in the Sydney Star Observer, which looked at a wide range of programs and occasionally gave a 'hetometer' reading of the fine channels' weekly output. The hetometer usually showed a 95% pursuit of the heterosexual audience. (44)

In this respect, queer criticism from early on had a wide-ranging brief in which the analysis of screen texts, of media cultures and of the corpus of available screen content at any one time was assessed for its relationship to – and distinction from – queer community and culture.

Activism, LGBTQ+ press and film/TV criticism

Popularly traced to the German newspaper *Der Eigene,* published by Adolf Brand in 1896, the queer press has a long and varied history around the world. Historian Florence Tamagne (2007) highlights that the period after the First World War was a golden era for homosexual associations and subsequent publishing in Germany where queer-oriented publishing grew substantially in the more liberal post-war era. However, it would be many decades before LGBTQ+ periodicals began printing in Anglophone nations. In the United States, the first gay and lesbian publications were printed in the late 1940s (Streitmatter 1998) and homophile groups such as the Mattachine Society began publishing newsletters in the 1950s while in the United Kingdom, the first publication was *Arena Three* in 1964 (Turner 2009). In Australia, the queer press did not emerge until the late 1960s with the first publication *Camp, the 'in' communicator,* v1 n1, published in July 1968.

Early contributors to Australia's vibrant LGBTQ+ print media scene were societies and organizations that produced newsletters and magazines such as *ACT Homosexual Law Reform Society Newsletter* (1969–70), *Daughters of Bilitis Newsletter* (1970) and *CAMP Ink* (1970–7). Emerging from activist communities in the late 1960s and early 1970s, these publications documented local and international news, political and social change, activist initiatives, manifestos and cultural life. Alongside these were more commercial magazines such as *William and John* (1972–3) and *Stallion* (1973–4), which featured news, reviews and erotica, and guides such as *Apollo* (1973). From the early days, LGBTQ+ publications in Australia explored issues related to screen culture. For example, the first issue of *William and John* issue 1 (1972), described in the editorial as 'the first issue of a camp Australian magazine' stated that the magazine aimed to: 'Campaign for the rights of homosexuals. Provide a voice and communication for the camp community. Provide entertainment and information. Publish great pictures' (William and John 1972: 4). It featured book reviews on LGBTQ+ titles such as *Sexual Latitude For and Against* (1971), *Tea Room Trade* (1970) and *Man into Woman* and film reviews focused on mainstream titles where readers could potentially find queer pleasures.

In the 1980s, 1990s and 2000s, Australian LGBTQ+ magazines, newspapers and newsletters shifted in emphasis as their communities and readerships responded to issues and events such as the decriminalization of homosexuality across Australia (between 1972 and 1997, depending on the state), anti-discrimination laws and adoption rights, the health implications of HIV and, much later, debates about marriage equality and increased acceptance of some LGBTQ+ identities within mainstream consumer culture. Publications such as *Campaign* (1975–2000), *OutRage* (1983–2000), *Melbourne Star Observer* (1985–2000), *Sydney Star Observer* (1985–now) and *Lesbians on the Loose* (1990–2019) were born within these moments of change, responding to shifting societal attitudes towards queer issues. Across these decades, many of them changed names, merged with other publications, adopted different publishing models and shifted from grassroots activist and political to commercial aims.

Different publications in Australia's LGBTQ+ print media history have differed, then, in their politics, publishing model and focus, and this has often shaped the commentary and critical reception of films and television series. For example, alongside Australian television's embrace of gay and lesbian identity in the 1970s through characters such as Don Finlayson in *Number 96*, film review sections of publications such as *CAMP Ink*, *Campaign*, and *Gay Community News* (1979–82) not only demanded more representation but also shaped discourse about how those identities should be represented. Reflecting their descent from activist groups and communities, these publications understood the media industry as profoundly political and became increasingly aware of the power of media to drive social change.

A notable instance of this was a commentary piece in the May 1972 issue of *CAMP Ink*, where writer Gary Dennison (1972) reflected on the politics of representation and his shifting perceptions of screen culture. He wrote: 'Two years ago I would have seen a camp film and cared little about its merit, just so long as it was about one of "us". Since that time, I've "come out", and am now more able to look at theatrical treatments from a rational point of view' (4).

Arguing that cinema should 'advance the cause' of Gay Liberation, Dennison called for mainstream film to promote a new, more 'authentic' image of gay identity that was less driven by camp stereotype:

> All these films do is pander to the conventional concept of homosexuality. If this was unharmful to causes such as the C.A.M.P it wouldn't matter. But it does matter because each time someone who does not know about homosexuality sees such a film an added layer of resistance is applied to their already difficult to penetrate mental block on the subject. (5–6)

Comments such as this are reflective of an evolving cultural sensibility around issues of representation in Australia, which in the 1970s began to value 'what was deemed to be "realistic" representation' of a newly formed socio-political identity (Matheson 2019: 17). Underpinning this was the understanding of cinema as a political tool, not simply for reflecting 'a newly forming "us" back to gay audiences', but 'to project – even advertise – this "us" to a heterosexual audience' as a means of accelerating change towards acceptance and equality (17). This aligns with Robin Wood's (1978) description of the gay film critic as a figure that emerges from the Gay Liberation Movement and appraises cinema through a rather narrow lens. Wood writes that for some gay critics, the emphasis is placed 'strongly, sometimes exclusively, on "gay," and concern[ed] . . . strictly with works that have *direct* bearing on gayness, approaching them from a political-propagandist viewpoint: do they or do they not further the gay cause?' (12). This sensibility would later be mobilized in the LGBTQ+ press in coverage around issues of 'positive' and 'negative' representation, the value of mainstream media and the perceived impact of screen media. John Lee (1972), for example, wrote in the *Sydney Gay Liberation Newsletter* about his experience leafleting at a screening of *Some Of My Best Friends Are* (1971), a film he describes as a 'exploitative'. He writes,

> we felt angry/depressed enough to produce a leaflet which was handed out to patrons entering the theatre, at several sessions . . . In the leaflet we tried to counter the film's 'objective', this-is-the-way-we-are style, by talking about gay liberation (the individual process) as the alternative to accepting the present definitions. (2)

LGBTQ+ press has also reported on direct action and 'zap' (public demonstration) activities related to issues of media representation. In 1973, *West Campaigner* printed an article about successful South Australian campaigns, identifying a particularly interesting moment when 'a local television compere who made disparaging remarks…was "zapped"…in front of his entire viewing and studio audience, to the vast embarrassment of his management' (West Campaigner 1973).

In addition to this coverage of activism, some LGBTQ+ print media sought to actively mobilize audiences in activist campaigns around issues of representation in the media. We discussed some of these campaigns in Chapter 4, when we explored the relationship between screen media cultures and Australian gay and lesbian activism in the 1970s, and traced similar ideas in the 1980s in our discussion of reception practices, policing and community change in Chapter 9. Extending this into the 1990s, TV writer Andrew Mercado of the *Sydney Star Observer* began a campaign for a boycott of television network Channel Seven in May 1998. The reason for this boycott was that Channel Seven had dropped the broadcast of US series *Ellen* (1994–8), denying Australian viewers access to the landmark 'Puppy Episode' of the series. This infamous episode saw the character Ellen come out and was broadcast in the United States to an audience of 42 million viewers the previous year. Creator and star of the series, Ellen DeGeneres, also publicly came out following the broadcast. Australian audiences were approximately one year behind the American episodes, so the response to this was not immediate.

In response to a tip-off that Channel Seven would never broadcast the episode, Mercado (1998) penned a full page article on the issue, titled 'From the closet to the shelf: Seven's big lesbian coverup' in which he called on viewers to participate in the boycott: 'Would everyone now join me in a nationwide, month-long boycott of Channel Seven, on the one-year anniversary of Ellen DeGeneres's coming out?' (9). The page featured a small coupon with big bold, all-caps lettering, 'REMEMBER ELLEN: BOYCOTT CHANNEL SEVEN DURING MAY', that readers were encouraged to cut out and mail to the Head of Programming at Channel Seven. Readers were also encouraged to phone Channel Seven all month and 'Fax this page to Programming (It'll clog up their fax)' (9). In the following issue, one reader wrote to the paper to support the protest, noting 'I have sent a fax…and I'll be getting everyone I know to refrain from watching their product' (Sydney Star Observer 1998: 13). Though the series was eventually picked up by pay TV provider Foxtel, Mercado worried how this would impact viewers that were not subscribers to the service, writing: 'I wish Seven had the courage to show it to you just once. You've not been allowed to see an award-winning show that's moving, touching, witty, groundbreaking television that made millions of people think' (9).

Lesbians on the Loose

In January 1990, the first edition of *Lesbians on the Loose* hit the streets of Sydney's Inner-West. Beginning as an eight-page black and white newsletter with distribution of one thousand copies, *Lesbians on the Loose* was hand-delivered to feminist bookshops, lesbian bars and women's health centres. *LOTL*, as it was affectionately known by readers, was founded by Frances Rand and Jackie Scherer, born from their desire to create a resource for Sydney's lesbian community. They wanted to provide readers with 'a regular source of information' about events, activities, venues and resources (Rand and Scherer 1990: 1) while also promoting lesbian perspectives on arts and culture, health, lifestyle, politics and news. To put it simply, as Rand and Scherer did in their first editorial, *Lesbians on the Loose* was 'by Lesbians on anything of interest to Lesbians' (1).

Lesbians on the Loose was the first lesbian magazine in Australia that was free of charge and fully supported by advertising that targeted Sydney's lesbian community. Unlike activist-driven, politically oriented magazines such as *CAMP Ink* or the earlier *Lesbian Newsletter* (1976–83), *Lesbians on the Loose* 'did not consciously seek to politicize or change readers' attitudes' (Calder 2016a: 425) and indeed adopted a neutral stance on controversial topics in order to maintain broad appeal. However, the magazine was not entirely apolitical. It fostered and developed lesbian community in Sydney through the inclusion of information about the lesbian scene – including community groups and event listings. At the time, the gay print publications largely focused on events for men and the lesbian publications were published infrequently (Calder 2016b), so *Lesbians on the Loose* filled an important gap.

Through the 1990s, the magazine's readership grew significantly, and it expanded its reach from queer enclaves in Sydney to national distribution. Its issue size peaked at sixty-four pages, and it gained a Circulation Audit Board figure above 16,000 in 2005 (Calder 2016a: 425). Notably, the increased size allowed for greater coverage of arts and culture, with more attention to entertainment media and celebrity gossip. Across this period of growth, *Lesbians on the Loose*

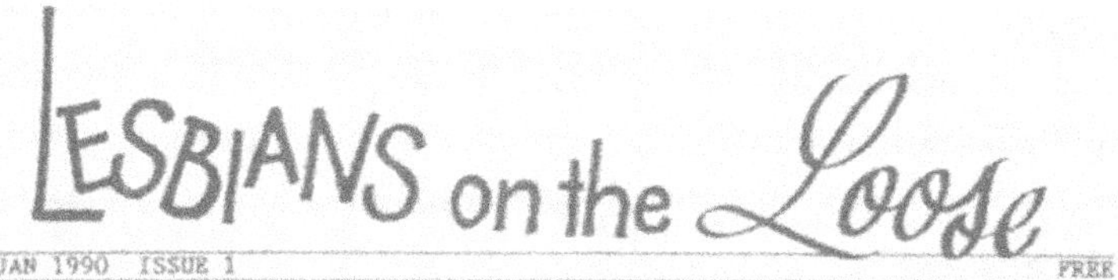

WELCOME!

Ever since we can remember Sydney Lesbians have not had a regular source of information about what activities and resources are available. Whenever a new venue's opened, or an old one's closed; whenever someone's held a dance or started a group we've largely depended on word of mouth to hear about them. There's been the gay press over the years but it's been either dominated by the boys or come out too infrequently. Sydney Lesbians need a publication that can be more accessible to dykes.

We are two dykes who have been active within the Lesbian community for a number of years and we are hoping to provide our community with an independent monthly publication. We hope that by charging for advertising space we can cover printing and administration costs and therefore distribute Lesbians on the Loose for free. So any dykes out there who want to take up this offer of advertising in such a prestigious journal, drop us a line!

Lesbians on the Loose will be distributed to all Lesbian venues, The Feminist Bookshop, The Bookshops, Women's Liberation House and some of the women's health centres. If your business or group wishes to be a distribution point please contact us.

Lesbians on the Loose will contain articles by Lesbians on anything of interest to Lesbians. In this issue we've included items about Lesbian Line and the struggle it has to survive, "Celebration 90" the international Lesbian & gay games to be held in Vancouver in August, and an article on the Lesbian & Gay Rights Lobby. We also have a listing of groups and activities available, ads for services provided by Lesbians and a classified section. In future editions we plan to publish features on wimmin prominent in the Lesbian community and articles focusing on different Lesbian groups to heighten visibility within our community. If your group or organisation would like to write an article about your activities

we would love to receive it.

Our prime objective will always be to keep you informed about existing nightclubs, venues, groups etc. and about upcoming events & activities. Lesbians on the Loose will only be as useful as the information we receive. Therefore we are relying on you, as individuals and groups in the Lesbian community to send us information on events, activities and news. But please don't send us anything racist, sexist or anti-lesbian. Write to us at Lesbians on the Loose PO Box 798 Newtown 2042. The deadline for Febuary 1990 issue is 12th January 1990.

We hope you enjoy reading Lesbians on the Loose.

Frances Rand & Jackie Scherer

Lesbians On The Loose

Jan 1990   1

Figure 7.1 Issue 1 of *Lesbians on the Loose*, January 1990.

writers grappled with shifting societal attitudes towards queer women's issues and the increasing visibility of these stories in the public sphere. *Lesbians on the Loose* rapidly became a significant community resource, providing readers with event information, venue guides, listings of community groups and services and a monthly calendar.

One of the important functions of *Lesbians on the Loose*, particularly in this first decade, was to identify relevant media for its readership, providing important information on how to access lesbian representations. One of the ways in which they achieved this was through the monthly calendar, a feature originally called the 'Fridge Calendar' and designed to be torn from the back page of the magazine to be used as a planner. Separate from the classifieds section, the calendar advertised upcoming events such as parties, festivals, conferences, community meetups, support groups and social clubs, theatre, music and recreation activities. Most event listings provided readers with necessary information to access these lesbian community activities: time, date, address, contact number and price (if relevant). Also highlighted on the calendar were film screenings and television broadcasts, which provided readers with information on what was relevant to lesbian viewers and how to access it.

A regular feature of *Lesbians on the Loose* was the film review columns, often drawing on puns for their names, such as 'Reel Girls' and 'Panning Out'. Reviews within the first decade of *Lesbians on the Loose* offer insight into the publication's aesthetic values and tastes, and also the boundaries of lesbian identity, lesbian culture and lesbian cinema as they were constructed and contested by the magazine. Notably, lesbian storylines in Australian film were not the sole focus of the magazine and often not commented upon by reviewers. Instead, reviewers largely focused on North American cinema. In this way, the magazine offered readers something of an outward focus, situating Australian lesbian communities within global movements towards equality and empowerment and media visibility.

Reviews during this era also revealed attitudes of the lesbian community towards increasing presence and recognition in mainstream spaces. In November 1991, contributor Catherine Lumby penned an article titled 'Stereotypes: Taking Control'. At the time, Lumby was a journalist, though she would later make the move to academia and the discipline of media studies. In 'Stereotypes' Lumby (1991) detailed not only on her experience with mediated stereotypes but offered an in-depth reflection on what stereotypes mean for the lesbian readers of the magazine, and how readers might begin to think critically about problems of representation and potential solutions. Describing mainstream media as a 'homogenous circulation of images and information', Lumby asserted that 'There is no denying that the media thrives on the stereotype. Television, radio and the print media are continually cramming the complicated and the contradictory into the tightest possible space' (12–13). Stereotypes, she wrote, function as 'shorthand forms which conceal social contradictions and prejudices' (12). With this in mind, Lumby noted the ways in which lesbian media representation was located in a complex juxtaposition between vilification on the one hand and invisibility on the other, suggesting that audiences found lesbian representation positioned somewhere between being ignored and being depicted as a 'recognised only as a curiosity' (12).

Tackling the problem, Lumby argued, 'requires a long term and concerted effort by sympathetic members of the media to break down the stereotypes. On the other . . . it requires an understanding of how stereotypes work and ability to bend them back on themselves. Interestingly, the lesbian and gay community itself is a mine of information on the latter' (12). Perhaps suggestive of a *queering* of stereotype as a potential strategy of resistance, this article offered a thoughtful and reflective response to negative stereotypes of lesbians that were all too familiar in Australian media in the preceding decades. These included some of the representation of lesbians that we discussed in Chapter 3 where lesbian and bisexual subjects were depicted as embittered men haters, devil worshipping witches (*Number 96*), murderous torturers (*Homicide*) and manipulative predators (*Hotel Story* (1977–8)).

While it primarily had a focus on mainstream cinema, *Lesbians on the Loose* also guided readers to relevant films at festivals, such as the Mardi Gras Film Festival and Sydney Film Festival. For example, in 1999, the magazine included 'Girls Own Guide' which was a three-page guide to the lesbian films screening at the Mardi Gras Film Festival. This included reviews of four feature films – *Relax, It's Just Sex* (1998), *High Art* (1998), *Blessed Are Those Who Thirst* (1997) and *Everything Will Be Fine* (1998) – alongside a range of short films and documentaries. Notably, the magazine highlighted short films as these are often only available in festival contexts and not afforded the same visibility and recognition as feature length cinema.

Beyond simply identifying relevant media for its lesbian readers, *Lesbians on the Loose* also fulfilled a need to help audiences make sense of newfound visibilities in media culture. The 1990s was an era of rapid transformation in lesbian representation. Lesbian and bisexual women's stories were featured internationally in films such as *Single White Female* (1992), *The Incredibly True Adventure of Two Girls in Love* (1995), *Bound* (1996), *Chasing Amy* (1997), *High Art, Wild Things* (1998) and *But I'm a Cheerleader* (1999). Lesbian and bisexual characters in were notable inclusions in US television series such as *Friends* (1994–2004), *LA Law* (1986–94), *Mad About You* (1992–9), *Ally McBeal* (1997–2002), *ER* (1994–2009), *Picket Fences* (1992–6), *Beverly Hills, 90210* (1990–2000) and *Ellen* (1994–8) to name but a few. This was also reflected in Australian media as the 1990s saw something of a resurgence of lesbian and bisexual women's television representation. Although lesbian and bisexual women characters were depicted with some regularity in the 1970s, the 1980s had seen a decline in representation, with little other than lesbian visibility on *Prisoner* until greater representation in the 1990s (Beirne 2009). Indeed, as we outlined in Chapter 3, the 1990s saw inclusion of lesbian and bisexual women as both supporting and main characters in a range of series including *Fire* (1995–6), *G.P.* (1989–6), *Breakers* (1997–9), *After the Beep* (1996), *Home and Away* (1988–present), *Raw FM* (1997–8), *Pacific Dive* (1996–7) and *Water Rats* (1996–2001). This newfound lesbian visibility was often both celebrated and critiqued in *LOTL,* and over time criticism noted the way in which lesbian and bisexual women were narrowly represented as privileged white, middle-class, femme-presenting cisgender women (Ciasullo 2001: 578).

Also notable through the era was the commodification of lesbian culture and identity (Clark 1993) through the popularization of 'lesbian chic', a pop culture phenomenon that 'combined sexuality with fashion, portraying lesbianism as a new trend or style' (Rand 2013: 124). According to Rand (2013), the film *Basic Instinct* (1992) marked the emergence of the 'lesbian chic' phenomenon, though as Ciasullo (2001) identifies, it gained significant traction in 1993 with several high-profile magazine covers declaring mainstream interest in lesbian culture. In May 1993, *New York* magazine's cover featured k.d. lang captioned with the headline 'Lesbian Chic: The Bold, Brave World of Gay Women'. The following month, *Newsweek* featured the headline 'Lesbians: Coming Out Strong: What are the Limits of Tolerance?' on a cover image of two women hugging and smiling. In August of 1993, *Vanity Fair* produced the famous cover image of Cindy Crawford shaving the face of k.d. lang.

While scholarship largely focuses on these issues in a North American context, this was a similar concern in Australia. For this reason, the phenomenon of 'lesbian chic' was debated in both academic and community media contexts with many writing about the politics of representation and visibility. For instance, in the one hundredth issue of *Lesbians on the Loose*, Frances Rand (1998) described lesbian chic as 'almost *de riguer*' (3) and triumphantly listed a dozen celebrity lesbians as evidence of the significant changes that had occurred since the magazine's launch in 1990. Two months later, in June 1998, the magazine had a celebratory feature 'Dycons & Bicons in New Word Order' on the potential inclusion of 'Dycon' (a portmanteau of dyke and icon that referred to iconic queer women) in the Macquarie Dictionary, claiming they first used the term over a year before its first reference in the mainstream newspaper *The Sydney Morning Herald*.

Conclusion: Community shaping audiences

This chapter has mapped the development of queer critical perspectives in community newspapers, magazines and newsletters, reflecting on these alongside significant moments of social change and activism. Reviews, commentary and criticism provide an important site for community *negotiation* of issues around media representation. Although published criticism of screen media texts is just one among a broad array of audience interpretations, they are framed in the context of queer publications which, for community members, provide a modelling for how to respond, interpret and appreciate such texts as audience members. From the 1970s to today, critics in the LGBTQ+ press have thus had a profound role to play in shaping local queer screen cultures. They guide readers to access relevant screen media, develop critical and cultural literacy about media representations, demand access to important screen content from overseas and call for better, more inclusive representation in Australian media.

Focusing on these contributions, we propose a new framework for understanding how community publications contribute to and develop Australian queer screen cultures. Our framework centres on three related themes: access, understanding and action. Though LGBTQ+ newspapers, newsletters and magazines have not directly shaped the screen industry in Australia, screen critics have actively contributed to social change by building publicity for independent and alternative films and their exhibition, establishing frames for film and television to be viewed and understood, carving a space of political action related to film and television. This perspective locates these publications and their writers as vital sources of knowledge about film and television. We also see the publications themselves as a site where communities have been very active in discussing and debating issues of media representation, mainstream recognition and the visibility LGBTQ+ communities on screen.

8

Gender-Diverse, Trans and Emergent Identity Frameworks in New Screen Contexts

Introduction

Trans and gender-diverse content in Australian entertainment media has shifted substantially over the decades. However, as we argue in this chapter, there remain both historical and contemporary problematic representations, and a lag in content that inclusively depicts the full range of trans experience and gender-diverse subjectivity. Those who have paid attention to local and international politics over the past decade will be very aware of the significant, well-organized and sustained backlash against many of the advances in gender healthcare, transgender rights and tolerance for gender diversity in expression, style and form. Whereas in the mid-1990s *Priscilla, Queen of the Desert* was more-or-less universally celebrated for representing a colourful, Australian expression of diversity through drag, in the mid-2020s drag performers are regularly threatened by violent, far-right activists (Kelly 2023). In the United States, literally hundreds of state legislatures have debated and passed laws to restrict the rights of trans and gender-diverse peoples to and healthcare (Human Rights Campaign, 2023). And where non-binary gender identities are represented, they are subject to active hate campaigns both in Australia and overseas (Cover 2024b). The fixation of many political, media and religious leaders in the 2020s on eradicating gender and sexuality diversity is difficult to fathom in the context of historical social change and increased positive media representation; hate has nevertheless has become a core part of the lived experience of queer, trans and gender-diverse people in Australia.

A significant element of the problem, as Judith Butler (2024) has noted, is the failure of those who oppose livable lives for sexuality- and gender-diverse subjects, to engage critically with the arguments, knowledge and facts at play; Butler argues there is an imperative for people not merely to protect the rights of their own identity claims but to engage critically from the perspective of the intersections all subjects have with gender diversity as interdependent bodies cohabiting the planet in endemic diversity (131–2). That is a call for greater critique, meaning not judgement of others' lives, but overcoming the ignorance that has been actively produced and maintained on gender diversity and the lives of gender-diverse people (Gilson 2011). Critique involves making sense of the historical, social and structural mechanisms that limit knowledge and thought in ways that open up innovative possibilities (Foucault 1977).

In the context, then, of queer screen media in Australia, that means not only making sense of *what* content about *which* gender-diverse subjects is absent, or could be done better, or *should* be incorporated into everyday on-screen settings, or *could* flesh out the lived experience of trans and gender-diverse people more fully. Rather, it calls upon media producers, scholars, distributors and audiences to understand and appreciate the historical formations and genealogies of gender-diverse representation so that what *is* depicted both historically and in the present can be understood in ways that lead to a more ethical, mutually caring, interdependent Australian society.

Although we discuss trans and gender-diverse representations, production contexts and reception throughout the book, this chapter investigates some examples of the specific content of young gender-diverse and trans people in Australian entertainment media from a perspective attentive to the shifting distributional frameworks and how they open up possibilities for more diverse content. We begin with a brief summary of some of the past representations of gender diversity – drag, trans identity and other diverse expressions of gender subjectivity – on Australian screens and the ways in which these both shift in focus and provide a genealogy on which more recent content has been generated. We discuss a number of key texts that have been widely hailed as 'breakthrough' moments in trans youth representation, including Georgie Stone in *Neighbours* and the ABC series *First Day* (2020–2). We then consider how post-binary gender identities that have emerged in the past decade are represented only in a nascent way to date, but argue that it is the shift in distribution from network television and cinema to transnational streaming content that enables a wider array of diversity in content.

Genealogies of gender play in Australian film and television

As Deb Verhoeven (1997) has outlined, there is a surprisingly substantial history of gender play – principally cross-dressing – in Australia's film history. These include diverse examples such as a woman cross-dressing as a man in *Jewelled Nights* (1925) in order to prospect for gold, and the film *Bitter Springs* (1950) in which a woman (affirmed by her mother) regularly plays with masculine identity terminology. Indeed, the depiction of gender play through cross-dressing has remained a common trope in much Australian and international media. There are a range of motivations given in screen narratives: sometimes it is for laughs, such as the apparent amusement or humiliation of a male character being forced to wear a woman's clothing or being mistaken for trans when subsequent to a cross-dressing mix-up, such as Dexter in *Home and Away* (1988–) in the early 2010s. At other times it is parody undertaken for satire, as was common in Australian series such as *Fast Forward* (1989–92) or the more sophisticated ABC political satires such as *The Dingo Principle* (1988). And sometimes it is for duplicitous reasons, such as in the Australian film *All Men Are Liars* (1995), whereby a man cross-dresses and impersonates a woman to gain the romantic attention of a singer in an all-girl group. From early on, then, gender play per se in Australian film and television was already diverse but a significant element of content across multiple genres.

Certainly, the most prominent gender-play fixture on Australian television screens for many decades has been the pseudo-drag character of Dame Edna Everage (played by comedian Barry Humphries). Dame Edna began as a satirical critique of the 1950s suburban domesticity with Humphries dragging up to present a drab, conservative and ignorant housewife. Drawing on Humphries' quick-witted humour, Edna became a fixture on much variety television in Australia and later in the United Kingdom. As with the formation of other kinds of drag theatrics, the depiction of Dame Edna moved from being the somewhat problematic parody of a certain kind of womanhood to become a parody of the character themselves, with Humphries satirizing the cult of celebrity and stardom as the Dame Edna character was represented as having gained global fame and worldwide influence (Lahr 1992).

Although sometimes mistaken for a drag performance (Cooper 2023), the gender representation of Dame Edna is neither quite gender-play in the sense of fluidity or gender critique, nor is it a part of queer drag culture as globally recognized (Edwards and Farrier 2020). Rather, as with many Australian film and television examples, it conforms to the kind of performance that Chris Straayer (1996) has identified as 'temporary transvestite' theatrics. The temporary transvestite figure is coded within a common on-screen narrative from at least as early as the 1940s, and remaining popular into the early 2000s. In fictional texts, a character would be for some reason required to cross-dress and would either learn something about themselves or their presumed 'true' gender identity, or be played entirely for laughs. What is important, according to Straayer, is that the audience is aware from the beginning that a person is performing in a gender not perceived to be 'their own' and that there is no expectation that this is permanent or done for any reason other than to gain something. In entertainment and comedy narratives we see this across a vast range of films such as *Tootsie* (1982) and *Birdcage* (1996). When it is undertaken by a non-fictional character such as in social comedy, parody, satire or hypermasculine humour, such gender play is framed as recognizably temporary because, either because the audience recognizes immediately that it is a person playing a part or presenting a caricature – again, with no expectation that that their cisgender identity is in question. In the latter, Dame Edna is a prominent Australian example if for no other reason than that Barry Humphries is widely known for other characters played in both fiction and non-fictional screen settings. Other, more recent prominent examples in Australia include Chris Lilley's cross-dressed performance of Ja'mie King to make a point about the ignorance of socio-economic inequality among some girls in elite schools in his mockumentary *Summer Heights High* (2007). The point here is this range of texts 'plays' with gender, but only in ways which are grounded in the 'temporariness' in either to satirize or amuse, eschewing any possibility of a critical reflection on gender's contingency.

Certainly, in the case of Dame Edna, it is not only apparent to the audience, but a key element in the humour that allusions to the 'wrong gender' are made throughout any performance, interview or event. Ultimately, gender play for the purpose of satire is not in itself problematic and is a key element of the television political and social comedy scene, both in Australia and elsewhere. What is more problematic in recent years is when the experience of gender play actively insults the gender being played usually through parodying womanhood, or that the performer capitalizes on gender play while disavowing gender diversity, contingency and multiplicity of gender identity. In the latter case, Barry Humphries was widely called out in 2018 for transphobic comments that betrayed the ignorance, perhaps, that stems from an octogenarian who has failed to engage with cultural change (Moran 2018).

The Adventures of Priscilla, Queen of the Desert (1994) remains among Australia's most celebrated films thirty years later, although it has often been criticized for its use of racist stereotypes (Riggs 2006), its problematic representation of rural Australia as homophobic and transphobic in contrast to the safety of inner-urban ghettoes (Cover et al. 2020), and for the subsumption of gender critiques underneath camp sensibilities (Padva 2000). Although notable for being among the texts of the mid-1990s that took queer and gender-diversity themes from the margins of art house screens into mass-circulation media, from a 2020s perspective *Priscilla*'s representation of gender diversity can be critiqued for the ways in which it insistently equates gender play with spectacle. Despite the presence of a trans character who is depicted as an elder of the Australian drag scene, the representation of gender play is only ever offset against the background of normative binary gender, simultaneously bringing gender play into the myth of national masculinity – as has occurred in many other queer texts in other national settings (Severiche 2020) – and offsetting it by narrating its distinctiveness from the masculine norm.

Although *Priscilla* actively challenges a number of norms by celebrating difference, including the constructive depiction of alternative queer families (Straayer 1996), the struggle against homophobia and transphobic rage, and the possibilities of cisgender/transgender relationships, its insightful critical content is subsumed by the spectacularity in which gender diversity is portrayed in opposition to more recent framings of gender diversity as part of Australian everydayness. In that sense, its content can be read as also representing an anthropological exercise for mainstream audiences into a particular perspective of gender diversity, much as a nature documentary might focus on the rituals and plumage that are still attached to actual birdlife. As with other forms of spectacle, that which falls under its banner is both the production of contemporary culture but also exonerates culture by representing it as radically separate from the norm. In this respect, *Priscilla*'s narrative, content and colour falls short of supporting gender diversity by setting up strict – and false – oppositions between norm/spectacle, normativity/diversity and seriousness/play (Debord 1967). In that respect, *Priscilla* makes an important contribution by representing forms of gender diversity to a wider, mainstream audience, but its narrative folds back on itself by isolating gender diversity to its categories and its ghettoes.

More recent Australian screen content addressing gender diversity has included the biopic for *Carlotta* (2014), which is among the first key Australian texts to place gender diversity and gender affirmation into a 'lived experience' narrative. Carol Spencer, also known on stage as Carlotta, is notable for being one of Australia's first widely recognized showgirls, and an early example of gender affirmation known and recognized by a wide, mainstream public. Spencer's drag persona and transgender identity are, of course, quite separate frameworks of theatrics and performativity, although the ways in which they disrupt conservative gender norms are related, as are the cultural spaces and settings through which both the theatrics of drag and the lived experience of being transgender are played out. The term 'showgirl' is more widely accepted today to describe persons who have transitioned and perform in the style of drag, while not actually being perceived as having 'cross dressed' for the stage performance.

The content and narrative of *Carlotta* do more than elucidate Spencer's biographical history. Rather, it is informational for a wider mainstream audience because it demonstrates that both becoming a performer in the drag genre and gender affirming are neither singular decisions nor involve singular instances that produce an identity change, but respond to the demand for subjective coherence *over time* (Butler 1993). Just as an authentic performance of gender stabilizes over time, the expert drag performer draws attention to this stabilization through the acquisition of expert ways of producing seamlessness (or, indeed, synchronicity) of a drag performance, while the language of transition or affirmation points to the contingency of gender and sexed bodies. Both of these narratives run simultaneously through *Carlotta* whereby we see the simultaneous story of Carol's gender affirmation, her settlement into forms of belonging among various communities, her resolution of her non-belonging of the past among family, and the related-but-separate framing of the development of her ultimate expertise as a lip-synching showgirl diva. Although we see the performance of a variety of drag numbers with different degrees of success across the film, it is in the final, closing scene that gender diversity is framed as a positive element of transition, process and becoming: Carlotta here performs against a rendition of the Shirley Bassey 1968 song 'This is my Life', an easily ecognized anthemic drag diva number which, like songs such as 'My Way', are re-signified in the context of drag as personal stories of agency, radical individualism and self-satisfaction as the pathway to personal happiness. In this respect, unlike the spectacular celebration of gender play of *Priscilla*, the biopic places transgender (as identity) and drag performance (as professional career) within an ethical framing of lived experience, notable as being among the first texts to represent a trans character leading a liveable Australian life among the community. That is, *Carlotta* contributes to the advancement of gender critique in Australian screen media by unpacking the Australian assumptions of lived experience of gender as normative and making the case for the diversification of lived experience of gender as a key aspect of contemporary Australian culture.

Finally, the contribution to contemporary gender diversity in Australian screen culture receives a significant advancement with the film *52 Tuesdays* (2013). Winning the best director award at the Sundance Film Festival in 2014, this Australian film focuses on a young woman's experience dealing with the gender transition/affirmation of her parent. Both presented and filmed across fifty-two weeks, daughter Billie is sent to live with her father for a year to provide space for her parent James' transition, only visiting James on Tuesdays. James has difficulties when it is found his body cannot tolerate testosterone injections, but does progress to top surgery. Alongside these developments, teenaged Billie experiments with her bisexual identity and polyamorous relationships, filming her sexual experiments with two older students, supported by her young uncle who lived in James' house while growing up. After a year, and some dramas after Billie's more extreme experimentation and partying threatens her education and her relationships and her father's life was temporarily more precarious after an accident, she moves back in with James to form a further development in their alternative family informed by new experience for all. The text is significant for beginning with diverse, contemporary family arrangements.

The experimentation in film, production and narrative in *52 Tuesdays* provides a code by which to read the context of gender affirmation in ways unbuckled from the individualism of *Carlotta,* the ghettoization of *Priscilla,* and the problematic temporary transvestism and parodic gender play of earlier Australian examples. Here, *52 Tuesdays* points to the radical interdependency in which gender affirmation occurs. Although almost all fictional narrative generates stories through representing intertwined lives, recognizing the interdependency of trans characters within frameworks of interdependent kinship has been less common in the Australian mythologies of gender diversity. Interdependency is, as Butler (2020) has theorized, an *a priori* condition of all identity, even though it is one that is often submerged by the cultural narrative of self-sufficiency and independence of the kind noted in *Carlotta.* What *52 Tuesdays* depicts, then, is the radical interdependency of the kinship group, represented as a contemporary family with estranged parents, extended family living arrangements, various lovers and supportive peers; the turmoil both James and Billie experience in their various transitions through different phases of liveability occurs as isolated from one another tests their capacity for resilience. Even in coming together through weekly visits, that interdependency is further strained through what Butler (2022) points to as interdependency's failure when it is not of the most ethical kind: that is, when it is acknowledged but not equitable. Although both their identities are always 'in process', a stability is found when it is understood they must live together again in a mutual and equitable respect for each other's changes as the only means by which they can recognize their interdependency as support for survival. Told primarily from Billie's perspective, gender diversity is at last depicted in Australian screen media in the context of everyday belonging.

Although only intended as a very potted, non-exclusive genealogy of gender diversity in Australian screen media over a very long period, we can discern a few trends over that time. The story begins with casual instances of gender play across a range of genres and inclusive of temporary transvestism tropes, drag used in satire and cross-dressing for humour. Moving beyond these sometimes problematic representations, *Priscilla* presents two forms of gender play and diversity (drag and trans characters) but does so principally through spectacle and demarcation from Australian norms, unwittingly bringing gender diversity into Australian mainstream culture. Later texts conceptualize trans identity and gender affirmation through more meaningful representations, including individualized lived experience and then locatedness within everyday kinship and social belonging. One way to read these is that gender-diverse subjectivity is slowly depicted over time with greater sensitivity and acknowledgement of lived realities, and a with a greater sense of dignity for trans and gender-diverse people. In that respect, it provides a powerful resource for social stability at a time at which such backlash against any gender play is occurring in other spheres.

The *Neighbours* breakthrough 2019

Mackenzie Hargreaves, played by actress, writer and advocate Georgie Stone, became the first transgender character on the prominent Australian soap opera *Neighbours* (1985–). A show that began as a snapshot of Australian suburban ordinariness, the series turned towards melodrama and sensational in the 1990s in order to enhance ratings (Ward et al. 2010). The ordinariness of the show's snapshot of the Australian 'everyday', however, has evolved over time to reflect the changing demographics of Australian and international audiences (Guiffre and Attfield 2022). Georgie Stone came to prominence in the Australian media, after she became the youngest person in Australia to receive hormone blockers. As a young person, she was a prominent campaigner for the rights of trans children, particularly around young people's access to stage one treatment and the Safe Schools Coalition. Through her advocacy, she featured on *Four Corners*,

The Project and *Australian Story*. The short documentary *The Dreamlife of Georgie Stone* (2022), written by Stone herself, was released on Netflix.

Mackenzie Hargreaves was originally introduced in a guest storyline in 2019 and featured in the online spin-off series *Neighbours: Erinsborough High*, becoming a regular in the main series from 2022 until September 2024. Stone's introduction was the result of activism attentive to media representation and screen inclusivity: she had written to executive producers about including trans representation in the series. 'As a trans person', Stone wrote at the time in a column for *Metro*, 'I didn't see people like myself on screen very often – it would often be a very tragic character, and never played by a trans actor. Because of this, I internalized the message that being trans was something to be ashamed of' (Stone 2019: 5). This was a considerable step in the representation of transgender characters in Australian scripted television where previous cisgender actors were cast in almost all trans roles in Australian scripted television (O'Meara and Monaghan 2024).

Mackenzie's character arc initially focused on her transgender identity and her gender affirmation procedures. Promoting the introduction of Mackenzie at the time, Stone was aware that there had to be drama surrounding her character but wanted her to be authentic:

> I really wanted to tell the story of Mackenzie being trans so people can learn, but I also wanted her to just be a regular teen at the same time, and get caught up with the teen drama which has nothing to do with her being trans (cited in McManus 2019: 7)

Stone worked with the show's writers to balance the need for drama and authenticity. Stone's portrayal of Mackenzie spoke to the larger trend of queer narratives that focused primarily on authenticity, agency and identity (O'Meara and Monaghan 2024), with many stakeholders in the Australian screen industry viewing the selection of Stone as form of ethical casting (Cover 2023b).

Mackenzie's first prominent storyline was her trying to track down her estranged father, Grant Hargreaves (Paul Mecurio), who had disowned Mackenzie – as well as her mother – due to her trans identity. She began as a new student at Erinsborough High and became friends with regular Yashvi Rebecchi (Olivia Junkeer) in order to get close to Shane (Nicholas Coghlan), who knew the whereabouts of her father. As their friendship developed, Yashvi accidentally outed Mackenzie, introducing a revealing storyline about transphobia, bullying and institutional issues preventing Mackenzie from using the female toilets (she was asked by the principal to use the accessible toilets as a compromise). Following the character's eighteenth birthday, Mackenzie is depicted as undergoing gender affirmation surgery. Significantly, Mackenzie's character arc progressed to concern more than just her transgender identity, with the character featuring in several romantic storylines. She went on to marry Hendrix Greyson (Ben Turland), who died after his body rejected a lung transplant. She then went onto start a relationship with Haz Devkar (Shiv Palekar) with whom she moved to Paris, ending her character arc on the show.

Neighbours, of course, represents a certain brand of Australian everydayness. Like most soap operas, it depicts a community of interconnected characters, families, geographical settings and storylines. As Alan McKee (2001) has noted, the boundaries of *Neighbours'* community are regulated and policed to demonstrate to the public who belongs to the Australian community who should be figured as a threat to that community. By agreeing to include a young trans character, *Neighbours* insistently changes the framework of trans inclusivity in Australia: a trans person is not something which happens outside its fictional suburb of Erinsborough or enters but must be represented as a risk or a disruption in the way both short-term and continuing 'bad' characters are regularly used in soaps. Rather, by creating a character who is depicted as having a good 'fit' within the *Neighbours* neighbourhood, casting a trans actor to play the role, and establishing the character's longevity over four years of episodes provides a powerful new way in which to represent trans identity within the soap-style storylines of radical interdependency and belonging.

The *First Day* breakthrough 2020

Acclaimed children's series *First Day* (2020–2) was Australia's first youth-oriented drama to cast a transgender actor as a transgender protagonist. Over one standalone episode that preceded the series in 2017, and two seasons of four episodes each airing on ABC in 2020 and 2022, the series follows twelve-year-old Hannah (Evie Macdonald) as she navigates her first years of high school, teenage identity and trans experience.

The first season largely focuses on Hannah's trans identity, narrating this through her move from primary school to secondary school. While grappling with typical teen issues at a new school such as making new friends, dealing with new social dynamics and the general messiness of selfhood in the transition between childhood and adolescence, Hannah also navigates her social transition, coming out to her friends and the greater school community, as well as transphobic hostility. Although the school principal speaks about the inclusive community at the school, like Mackenzie in *Neighbours,* Hannah finds she is not permitted to use the girls' bathrooms and is bullied, threatened and publicly outed on social media.

One of the unique aspects of this series is that the creator, Julie Kalceff, placed significant emphasis on giving Hannah the agency to solve problems and resolve conflicts. As a result, she is a notably resilient character, overcoming every challenge with the support of friends and family. In the first episode of season one, she is anxious about being outed and worries about the year ahead. Throughout this first season, Hannah achieves her goals to fit in: wearing the girls' uniform, using the girls' bathroom, having sleepovers with her friends, going swimming, and attending school camp. By the end of this first season, Hannah is proud of her identity and becomes a role model for other trans students.

First Day's second season deals with typical teenage conflicts, such as feeling left out when friendships change. This season builds towards a school dance, where Hannah tells her crush that she likes him. Alongside this narrative, she becomes a leader for LGBTQ+ communities at the school. In contrast to the first season's emphasis on passing, the second season focuses on Hannah building a queerer, more inclusive community at the school. To achieve this, she creates a 'Pride' support group for LGBTQ+ students and stages a campaign to abolish the school's gendered uniform policy.

What makes *First Day* most significant is that, in addition to its inclusion of a transgender actor as a trans protagonist, the series was aimed at a youth audience. Although *First Day* often relied on transnormative conceptions of identity and affirmed a binary understanding of gender, depicting character complexity, resilience and engagement in a text primarily made for child audiences broke new ground in gender-diverse representation in Australia (McIntyre, Riggs and Bartholomaeus 2023).

We have described both the *Neighbours* and *First Day* depictions of trans characters as 'breakthroughs' that have radically shifted the corpus of gender diversity on Australian screens. While earlier depictions across film and television of the twentieth and early twenty-first centuries reflected broader cultural frameworks of gender norms and perceived 'transgressions' of their time, both of these texts framed trans characters not as spectacle to be investigated but as core parts of the tapestry of Australian everydayness and cultural life. As we discuss in later chapters, the impact of 'positive' representation is typically only meaningful for both the well-being of gender- and sexuality-diverse audiences and for social and attitudinal change among mainstream audiences when it depicts engagement and ordinariness, rather than difference and sympathy. It is significant, then, that it is primarily in television – with perhaps the rare exception of *52 Tuesdays* in film – that achieves this ordinariness. Here, accounting for the medium that, itself, is marked by domesticity and promotes spectatorship in the everyday surroundings of domestic life (Barker 1999) is important.

Post-binary identities and streaming media

In thinking about how gender- and sexuality-diverse characters are represented on Australian screens, it is important to consider not just identities that fall under the 'LGBTQ+' umbrella such as trans, but to engage critically with new, alternative ways of describing, experiencing and being gendered subjects. Over the past decade, the affordances of digital and networked platforms facilitated young people (initially) to engage creatively in defining their own sense of sexuality and gender, and this included the production of new, diverse gender categories, labels and descriptors that worked against binary oppositions such as masculine/feminine, cisgender/transgender and hetero/homo. For some, this was about finding new ways to describe, articulate the experience of genders and sexualities that fell outside the ordinary expectations, behavioural norms and constraints of lesbian, gay, bisexual and transgender subjectivity and for which their own sense of subjectivity fell into a 'gap' in that identity language. For others, it was about finding a post-binary way of describing the lived experience and meaningful feelings of their gender or sexuality.

In many ways, what we have witnessed is a powerful new language of gender and sexuality identity and an emerging typology of attraction that has actively challenged and contested older norms and stereotypes. What has been referred to as an emergent and popular taxonomy of gender and sexuality identity (Cover 2019) is still relatively absent from overt screen entertainment representation. This was not, of course, the first significant reformulation of gender and sexuality since the nineteenth-century institution of sexuality as a discrete and innate personage (Foucault 1990). Rather, we have previously witnessed such challenges in the psychoanalytic Marxism of the 1960s and

1970s (Marcuse 1969), the Gay Liberation Movement's anti-establishmentism of the 1970s (Altman 1971), the French Feminism of the 1980s (Irigaray 1985) and, during the 1990s, queer theory's poststructuralist and anti-essentialist critique of the masculinity/femininity and hetero/homo binaries as constructed, narrow and normative (Sedgwick 1990, Butler 1993). What these earlier alternatives offered were greater agency in how genders and sexualities were expressed and described away from stereotypes or 'expert' medico-psychological approaches, and a strong embrace of fluidity, contingency, multiplicity and diversity that was expected to revolutionize gender, sexuality and human life. However, such accounts of gender and sexuality were never quite picked up as part of everyday popular culture, remaining broadly an expression of the avant-garde, radical queer politics or of scholarly critique.

The post-binary identity frameworks that emerged in the 2010s were, however, an expression of grassroots community needs. Beginning principally online in settings like Tumblr, where those who felt terms such as masculine, feminine, trans, LGBTQ+ and straight did not capture the lived experience of subjectivity began to develop hundreds of new terms, practices and descriptions. Online dating sites soon provided lists of multiple new genders and sexualities (Kellaway 2014, Wong 2014), and some social media platforms altered their gender and pronoun interface options to encompass fifty or more different genders that were more inclusive of transgender, intersex and other gender-diverse persons (Molloy 2014). Although there are now (literally) hundreds of gender and sexuality identity labels or descriptors in increasingly regular use (Cover 2019), among the more common are asexual, bisexual or bi+, demisexual, homoflexible, heteroflexible, pansexual, sapiosexual, omnisexual, maxigender and, perhaps most regularly used to describe genders outside the older dichotomies, non-binary. The production of new terms of gender that fall outside masculine/feminine, and new terms for sexualities and relationships that are not based on attraction of one gender to another gender, continues to expand (Mardell 2016).

However, screen entertainment media have been relatively slow to catch up, both in Australia and internationally, tending to preference more simplified LGBTQ+ subjectivity that is more quickly recognizable to audiences. Certainly, some interviewees in the *AusQueer Screen* project noted the relative absence of these alternative and post-binary gender and sexuality frameworks in Australian screen entertainment which, they argue, remains too firmly rooted within liberal-humanist LGBTQ+ norms. As one participant put it:

I guess to help future generations, like, there is a lot of gay, gay, gay, gay, everything gay, so I think probably can do without another gay character for now. I think nonbinary and asexual are really, really underrepresented, even compared to, like, you know, bisexuality.

There are, however, a small number of Australian examples that show the way forward, including *Starting From Now* (2014–16), *Homecoming Queens* (2018), and the latest iteration of *Heartbreak High* (2022–). These titles, produced for distribution on YouTube, SBS On Demand and Netflix, have featured several post-binary characters, including trans pansexual and non-binary subjectivities. This, we argue, is just as much about emergent forms of distribution such as streaming platforms as it is about attempting to be inclusive to a wider range of gender diversities.

The proliferation of digital platforms has had a profound impact on the screen landscape, the experiences of audiences, and broader screen cultures. Australian queer film and television now includes social media and video platforms such as YouTube, Instagram and TikTok, and Broadcast Video on Demand (BVOD) and Subscription Video on Demand (SVOD) services, which are often grouped together as 'streaming platforms'. Within this contemporary streaming environment, operators employ varying business models, industrial practices and emphases with regard to programming, curation and categorization of film and television content (Lotz 2022). Broadly, social media platforms host user-generated content and serve this to audiences algorithmically, while BVOD services are advertiser-driven with libraries consisting of content originally distributed elsewhere, such as broadcast television or cinema-released texts. SVOD services are subscriber-driven, offering users access to a library of on-demand content that is often exclusive to each platform. While these streaming platforms differ, they collectively contribute to the experience of engaging with screen culture today. BVOD and SVOD services in particular have similarities in their categorization of queer media, which contributes to our understanding of what constitutes queer film and television, and more expressly, what constitutes Australian queer film and television. Our argument here is that not only has the advent of digital platforms and streaming services changed how queer screen media is *accessed, categorized* and *engaged with* in Australia and elsewhere, but that it has opened new frameworks for making sense of content and for representing a wider array of stories and more diverse subjectivity. Significant in streaming services is that it has further expanded the range of television and film access and diversified the audience in ways which enables more diverse content that may be less palatable or easily understood by mainstream audiences. In itself, distributional diversification is not new: Reeves and colleagues (1996) found, in the North American context, that the proliferation of cable channels enabled more diverse content and more diverse viewing practices, producing casual, devoted and avid fan viewers, as well as more complex series narrative and more challenging stories in ways which were less possible in a limited network broadcast framework. These, arguably, advanced television's depth beyond the simplistic, clichéd and episodic that had marked much North American television for many decades. The same can be said to have occurred with the introduction of streaming: a reduced need to capitalize on an audience market share allowing for 'niche' television with challenging character identities and themes.

Just as significant is the fact that streaming services have not limited themselves to distribution but to production. Again, as in the cable era in North America whereby cable services such as HBO and Showtime produced significant advances in on-screen diversity for, particularly, lesbian and gay representation, we are seeing similar advances in content made for and by streaming platforms. For example, Amazon's *Transparent* (2014–19) would likely not have been possible on traditional network television of the 1980s in the United States of America, nor would such a show have received international syndication. And despite the growth of cable television networks and their wider range of subjects, trans issues would still not necessarily have appealed to those audiences that were cultivated by each cable network. Rather, the further shift towards niche audiences enables greater experimentation with breaking the bounds of normative characterization.

This, we note, has actively enabled the diverse sexuality and gender identity content in a range of series including the new iteration of *Heartbreak High* which has foregrounded a non-binary character among its broad cast: sixteen-year-old Darren Rivers. Using they/them pronouns, Darren identifies as queer and non-binary, and of intersectional African-Australian identity. Portrayed by Australian actor James Majoos who themselves identifies as non-binary, Darren is considered a 'breakthrough' character who, arguably, is 'rewriting queer stereotypes' (Millar 2022) by breaking with the presumption that all non-heterosexuality is performed by a gay-identified, masculine self. Although Darren is portrayed often through a camp sensibility, the characterization provides a complexity and depth beyond the more typical 'sassy' gay friend with cutting one-liners, and this is at least partly due to the storylines in which their gender-diverse subjectivity is foregrounded. This complexity is added to by Darren's relationship with Ca$h who struggles with his identity as asexual (or ace) but not aromantic – that is, desiring to be in a relationship but not desiring that the relationship is sexual. There are also tensions resulting from the differential class demarcations between the two which have resulted in broadly divergent cultural attitudes. The messiness of navigating complex, conflicting and contingent desires, genders, sexualities and intersectionalities is represented not through individualized agency, personal resilience or radical rejection of norms but through the support networks of interdependency in which Darren's well-being as a non-binary character is located.

As with *Neighbours*, the inclusion of a non-binary character in *Heartbreak High* is a marker of ethical diversity programming, not merely because it represents advancements in the taxonomy of gender subjectivity and descriptors increasingly meaningful among younger people, but because it locates that character within an interdependent framework of other characters, both with tension and acceptance that is very much the 'everyday' of secondary school culture. Darren's identity is complex and their relationships are difficult and intricate, but the distributional frame of streaming enables characters whose trajectories and identities do not need to be easily categorized, stereotyped or made instantly recognizable as was long the case in broadcast television. By embracing complicated storylines, subjects and characters, streaming platforms engaged in creativity have overcome the hurdle of traditional network ratings to present content that is more up-to-date with contemporary gender diversity practices.

Conclusion

Gender diversity, non-binary identities and post-binary experiences are, as Sebastian Cordoba (2023) as much an emergence of popular media culture as they are an articulation of a felt sense of being and relationality among individuals. At a deeper level, arguably, it is not that gender diversity is either *caused* by screen media or first *appears* in screen media; rather, it is that screen media has always set the conditions through which the transformation of identity norms becomes possible (Barker 1999). Our genealogy of on-screen gender diversity, then, reflects not only shifting cultural norms, but contributes to the matrix of historical change that makes emergent ways of performing and being gendered subjects both thinkable and acceptable. We have witnessed the exclusion or ridicule of so-called 'breaches' of gender norms in past Australian texts, we have seen gender play deployed on-screen as both drama and humour, and we have watched as trans subjectivity has been made 'ordinary' in broadcast television, while non-binary and post-binary identities became representable in contemporary streaming media. All of these reflect and, importantly, *shape* the Australian knowledge frameworks of gender subjectivity, opening new ways of being for understood and conditioning a future in which the meaning of gender is simultaneously more complex but more approachable for many.

9

Historical Reception Practices, Policing and Community Change

Introduction

Understanding how screen media is interpreted, received and incorporated into lives is not just a matter of figuring out the meanings the everyday audience member makes. Rather, it acknowledges that how we make meanings and our practices of viewing are at least partially conditioned by community audience customs developed in the past. That is, where we find something appealing or something homophobic is not only up to the individual but cannot be disconnected from the ways in which different audiences in different times made sense of high-profile film events of their era.

This chapter takes on this task by examining some of the ways in which local contexts of criminalization, policing and anti-LGBTQ+ violence provide frameworks for queer Australian audience reception practices and cultures of spectatorship today. We focus here on a very important case study for Australian queer audiences: the relationship between policing and criminality in Sydney, New South Wales and the reception at the time of the American police thriller, *Cruising* (1980), written and directed by William Friedkin, based on a 1970 novel by New York Times journalist Gerald Walker. This popular albeit sometimes controversial film tells the story of heterosexual police officer Steve Burns (Al Pacino) going undercover to investigate the murders of gay men in New York. *Cruising* positions the city's corrupt, violent police force and its underground gay leather scene as mirror images; perverse reflections that cohere into a disturbing vision of a dystopic world (Young 2018).

Our aim in this chapter is to reveal a critical element in Australian queer film cultures; namely, that the history of queer film in Australia is frequently a story of local audiences making meaning of movies created overseas in ways that reflect back on how everyday institutional and governance practices are at play

(McKinnon 2016). We argue that, far from replicating the response of North American audiences, Australian cinemagoers have interpreted and responded to these movies in ways that are shaped by specifically local histories, identities, spaces and viewing practices. In the case of the Sydney reception of *Cruising*, those contexts included an urban gay community grappling with homophobic violence and police corruption amid a campaign to decriminalize sex between men (McKinnon 2014).

If we are to understand how Australian audiences interpret, comprehend and engage with queer screen media, the case of *Cruising* provides a powerful historical case study. Audience discourse about the film highlighted community discord over modes of political activism, while simultaneously generating forms of unified activism against routine police violence and for legislative reform to decriminalize homosexual sex. We begin with a brief summary of the context of *Cruising* both as a film and the Sydney setting in which queer audiences interpreted its meaning and impact. We then consider how relationships between the 1980s Sydney gay scene, policing and criminality can provide a deeper contextualization of the issues activism was facing around the time the film was screened. This is followed by two, interconnected histories of the reception of queer screen content in the 1980s – the issue of violence, and the issue of police raids on queer venues. Significant here is that it is not only the problematic film that generated reception discourse, but also the cultural milieu in which that discourse was ready to emerge in ways which demonstrate how screen culture participates in socio-political shifts.

Cruising

In *Cruising*, patrons of New York's gay leather and S&M nightclubs are being targeted by a serial killer. Steve Burns, who bears a physical resemblance to the victims, is recruited to find the murderer. Leaving his girlfriend Nancy (Karen Allen) behind, he moves to a gay neighbourhood, befriends his gay neighbour Ted (Don Scardino) and spends his nights in a series of real-life clubs in New York's Meatpacking District. Burns visits spaces crammed with leather-clad bodies cruising, dancing and fucking in sweaty, blue-lit abandon. If the Hays Production Code had famously forbade representation of homosexual desires on-screen, *Cruising* demonstrates some of the ways in which the post-Code production of the 1980s was willing to present queer sexuality as anthropological spectacle, with images of men in a range of sexual acts including passionate kissing, fellating a police baton, rimming, anal sex and fisting (Miller 2007).

When *Cruising* reached Sydney screens in 1980, homosexual activity was criminal. At that time, the New South Wales Crimes Act provided that: 'Whosoever commits the abominable crime of buggery . . . shall be liable to penal servitude for fourteen years', while attempted buggery or attempted indecent assault on a male was punishable by up to five years, and consent of both parties was not a legislated defence. Public opinion was largely in favour of reforming this law (Bull et al. 1991) and gay sex had already been decriminalized in South Australia in 1975 and Victoria in 1980. Yet, law reform remained a significant hurdle that local activists had yet to overcome, with the NSW police force among the politically powerful groups actively resisting legislative change. The attitude of police was made clear by the devoutly Catholic NSW Vice Squad chief, Detective Inspector Ernie 'the Good' Shepard, who argued that 'paedophiles' 'are turning young children, the adults of tomorrow, into sexual deviates. This might be a big statement, but I think this is why the number of homosexuals in our community is increasing' (cited in Lowe 1984: 97).

Although arguably less of an active presence in the lives of gay people than in previous decades, the NSW Vice Squad, under Shepard's direction, continued to see enforcement of anti-gay laws as an important part of its duties. Activists complained, with good reason, that a police force inclined towards punishing queer people was unlikely to take seriously its duty to protect those same people from violent crimes. In that respect, spectatorship of *Cruising* prompted concern among Sydney gay activists in part because the horrific anti-gay murders the film depicts had real-life local parallels. From the 1970s to the 1990s, dozens of gay men and trans women were murdered in Sydney. In 2023, a commission of inquiry into these still mostly unsolved murders found that 'the NSW Police Force failed in its responsibility to properly investigate cases of historical gay and transgender hate crime' (Sackar 2023: 5).

The pre-AIDS era of the early 1980s was a time of flux in Sydney's queer activist history, in which the community was reflecting on its recent achievements and debating strategies for continuing to move forward. As we discussed in Chapter 4, since the origins of the Australian lesbian and gay activist movement in 1969, there had often been conflict between gay liberationist politics, which advocated for social and sexual revolution, and liberal reformists, who sought equality and mainstream acceptance (Reynolds 2002, Willett 2000). By 1980, reformism was dominant, based in no small part on the emergence of an identifiably and proudly gay neighbourhood centred on dozens of bars and other gay businesses along Oxford Street and the surrounding residential areas of Darlinghurst and Paddington. Some of these venues, with names like The Barracks, Signal and Club 80, modelled themselves on the New York leather scene of the 1970s depicted in *Cruising*.

From the viewpoint of the anti-capitalist gay liberation movement, the bars of the gay scene were sites of oppression formed through a collaboration between exploitative business owners, corrupt police and unliberated gay consumers. While there is an argument to be made that the partying, cruising and fun of the bars empowered queer identities, it is also true that the NSW Crimes Act created conditions for the exploitation of homosexual people. Through the 1960s and 1970s, many of Sydney's gay venues were run by a syndicate with widely discussed links to the criminal underworld. The syndicate purportedly kept their doors open through the payment of regular kickbacks to police. While liberationist and reformist activists campaigned for the decriminalization of gay sex, some bar owners and corrupt cops likely feared the loss of income that would result from a gay community no longer fearful of arrest. If gay sex was decriminalized, bar owners would neither be paying for police protection nor relying on underworld finance to operate, potentially realigning long-standing tacit arrangements of Sydney nightlife (O'Grady 2013).

Into the 1980s, with more businesses owned by openly gay people and with residents of gay neighbourhoods forming a significant electoral bloc, that realignment was looking inevitable and the criminalization of gay sex increasingly absurd. Homosexual people were developing an open place in the political, social and cultural mainstream, with increasing representation on television and in movies very much a part of this new mainstream visibility.

Cruising was just one of many films centred on or featuring gay characters that screened in Sydney in the first years of the 1980s, including *Taxi zum Klo* (1980), *Fame* (1980), *Deathtrap* (1981), *Victor/Victoria* (1982), *Querelle* (1982), *Partners* (1982) and *Making Love* (1982). Fighting for legislative reform, gay activists were highly alert to how gay lives were represented on screen. In the flourishing LGBTQ+ press, film critics continued to demand 'positive' imagery of homosexual people that would support the community's arguments for greater tolerance and would reduce their vulnerability to violent crime. With the arrival of *Cruising*, questions were raised as to whether big screen images of uninhibited leather sex would help or harm the fight for acceptance among the greater public.

Intriguingly, events in Sydney just three years after the release of *Cruising* closely replicated issues presented in the film. As we will explore below, three police raids on Sydney leather and S&M sex venue Club 80 ignited outrage among the gay community. Skilfully transforming community anger into political action, activists rejected the idea that leather sex clubs comprised a hidden world of shame and horror righteously exposed by brave police. Instead, they celebrated gay sexual pleasure as a form of joyful resistance to ugly and shameful repression by the state. In so doing, they specifically rejected *Cruising*'s vision of a queer world inextricably tied to criminality, corruption and violence. Director William Friedkin's film was shocking in its portrayal of some gay men's sexual lives, yet the film failed to capture the counter-public imaginary that was already in development both in New York and Sydney. Specifically, *Cruising* presented criminality and corruption in queer spaces otherwise defined by liberation, kinship and community interdependency.

Undercover cops and out gay men in *Cruising*

Cruising first depicts New York's gay spaces through the eyes of two police officers driving their squad car through city streets on a steamy summer night. The police view sidewalks crowded with gay men and see not pleasure and partying but criminality and violence, bemoaning the fact that an area in which children had once happily played is now 'lost' to uninhibited queer sexuality. Rather than positioning the police as moral arbiters seeking to restore the neighbourhood's innocence, *Cruising* presents the two officers – and, by extension, the police force they represent – as violent misogynists and sexual abusers. Both men notice two trans sex workers walking along the street, whom they harass before coercing both into the squad car and demanding oral sex.

Far from operating as society's protective shield from the queer sexual underworld, therefore, the police of *Cruising* are an alternate vision of that world seen reflected in a horror film's funhouse mirror. Indeed, the film muddily blurs together the violence of the murders, the actions of the police and the sexual acts of the gay scene, allowing for no easy visual, political or moral distinction between each. In *Cruising* queerness is not, then, the exception to normative masculinity but, as one scholar has put it, 'the latter's shadow side, its omnipresent mirror image' (Young 2018: 131). Killers and victims look so alike that it is sometimes difficult to tell which is which or how many victims and perpetrators there might be. The identity of the murderer is never fully resolved, with the same actor playing a victim in an early scene then a killer in a later one. Of the constant parallels between queer sexual subculture and anti-queer violence, perhaps the most disturbing is a scene in which penetrative male-male sex is mirrored with depictions of a knife being thrust into bare male flesh. The film develops a narrative of degradation and corruption, entirely ignoring the ethics of mutual pleasure, consent, care and kinship central to queer communities.

Unsurprisingly, the fact that the film so specifically equates the sex lives of gay men in the early 1980s (dark and criminal *or* liberatory and joyful) with the actions of police (oppressive and violent) was responded to with anger and dismay by many in the gay community (McKinnon 2014). These concerns were only exacerbated by the film's positioning of a violent murderer as the seemingly inevitable final product when the policing/homosexual mirroring coheres into corporeal singularity: Burns' journey through the film charts this conjoining as he transforms from fresh-faced, heterosexual rookie cop to a pale, frightened wraith who may well be a murderer and who, if not gay, has almost certainly become more than just a casual observer of the gay S&M scene. The narrative, as some have argued, actively queers him to the point it is never clear whether or not he is – or has become – homosexual (Miller 2007). In the film's final scenes, the bloodied corpse of Burns' gay neighbour is discovered. Ted has been brutally stabbed to death, perhaps by Burns himself. We last see Burns staring into a mirror, where his haunted eyes meet the gaze of the camera, possibly, if ambiguously, conveying horror at what he has become.

The anti-policing themes in *Cruising* have, interestingly, rarely been acknowledged by critics but nevertheless serve as an indictment of the relationship between police and queer communities (Petrychyn 2022). While Burns expresses some sympathy for gay people and develops a seemingly genuine affection for Ted, by the end of the film he has most likely become a murderer, with Ted his apparent victim. *Cruising* offers little hope that reform would improve relationships between the police and the gay community. Instead, corruption and violence are presented as the inevitable product of interactions between the two.

The anti-police perspective of *Cruising* was only rarely mentioned in the responses of Australian gay critics and activists in the early 1980s. Although the homophobia of the police was a central topic of conversation among the activist movement at that time, particularly in relation to the cause of decriminalization, *Cruising* was never applauded for bringing police bigotry to wider public attention. Instead, gay critics and audiences feared that the film's homophobic depiction of queer people would only encourage more homophobia among the police and worsen the dire problem of anti-queer violence on the city's streets.

Contexts: Police, gay activism and illegal sex in early 1980s Sydney

To many gay men in early 1980s Sydney, *Cruising*'s hyper-masculine, violent and homophobic police force would have been deeply familiar. At lesbian and gay protests through the 1970s, a commonly deployed chant was, 'Stop police attacks on gays, women and blacks!' The chant neatly summarized the fact that homophobia, misogyny and racism were inherent to policing, revealing the ways in which the political, social and cultural dominance of white, heterosexual men was enforced, at least in part, by and within the state's police force. Describing attitudes among his colleagues in the 1980s, former officer Duncan McNab (2017) has argued that an 'ingrained culture of thuggery against gay men [had been] mentored into the NSW Police for generations' (27).

Held just two years before the film's Sydney release, the 1978 Mardi Gras is the best-known example of police violence in the pre-decriminalization era. Despite the obvious brutality of police actions at the event, the state's premier Neville Wran supported the police. Although personally in favour of the decriminalization of homosexual sex, Wran faced significant resistance from members of his own Labor party, many of the Liberal party opposition, religious leaders and the police. He appeared unwilling to risk political capital on the issue, arguing instead that, through the reforms he had been able to manage, the public place of homosexual people had been vastly improved by his government. In 1981, for example, he claimed that he had ended the previously common practice of police entrapment of gay men at beats, telling reporters, 'I'm always intrigued by this talk about harsh treatment of homosexuals in Sydney . . . . Homosexuals can walk up and down Oxford Street day or night without any trouble from the police at all' (cited in Chaples 1985: 47).

For gay bar-goers with little connection to or interest in the activist cause, Wran's words may well have carried some truth. The gay bar scene was no longer a hidden world. Homosexuals did walk up and down Oxford Street most nights without any interaction with the police. The number of men charged under the anti-gay provisions of the Crimes Act was small and, partying and cruising in an area of the city in which there were dozens of gay venues to choose from, it was often easy to forget about the law's supposed constraints. To activists, however, many of whom were dealing with the physical and psychological impacts of police violence at multiple protest events over the previous decade and/or were carefully monitoring reports of aggressive policing at beats or in other queer spaces, Wran's statement fell significantly short. Working hard to advance the cause of decriminalization, many activists were frustrated at the apolitical complacency of the gay bar scene.

In downplaying the likelihood of police intervention in gay lives, Premier Wran was implicitly suggesting that troublemaking activists blocking traffic or otherwise creating havoc only had themselves to blame if the police responded harshly. Well-behaved homosexuals, from this point of view, were unlikely to face any problems from the police, regardless of the law. Presumably, Wran was hoping to keep the issue of decriminalization quietly out of view.

For this fragile peace to sustain, however, Wran needed the police to behave themselves. Any more widely witnessed acts of police violence would risk (re)radicalizing the gay community. The argument that homosexuals had the freedom of Oxford Street would fail if police made regular arrests or were too obvious in their harassment of queer people in the city's gay bars, pubs and beats. Activists worked hard to encourage anger among gay men at their continued criminal status, aware that change could only be produced by significant community action. However, by the time *Cruising* was screened in 1980, the issue of homosexual law reform was fading from the minds of those content to accept the status quo.

Historical reception: Police raids, leather sex and decriminalization

To convincingly go undercover in *Cruising*, Steve Burns pumps iron and squeezes his muscular physique into body-hugging denim, t-shirts and leather. The 'clone look' that he adopts served a range of purposes for its many gay devotees in New York, Sydney and elsewhere. First, it publicly marked adherents as gay, representing the drive to be visibly recognized as a member of a more visible community. Secondly, it rejected the stereotypical alignment of male homosexuality with femininity, displaying an identity that explicitly rejected effeminacy. Thirdly, the look was deliberately sexual (Edwards 2005).

In 1981, Melbourne-based gay newspaper *Klick!* reported on Sydney's gay scene: 'The big thing in the Gay Capital of the South Pacific is the clone look . . . everywhere one goes these days the San Francisco butch image of T-shirt – check shirt – jeans is to be seen' (Kay 1981: 46). Not all clones were involved in the leather and S&M scene into which Burns so enthusiastically launches himself in *Cruising*, yet there was substantial crossover between the masculine performativity of the clone and its hypermasculine leather extension. *Klick!* noted that, 'The leather scene [in Sydney] has boomed as well . . . those who have not been to Sydney for a while will certainly notice the changes' (Kay 1981: 46). Sydney's leather scene incorporated bars and pubs like the Barracks, along with unlicensed 'backroom bars', also known as 'fuck clubs', like Club 80.

Clones and leather sex were the subject of enormous debate in late 1970s and early 1980s Australia, with frequent opinion pieces and letters to the editors in LGBTQ+ community newsletters, newspapers and magazines either applauding or decrying this new model of queer masculinity. Michael Glynn (1995), editor of Sydney's first gay newspaper *The Star*, was an advocate of the clone look and of Sydney's leather scene, who argued that clones signified a cultural moment in which gay men had ceased performing their gender in an effeminate fashion and had embraced an 'authentic' maleness. Many left-wing activists, however, identified a worrying conservatism and embrace of misogyny in the look. Activist Terry Stokes (1980), for example, argued that 'The Macho Clone strives to distance itself from any association with femininity, effeminism and feminism. It attempts to adhere in all externals to the icon of a man foisted upon us by patriarchy; to be more manly than straight men' (4). To Stokes, the misogyny of the clone was not 'incidental but, rather, intrinsic' (4).

Stokes was responding to an essay by fellow activist Phil Carswell, in which Carswell analysed his own recent adoption of the clone look. Carswell (1980) described a re-evaluation of his relationship to the gay movement. Activists, he argued, were making themselves irrelevant by refusing to embrace the pleasures and politics of the gay bar scene. The activist movement, he stated, 'must gain more political sophistication in dealing with our oppressors and more sympathy in dealing with our homosexual compatriots' (25). To Carswell, the clone look as articulated in gay bar culture was 'the avenue where I can express my personal needs and desires with other gay men . . . bars are the one area where a lot of us receive our introduction and an ongoing interaction with gay life.'

While activists of the radical left criticized the clone's gender politics, those towards the political centre worried that the visibility of an unapologetically promiscuous gay sexual culture would harm efforts to gain mainstream acceptance. This liberal-humanist politics of respectability and tolerance was at odds with the Gay Liberation movement's anti-establishment flouting of conservative domesticity and monogamy, and those advocating a civil rights reformism broadly rejected what was seen as the queer community's excesses (Boucher and Reynolds 2018). Indeed, among Sydney's community, there was an active debate over whether, in order to achieve decriminalization, it might be necessary to disavow the leather scene.

This debate directly influenced the local reception of *Cruising*. To those who hoped that the aggressively sexual gay leather world could be safely kept away from the heterosexual gaze, the fact that a film comprising images of slings, harnesses, Crisco, fisting and fucking was playing at the local multiplex was of concern lest it be seen to encapsulate the totality of queer life and culture. To some, Friedkin's explicit depiction of the leather scene was homophobic propaganda, designed to limit the claims of gay men to middle-class respectability. Ken Lovett (1980), for example, described *Cruising* as 'playing into the sweaty hands' of anti-gay Christian activists (7).

To many in the leather scene, however, the real shame should be attributed to those people, gay or straight, who were too sexually repressed to understand the radical pleasures of S&M sex and sexuality outside of domestic relationships. Interviewed in the mainstream media about the gay community's response to *Cruising*, Michael Glynn argued that the film had misrepresented a sexual subculture that, far from violent and immoral, was instead a site of joyful, liberated pleasure. According to the *Sydney Morning Herald*, 'Glynn believes there is more to the leather scene than was portrayed in the film. Aspects such as respect, trust and love' (Stewart 1980: 15). Glynn argued, 'Everyone has sex fantasies, but a lot of people have tension because society places such a taboo on these fantasies.' Rejecting the pathologizing of leather sex in *Cruising*, Glynn celebrated the possibilities the scene provided for pursuing sexual pleasure free from the hang-ups of the broader society. From this point of view, Burns was not going undercover into a world of shameful degeneracy otherwise hidden from the mainstream but was instead witnessing a community liberated from the shameful constraints under which the mainstream continued to limit itself.

Witnessed in the local reception of *Cruising*, this reversal of shame, rejected by the gay community and reapplied onto the repressive state, became the centre of a battle between gay activists and the NSW police in 1983, when members of the Vice Squad conducted a series of raids of the leather sex club, Club 80.

Across the course of three raids, police arrested twenty-eight men, charging with them with crimes under the anti-gay provisions of the Crimes Act, as well as a little used misdemeanour of 'scandalous conduct'. In the process, police sparked an extraordinary wave of anger among previously apolitical gay bargoers, who were forced to confront the possible loss of their newly found sexual freedoms.

In the context of audience debates about *Cruising,* the Club 80 raids provided exactly the trigger activists needed to radicalize the gay bar scene and reinvigorate the campaign for law reform. In the campaign that followed, any ambivalence the gay community might have felt about the politics of clones and leather sex was entirely absent. Instead, activists framed the raids as an invasion by police into gay spaces, arguing that it was the actions of police that were shameful, not the men in the club. Twenty-eight men subsequently signed statutory declarations stating that they had 'in the last two years participated, on a number of occasions, in acts of mutual masturbation, fellatio, anal intercourse and other sexual acts with male persons'. In other words, they had committed the same crimes with which the men at Club 80 had been charged. The declarations were presented in-person to the Vice Squad chief by two activists, Lex Watson and Robert French, who demanded to be arrested. Sensing a public relations scandal, Shepard declined.

Watson and French subsequently appeared on a popular morning television programme to explain their campaign. Watson told the show's host:

> The Vice Squad has this notion that homosexuality is all something that happens obscurely out there and it's all sinister and they have to chug out in the middle of the night and uncover it and go, 'Shock, gasp!' . . . We were just saying to them, 'Look, if you want to do that, we're doing exactly the same thing, in effect [as the men at Club 80], why not arrest us?' And they can't understand this (Kennerly 1983).

This argument was, in essence, smashing the mirror *Cruising* had placed between the queer leather scene and corrupt police, showing blatantly from our perspective today the extent to which reception practices and screen public controversy lean into local politics and sociality. If Friedkin had aimed for verisimilitude in recording the sex of the Meatpacking District clubs with seemingly frank detail, he had failed to notice critical elements. The men he watched were engaged in sexual play that centred on mutual pleasure, care and consent. Rather than accepting the direct alignment of their desires with violent, degraded and shameful behaviour by repressive forces, gay men in Sydney found political value in claiming the normative centre for themselves. Far from disavowing some sexual practices in order to seek acceptance on terms set by the heterosexual mainstream, they instead declared that it was the police whose perverse ideas should be disavowed.

Conclusion

In May 1984, the NSW Crimes Act was reformed to decriminalize gay sex. While the amended law continued to apply a discriminatory age of consent – 16 for heterosexual sex, 18 for sex between men – it was nonetheless a significant achievement for the activists who had been campaigning for more than a decade. Some identified the police raids on Club 80, along with the community response, as the tipping point that finally forced Wran and his government to act. Describing the raids as a 'watershed moment', Gay Rights Lobby member Barry Charles has remembered them as 'what got us law reform in a really reverse logic kind of way, because at the moment those efforts to unite the activist community, the bar community, the bar owners . . . all came together' (Charles 2022).

Importantly, however, that activism had earlier been apparent in reception practices and audience debates about this North American film and its problematic representation (to some) of elements of 1970s and 1980s gay male culture. The perception that *Cruising*'s spectatorship by a wider cisgender and straight population would misrepresent gay sexual cultures as violent and uncaring rather than as communal, liberatory and consenting was a clarifying moment for activists debating how those sexual cultures should or shouldn't be publicly represented. *Cruising*, meanwhile, has developed a cult following subsequent to reappraisals by queer critics, although debates continue as to whether or not this is a misunderstood masterpiece or a muddled mess. Exploring the historical reception of *Cruising* provides us with important insights into how queer audiences perceive a film in relation to socio-legal contexts, and how community debates over interpretations of the film have highlighted internal political differences but also engendered unities in the struggle against violence. Significantly, it calls upon us to think about how our response to various texts – international, local – are framed by past controversies that may not be memorable but shape the queer collective unconscious in the act of media spectatorship.

Part Four

Audience, Identity and Culture

Australian Queer Screen Audiences

Place, Time and Memory

Introduction

International queer scholarship over the past couple of decades has been attentive to the ways in which LGBTQ+ adults reflect on queer screen representations they encountered while 'growing up'. Some of this literature notes the ways in which on-screen characters, narratives and themes may be significant in identity formation and practices of self-identification (Padva 2004, Lipton 2008), as well as the formation of a sense of shared culture for LGBTQ+ subjects, who are sometimes perceived as growing up without knowing other LGBTQ+ people (Horvat 2021). However, there is still only limited empirical research on the experiences of LGBTQ+ audiences (McKinnon 2016, Cover and Dau 2021), and the broader social significance of queer screen representation in Australia over time. This chapter seeks to explore the recollections of gender- and sexuality-diverse people born in the 1970s and 1980s in relation to place and the temporal and spatial dimensions of accessing and engaging with queer screen content when they were younger.

This chapter focuses on an analysis of audience interviewees' discussions of their experiences and memories of encountering and engaging with LGBTQ+ on-screen representation while growing up, drawing on thirty-eight audience interviews conducted by the *AusQueerScreen* study. The study interviewed Australians born between the 1970s and 2000, twenty-one of whom were born in the 1970s and 1980s. This chapter focuses principally on those born in the 1970s and 1980s – that is, those who were in the late teens and early twenties between 1990 and 2005 – to draw out new ways to understand how the transitions in queer screen representation in the 1990s were experienced by audiences. In the context of LGBTQ+ history, media representation, education and policy, this period was pivotal for a number of reasons: first, it pre-dates the introduction of Web 2.0 internet, marked by broadband access to video, social media and discretely accessible resources, information and texts on LGBTQ+ life, health and politics; secondly, persons coming of age in that period had generally become sexually active after the advent of HIV and thereby had access to knowledge about its transmission (Hillier et al. 2010); decriminalization of consenting same-sex sexual acts was completed in all parts of Australia during this period reflecting the growth of a liberal-tolerance framework (Altman 2013); mass-circulation film and television were beginning to representation lesbian and gay characters in 'mainstream' film and television media, albeit often problematically and stereotypically (Cover 2000). Participants born from the 1990s onwards often discussed their experience of film and television in the context of internet access and social media – as the contrasts are substantial, we have chosen to keep that separate from the present analysis in order better to evaluate the ways in which memory and place are utilized and intersect in an era prior to the introduction of Web 2.0 social media.

Key to understanding audience experience involves making sense of how memorial accounts of the past are narrated, including particularly periods of transition we ordinarily refer to as 'growing up' or 'coming of age' (Cover and Prosser 2024) and the significance of key queer cinema texts or films and series broadcast on television. We use the term 'growing up' liberally, acknowledging that a sense of self-identity is recognized, develops or representation stabilizes over time in a non-linear and gradual way (Horley and Clarke 2016). We also point to the need for framing LGBTQ+ growing up in ways that acknowledge the shared experiences of growing up without insisting on a uniform or stereotypical narrative (Marshall et al. 2019). Additionally, in the homophobic and transphobic conditions of many queer people's childhoods in the 1980s and early 1990s, the significance of particular film memories, tastes or fandoms is often recognized only retrospectively later in life.

Two very significant themes emerged in our interviews with Australians discussing their memories of engaging with queer screens while growing up. The first was the significance of *place* and *space*. Physical spaces of media engagement such as the domestic living room, video shops, and cinemas were all important contexts for understanding how queer film and television were experienced and for how it played a role in constituting gender- and sexuality-diverse subjectivities. Likewise, concepts of place marked by rural/urban divides and mobility towards the city were significant in participants accounts. The second was *time.* Our interviewees engaged with the temporal dimensions of navigating place, identity and belonging in ways which intersected with the narratives they encountered in media.

We begin with a brief summary of the significance of a turn to audience. Much as our discussion of the significance of production perspectives was important in Chapters 5, 6 and 7, the final four chapters of this part take audience and reception as necessary focal points for understanding queer screen media in Australia. We follow this with some remarks on the role of memory in the context of identity before discussing our interviewees' framing of their experiences engaging with queer texts in the domestic space of the family home. We interweave these discussions with their considerations of temporality. While contemporary young people experience media engagement, viewing practices, growing up LGBTQ+ and frameworks of place and time in ways markedly different in the contemporary digital era, the experiences of our study participants are important not because they reveal cultural formations of past generations but because they play a constitutive role in the lives of this age-group as they navigate their lifecourse, and thereby inform on the experiences of a discrete social generation.

Refocusing on the audience

As we discussed in Chapter 5 and elsewhere throughout this book, one key historical fixation of queer media scholarship has been on questions of visibility and representation, and on the use of textual analysis as a method. These are important and worthwhile topics and tools, and they are the more likely ones given that production and audience/reception research often has substantially higher costs, requires co-located team-work that is difficult in a small scholarly field, and typically requires a much greater investment of time without necessarily producing greater returns in the key areas on which scholarship is measured: publication and engagement with wider communities.

We have been arguing that more attention is needed on audiences, but that means particular kinds of attention. One problem with some international queer screen scholarship is that it relies on assumptions about audiences, interprets on their behalf and argues for audience needs without actually talking to audience members and analysing their responses to know the actual conditions of queer audiencehood. This is something on which our field tends to lag behind other advances over the past few decades (in areas of scholarship admittedly better resourced and more widely staffed), and particularly since the 1990s.

The 1990s was an important decade in cultural, film, screen and television studies for a number of reasons, most particularly for the increasing turn towards reception studies, building on the frameworks developed by cultural studies in the United Kingdom, particularly David Morley's (1980) testing of Stuart Hall's (1980a, 1980b) encoding/decoding models of audience interpretation and the production of meaning. John Fiske's influential *Understanding Popular Culture* (1989a) and *Reading the Popular* (1989b) and Janice Radway's *Reading the Romance* (1984) exemplified the movement towards making sense of both texts and the cultural circumstances of their reception and/or consumption by overcoming an arbitrary dichotomy of art versus popular culture, and positing the important view that popular culture, including texts that may not convey 'artistic value' in the subjective and discriminatory sense of high art, are sometimes more valuable, and thus merit analyses that take into account the views, understandings and uses of the text by popular audiences. Cultural studies approaches that drove scholarship towards a necessary focus on the audience also included the reconceptualization of the audience as active, self-conscious, multiple, fragmented and engaged (Ang 1991).

The various historical shifts towards audience scholarship exemplified by cultural studies, however, were not as pronounced in queer film/television studies. Rather, the field is broadly dominated by scholarship which undertakes important examinations of representations, cultural contexts of meaning, and visibility, but in ways which are not matched by as much scholarship that tests such knowledge frameworks among audiences, and some of which reads film and television texts on behalf of audiences in ways which assume universality of meaning. Arguably, much of this has to do with the cost of audience research and the relative historical scarcity of major research funding for queer media topics until the past ten years in the United States, United Kingdom, Europe and Oceania. The combination of funding flows and the establishment of much gender and sexuality scholarship with the humanities rather than the social sciences results in work which has, by necessity made assumptions about audiences. The following quote is an exemplary phrase which indicates how a textual reading is sometimes seen to represent audiences: 'Agitation, repulsion, and attraction are not only sensorial and emotional states that Max stimulates in the audience; his fictional friends also perceive his sublimity, but they are not quite sure how to manage it' (Ciamparella 2016: 86). While grounded readings are, of course, very valuable to making sense of textuality, and an argument that the character of Max in *The L Word* invokes mixed reactions by virtue of a complex identity depicted through the pregnancy of a trans man character, the assumption that this is the reaction of 'the audience' is more problematic – studies which empirically test reactions in fan communities such as Edwards (2010) present an alternative account of nuance and complex audience meaning-making.

There are two areas of assumption about audiences that emerge here. The first is that what comprises the figure of the audience is very often 'straight people'; the second is that even when audiences are understood to be diverse or queer, identity is viewed as being fixed, essentialist and always preceding the encounter with the screen text. We will address these two assumptions in turn. In regard to the former, much queer scholarship on mass-circulation film and television has assumed that the creative outputs of these industries are designed with a straight audience in mind and, as described in our discussion of different kinds of 'visibility' above, the presumed needs or tastes of straight, cisgender, normative audiences are often believed (in very simplistic terms) to have directed the characterization or use of 'safe' stereotypes of, particularly, gay men and lesbians (Verhoeven 1997). It has, indeed, been argued that the focus on heterosexual audiences indirectly marginalizes or at least minimizes the reception of queer media by queer audiences. As film theorist Brett Farmer (2000) argues, scholarship aimed at identifying and castigating the effects of Hollywood's heterocentric agenda is undoubtedly valuable, 'but with its exhaustive taxonomies of pernicious stereotypes and its impassioned diatribes against an alleged universal filmic heterocentrism, it has effectively marginalized gay spectatorial desires out of existence' (4). In other words, academic film theory might effectively closet gay spectatorship, like so many other forms of queerness, though, as Farmer acknowledges, this occlusion of gay and lesbian spectatorship in film theory and criticism is being increasingly challenged (5).

To label a queer movie as one intended for straight audiences is to ignore its queer audiences and their reception of the film, along with the pleasures these queer audiences might receive in viewing the movie (McKinnon 2016: 149). McKinnon's study of gay men's film reception in Sydney draws on empirical engagement with audience members' own experiences and practices of storytelling to argue that 'many gay men may take pleasure in a story that is specifically centred on a romance between two men' (149). Thus, by suggesting that such a film is for a straight audience, one implies that queer subjects are still required to undertake 'perverse' viewings even if the story is about lives (somewhat) like their own – that they are only incidentally involved as viewers 'even when centrally located on-screen' (149). McKinnon's critique here draws on Janet Staiger's (2000) concept of 'perverse spectators', viewers who do not interpret the text as expected. One example Staiger uses is of gender- or sexuality-diverse subjects who have inserted their lives and interpretive frameworks onto heterosexual cinematic storylines (37). Staiger's argument is similar to Alexander Doty's (1993) claim that traditional narrative films that are ostensibly addressed to, and are assumed to be for, straight audiences, yet which contain 'intense tensions and pleasures generated by the woman-woman and man-man aspects within the narratives', such as *Gentlemen Prefer Blondes* (1953), *Internal Affairs* (1990) and *Thelma and Louise* (1991), 'often have greater potential for encouraging a wide range of queer responses than such clearly lesbian- and gay-addressed films' (8). In Staiger's (2000) exploration of the perverse spectator, she maintains that context – including viewers' interpretive strategies such as aesthetic preferences and practices, prior knowledges and expectations, and experiences of the screening location – is more significant than textual features in explaining interpretive events. This particular strand of considering the context of audiencehood is, as we show in the next section, limited to a small number of texts, although it has been influential in helping to address assumptions by queer researchers that the texts being analysed for their narrative, discursive foregroundings and broader textuality are created and produced for particular 'types' of audiences, opening the field to consider audiences in more nuanced ways in line with earlier cultural studies work.

Queer screen, memory and identity

If we are to make sense of audience experience told to us retrospectively, then we must from the outset take into account the operation of memory not as a repository of actual experience but a discursive framework that shapes the accounts and narratives of the past (Cover and Prosser 2024). Recent scholarship on gender- and sexuality-diverse characters, themes and stories in film and television has often utilized memory as a central framework for understanding the relationship between screen representation and LGBTQ+ identities and cultures. Horvat, for example, draws on the utopian queer theory of Muñoz and the 'world-making potentialities' of 'our remembrances and their ritualised retellings' (Horvat 2021: 12) understanding memory as broadly unstable. For Horvat, queer screen memory is valuable less for individual recollection and more for what it can reveal about how the LGBTQ+ community understands itself and is remembered by others in the present. Horvat argues for the uniqueness of screen culture's relationship to LGBTQ+ community, suggesting that recollection is more often shaped by queer screen interpretations than by other settings of memory such as face-to-face encounters in community space.

At the same time, memory is central to the reflective framework by which minority gender and sexual identities are articulated in the present, lending an identity consistency by recalling the past as 'always having been' a queer past, including particularly a queer childhood (Sedgwick 1993: 42). Often this involves a form of painful nostalgia in which a subject refers to a knowledge of difference or marginalization without have necessarily had access to the cultural logic, symbolic language or terminology to understand and describe that difference as a matter of gender or sexual identity (Probyn 1996: 110).

Typically, memorial accounts of a gender- or sexuality-diverse childhood involve three core tropes: firstly, a reaction to the unpalatability of gendered scripts utilized in education, media and family settings; secondly, a trope involving an 'encounter' with the discourses of gender and sexual diversity that made available a cultural logic by which to describe, understand and articulate an LGBTQ+ identity (Cover 2002); and finally, a recalled instance of 'coming out' both to the self (recognition of the self in comparison with a similar other, which may a screen other) and to other people, very often recognized through narratives of coming out to family and friends at particular points in a normative lifecycle (Cover and Prosser 2024).

The pivotal moment, then, is the encounter with discourses of gender and sexual diversity, and this is often discussed as both a pedagogical and formative moment. That is, the narrative by which childhood memory as an LGBTQ+ childhood is articulated involves the suggestion that one *really did know* but nevertheless required the 'resource' of sexuality discourses in order to name oneself and thereby articulate oneself as lesbian or gay. This is a claim that there is indeed an 'inner core' of sexuality and one knows this for having 'always been' in spite of the gap between birth and the moment at which one encounters the discourses providing the necessary cultural codes for the 'outer' denoters of that sexuality, serving later as shared experiences that denote belonging among a minority community (Probyn 1996).

This is a media-saturated culture that consists of not just a screen culture of television broadcast flows and engagement with cinematic screens but also a discourse about those screen settings. Pivotal moments in identity formation involve the recalling of an 'encounter' with LGBTQ+ discourses on screens. Several Australian interviewees who were born in the 1970s and 1980s and grew up in Australia's media culture of the time noted the significance of the 'encounter' with discourses of gender and sexual diversity as occurring in the context of watching films and television. They often remember it as a pivotal moment of identity formation, articulating how it confirmed a sense of selfhood and difference that was otherwise not available in other forms of everyday communication, education or discourse. For example, one participant noted their first viewing of bisexual and pansexual characters in the Australian television series *The Secret Life of Us* (2001–5):

> so that was like my first memory of seeing, I guess, like a bisexual or pansexual female character at a time when I identified that way . . . in sort of later high school.

Likewise, Jess, who was born in the 1970s, seeing a same-sex relationship for the first time on television as a child in the Australian soap opera *Number 96* (1972–7) was subsequently able to put a language to perceptions of norms:

> And in terms of the impact that might have had it was just, oh, here's a representation of homosexuality. And I know that that was discussed in my family as, oh, this is very, you know, this is sort of out there for this to be on TV . . . . So, in terms of the impact, obviously not identifying as homosexual, gay male. That is, it didn't really impact me, but I knew it was something that was different, that was not normalized, normal, not perceived to be normal as a child.

What we witness here is a memorial reflection on the encounter with a screen media text that provides a framework for social norms. The fact that a sense of normativity is produced in the context not of the relationship between the viewer and the text but in the interactive triangle of viewer, text and family is significant in demonstrating the ways in which memorial accounts of growing up in relation to media texts often implicate the domestic viewing space of the living room as performing a central role in the production and inculcation of norms.

At other times, interviewees discussed some of the ways in which the encounter with international film and television texts broadcast on Australian television was something to which they could relate from the perspective of a minority gender or sexual identity, even though it was the first time it was encountered. For example, Kristin (who was born in the 1970s) noted that watching LGBTQ+ characters in *Degrassi Junior High* (1987–9) was 'the first time where I saw that stuff represented, and I could relate to what was going on . . . I probably picked up on some queer vibes along the way there somehow, but it wasn't explicit by any means.' Similarly, Andrew (trans non-binary, born in the 1980s), recalled a moment of recognition in the first encounter with representations of a trans man in the film *Boys Don't Cry* (1999): '. . . when I saw *Boys Don't Cry*, I was like, "Oh my God, that's me." That was the first time I saw myself and went, "That's me."'

The memorial accounts of an individual 'remembering' the first encounter with discourses of gender and sexual diversity on Australian screens, and how that came to produce a realization of one's identity, are thus often described by participants as a *deeply meaningful* instance of growing up, putting the screen experience very much at the centre of the recollection of identity formation. From a queer theory perspective, of course, that temporal instance can be theorized not only as a moment of recognizing the self in the screen text but as a re-orientation (Ahmed 2004) of identities of difference and an 'entry' into discourses of sexuality and gender. Memory, of course, is meaningfully described but, in the act of describing it, it always deploys the discourses that have *subsequently* become available to the participant making the description as Jacques Lacan (1968: 17) noted, 'doubtless a reproduction of the past, but it is above all a spoken representation – and as such implies all sorts of presences'.

Those presences include, therefore, the ways we are encouraged to speak about (and recollect) queer media content of the past as significant not only because they may be a moment of remembering identity formation or naming or explaining difference to the self, but also because the assumed scarcity of queer screen representation has often made those moments of depiction more pivotal in community discourse. This thereby feeds back to the ways in which we tell stories (Plummer 1995) of our Australian queer encounters simultaneously as stories of community record and as stories of individual subjectivity. As these stories recollect experiences that occurred in the temporal setting of the pre-digital and pre-networked era of broadcast and analogue media, the physical and geographic settings emerge as central tenets of those memorial descriptions when the story is weighted towards individual engagement. We describe in the next sections some of the ways in which place and space are foregrounded in the discussions of that screen media encounter by the participants in the study.

Domestic screens: Young queer audiences at home

A common experience among our participants born in the 1970s and 1980s was a sense of scarcity in media content with gender- and sexuality-diverse they had access to as kids or teenagers. Many interviewees in our study described growing up with very little or no LGBTQ+ screen content – Australian or international – with their viewing access limited to broadcast television, video rentals and mainstream cinema releases. Although as we have discussed throughout this book that was not exactly the case, it remains true that many people including the *AusQueerScreen* audience interviewees remembered general queer invisibility on screens in contrast to today. In this context, the domestic and familial space of television viewing was therefore often recalled as a space of cisgender heteronormativity whereby it was a rare experience to encounter texts with gender- and sexuality-diverse themes, characters and stories. Such rare encounters were often memorable because, on the one hand, they invoked a sense of deep attachment and meaning and, on the other, they were radically juxtaposed to the otherwise cisgender and heteronormative space of the living room and the space represented by the television screen.

However, several of the participants also described attachments to ostensibly 'straight' texts whose characters or scenarios could be 'read' by the viewer privately and tacitly by Australian LGBTQ+ audiences as queer. In this sense, a practice of 'passing' in the domestic space of viewership through one's reading and appreciation of ostensibly cisgender and heterosexual storytelling indicated that the living room space and the temporal act of viewing were not always, in itself, an exclusively cis- and hetero-activity. Leo, a gay cis male participant, spoke about seeking out films with strong female characters or proto-feminist themes, such as period films about constrained women's lives. Clea, a bisexual cis woman, noted that female film and TV characters who were strong-willed, 'alternative', 'outrageous' or 'bad girls' were coded as bisexual in a sometimes positive and admiring way by herself and her school friends. Indeed, several participants noted that an interest in independent, alternative or 'grunge' cinema could disguise the pursuit of queer screen content to others. Australian film in the 1980s and 1990s was also noted by interviewees for its characters who, while not LGBTQ+, were transgressive or resonated with a queer sensibility, such as Noah Taylor in *The Year My Voice Broke* (1987), or Rachel Griffiths in *Muriel's Wedding* (1994).

The Australian public broadcast network SBS played a significant role in our interviewees' young viewing lives, with many participants mentioning its screenings of *Queer as Folk* (1999–2000) or the curated short films of *Eat Carpet* (1989–2005) that were screened by SBS late on Saturday nights. As one interviewee said, these films 'always had glimmers of other types, kind of mind-expanding types of experience . . . people and bodies that weren't the ones that primetime mainstream TV was offering you'. SBS was the place to view foreign language films and campy genre films: as Liza noted in their interview, 'they were appalling, terrible movies, but you never watched them for the quality of the movie, you just watched them for representation'. For participant Stevie, SBS provided her first exposure to the Sydney Gay and Lesbian Mardi Gras:

> I've got a pretty strong memory of the Mardi Gras being on SBS and that being – very large protests about that, people saying that it shouldn't be screened. I was quite young, I was in primary school . . . and then being like, well, that's not – I was thinking maybe I was gay, but that's not me. I'm not that. Which is ironic, because I've grown up to be exactly that.

However, for one interviewee, SBS film and television programming compounded a sense that queer people were *elsewhere*: as Benjamin noted in his interview, 'SBS became an absolute lifeline . . . international queer directors like Almodóvar and Todd Haynes . . . [yet] Australian content, local content was so sorely lacking.'

In the context of encountering queer content on screens in the domestic space of television viewing, several participants perceived the act of viewing in substantially anti-normative terms within households and kinship systems. Some participants commented on how queer screen representation was often perceived as being 'sexually explicit', particularly given the absence in that period of LGBTQ+ screen texts made for pre-teen or younger teenagers prior to the 2000s. The decade of the 1990s was a transition period in the design of Australian housing and in the availability of multiple television sets, screens and VCRs per household. While those with greater household income were beginning to separate the entertainment and living spaces of a household's adults and children, and provide older children with private spaces for viewing in other parts of the home (Davis 1997: 2), most households continued to share television viewing spaces as the household place shared by whole families whereby public discourses entered the private home in the form that became normalized in the 1960s and 1970s (Williams 1975). That is, for many of our participants the physical space of the family home and the practice of shared viewing was, during the teenage years, the most common setting for encountering gender- and sexuality-diverse screen content. The shared entertainment space and singular household television sets and VCRs meant, therefore, that many interviewees recalled the encounters with LGBTQ+ screen content as awkward and embarrassing when other family members were present, and in some cases resulted in painful interactions with family members. Many of our interviewees sought out and watched LGBTQ+ content alone late at night, because of the discomfort of watching with family.

Indeed, only two participants mentioned parents' attitudes to LGBTQ+ themes on-screen as affirming or neutral. Much more often, interviewees described homophobic or awkward comments by family members – for example, several described family members making 'disgusted' noises or 'tutting' at the screen during SBS's annual coverage of the Sydney Mardi Gras parade. Sex scenes between women in films broadcast on television could prompt homophobic responses from mothers or 'gross' comments from fathers. Family members' comments about television personalities recognized as gay – such as Australian music journalist Ian 'Molly' Meldrum – were often derogatory, and some participants spoke about the presence of camp characters and drag queens on television as comic relief, and the difficult experience of watching these characters with family. Those who grew up during the HIV/AIDS epidemic of the late 1980s recalled family attitudes to gay lives as aligned with HIV risk, 'paranoid' or tinged with 'tragedy and judgment'.

Like the shared lounge television, the video cassette recorder (VCR) was a nexus for the complex negotiation of shared living space with family members while growing up. The development and widespread uptake of the VCR in the late 1980s and early 1990s prompted a significant shift in the cultural practices of screen entertainment, primarily because it provided the facility to break the dominance of television programmers' flows of entertainment and control over the time of viewers, allowing viewers to time-shift viewership (Cubitt 1991), develop new configurations of viewing such as recording, binge watching and either increasing or decreasing the company of others while watching a television programme or film (Cover 2005), play with texts through crash editing (Cubitt 1991), and watch films that were otherwise primarily available in the public space of the cinema in the private domestic space of the home (O'Regan 1991).

The video shop or library has also been noted in scholarship as a key site of identification for participants, with the 'foreign' or 'arthouse' section being the place to find local and international queer or queer-adjacent film. Prior to the introduction of Web 2.0 broadband networks that made downloading films and television possible, video stores were important points of access for arthouse, international and independent film. Williams (2018) notes that the physical space of video stores, and the potential for browsing and receiving recommendations from clerks, are central to the way video stores are memorialized. Scholars have noted the significance of the VCR to young LGBTQ+ adults as a tool for exploring identity (e.g. McKinnon 2016: 215). Several interviewees named specific arthouse video shops with a good queer selection they recalled as spaces in which they discovered or first encountered gender- and sexuality-diverse screen content on VHS during the 1980s and the first half of the 1990s.

The physical tangibility of VHS cassettes is also key to these memories. Unlike digital and streaming content that is marked by its very intangibility, the VHS cassette was an object that was geographically located, moved, engaged with physically and vulnerable to destruction. This tangibility and vulnerability were reflected in our interviews. For example, one participant described a significant moment in her queer identity formation, when an attempted viewing of *The Devil's Playground* (1976) was thwarted by the VHS getting stuck in the household video player. Another spoke about housesitting for an older gay couple as a teenager and finding a lesbian-themed film on the video shelf, hidden with the spine inwards, and then secretly ordering a copy for herself. As these examples make clear, showing interest in queer or queer-adjacent content risked rendering their queerness visible, and the material object of the VHS cassette thus took on heightened significance. Laura, a queer cis woman, recalled the presence of a rented copy of *Head On* (1998) causing tension in the family home:

> it resulted in an enormous amount of angst. And it was with some relief that that VHS was returned to Blockbuster . . . I think once it was out of the house, my mother felt like we could move on from that – from an episode of – I don't know, queer performativity or something, like you know, trying on hats – I think this is how it probably felt for her . . . So yeah, the object itself had a certain power, and not just the film, in my home.

In this anecdote, the physical artefact of the VHS cassette discovered in the physical space of the home signals to the parent her daughter's possible queerness, albeit in this case one that is understood as a 'phase' that is both trivialized and seen as potentially dangerous. It is thus notable that in recalling their engagement with gender- and sexuality-diverse content and discourses, the video cassette was not always a solution to the difficulties of family viewing but could, in some instances, solidify a sense of non-normativity by providing the physical trace of a non-normative sexuality or gender.

While many of our participants utilized a discourse of cultural and social generationalism to understand their experiences growing up in contrast to their expectations of those presently growing up in a post-digital era, several drew on cultural generationalism's alternative understanding of youth transitionalism (Wyn and Woodman 2006) in order to describe periods of change that were marked by shifts in their viewing practices. For many, in the process of transitioning from teenager to young adult, young adulthood also signalled a welcome shift away from watching queer(-ed) content when alone, or anticipating negative reactions from relatives: as Benjamin said of watching TV in his first share house, '[not] having to change the channel when I heard someone coming into the room was just so fucking liberating'. This made the experience of domestic viewing of gender- and sexuality-diverse content in the family home more marked as a painful experience and the possibilities of viewing in private or among peers a more palatable experience, showing the ways in which the figurative concept of domestic and familial space dominated their recollections of growing up and screen media encounters.

Conclusion

In this chapter, we have presented one of the more interesting themes raised by the audience interviewees from the *AusQueerScreen* project. Accounting for the ways in which participants in a study of Australian queer screen media not only describe their experiences of audiencehood but do so through narratives that highlight how memorial accounts are shaped by prevailing discourses is significant to making sense of the importance of queer screens in everyday lives. Although memory is always subjective, the childhood and young adult memories of participants in this age group were articulated both as formative and futural, giving a sense of the significance of media engagement in the formation of identity and belonging, and in their current understanding of subjectivity.

And, as we have highlighted, these memories intersected with important concepts of both place and time. Place varied across interviews and ranged from expressions related to the difficulty of viewing gender- and sexuality-diverse stories on screens in domestic settings in the 1980s and 1990s. The experiences described by our participants relating to growing up, viewing television and film, communicating with their peers and access to LGBTQ+ content in screen media are substantially different from those of young people today who grow up in an era of networked connectivity, digital downloads, greater social tolerance and acceptance of diverse sexualities and genders and marriage equality. The accounts of earlier generations do not necessarily speak to the experiences of young people today – indeed, we caution against any assumptions that contemporary LBGTQ+ youth experience things in universal rather than generation-specific ways. While this particular group of study participants are now aged in their thirties and forties, they comprise a social generation who, in some respects, experienced greater vulnerability and marginalization while growing up in ways which continue to frame their views on the utility of screen representation and their practices of viewing LGBTQ+ media content.

11

Young Audiences, Mental Health and Identity

Introduction

An understanding of the role of culture, media representation and society in the mental health of LGBTQ+ young people emerged in the late 1990s and early 2000s, particularly around questions of socially induced stress and suicidal risks related to depression (Hegna and Wichstrøm 2007, Walls et al. 2008). Bolstered by a simultaneous public discourse that framed evidence of increased social anxiety among the general youth population as a global mental health pandemic (Goldberg 2018), it opened an important window on the ways in which cultural norms, marginalizing practices, problematic stereotypes and discourses of hate actively vulnerabilize gender- and sexuality-diverse young people. Widespread public attitudes incorporated a mental health focus as a component of how we discuss queer culture. This has had implications for how we think about the role of queer screen media in relation to audiences, providing a very important 'lens' for thinking through the ways in which screen media plays a role in well-being on the one hand, but on the other may sometimes exacerbate harms for audiences, both individual and communities. For example, 1990s films which associated queerness and trans identity with criminal psychiatric illness, such as *The Silence of the Lambs* (1991) and *Butterfly Kiss* (1995), are well-known for the ways in which that association actually damaged well-being among audiences.

Despite the public turn to a mental health focus in relation to gender- and sexuality-diverse young people, there remains an uneasy relationship between mental health and LGBTQ+ discourses for two reasons. Firstly, a continuing – albeit residual – suspicion of psychiatric discourses remains at play. Discussing mental health concerns around queer youth often risks re-invoking the now-disparaged idea that homosexuality and trans subjectivity are themselves symptoms of mental illness, allowing a return to the idea of gender and/or sexuality diversity as psychological problems that can be treated. Queer culture has long maintained a deep suspicion of psychological approaches in order better to combat the still-powerful conservative rhetoric that seeks to dismiss the reality and lived experience of queer and trans lives as legitimate identities. The American Psychiatric Association (APA), which first drew up its classification of diagnoses in 1952, categorized homosexuality, for example, as a sociopathic personality disturbance. Although a 1968 classification revised the entry on homosexuality, it continued to characterize it as a mental disorder. It was only in 1973 that the APA declassified homosexuality as a disorder *per se* (Murphy 1997). Certainly, the APA classification has remained strong in the cultural memory of queer discourse; opposition to any psycho-pathologization of diverse sexualities and gender identity and is thus equally strong, resulting in the care needed when mental health issues are discussed in relation to sexualities and genders. Whether or not queer screen texts represent a link between mental health and diverse gender/sexualities unproblematically or in ways which reinforce outdated psychiatric explanations of diverse identities is a key consideration if we are to understand how audiences are shaped by the media with which they engage.

Secondly, many community advocates, scholars and activists became increasingly concerned about the ways in which a stereotype of LGBTQ+ young people as suffering very poor mental health – regardless of the socio-cultural causes – was overwhelming the public circulation of stories of resilience, well-being, happiness and successful lives (Driver 2008, Harvey 2012). Again, making sense of the balance between resilient characters who cope with the stresses of minority identity or other aspects of life depicted on screen is significant to audience members who benefit from role-modelling by queer and trans characters who express resilience, bounce back from adversity and are not mentally harmed by the conditions of liveability articulated in a screen narrative.

This chapter draws on audience interviews undertaken in the *AusQueerScreen* project. Although we did not ask interviewees about their experiences or knowledge of mental health, many raised the topic in their discussions of specific film and television texts, in the context of the practices as audience members, and in their perception of the role of queer screen media in shaping healthy identities, particularly among younger people. We begin with a brief discussion of the contemporary context of gender and sexuality in relation to well-being in Australia, followed by some of the key themes raised by interviewees in relation to the importance of 'positive' images, depictions and representations on-screen. This is followed by a discussion of two aspects of Australian queer screen media our interviewees found likely to have a negative effect on the mental health and well-being of queer and trans audiences: the continued and regular depiction of queer suicidality in Australian screen texts, and the 'bury your gays' trope in which queer and trans characters to whom audiences form an attachment are killed off. We end with an analysis of the ways in which interviewees talked about the positive mental well-being that comes not from watching queer screen media but from discussing it with other audience members.

Young gender- and sexuality-diverse Australians and well-being

Screen representation plays a potentially significant role in both supporting LGBTQ+ young people and in framing the ways in which well-being is understood, particularly at time in which there is greater nuance in the public awareness of LGBTQ+ mental health. LGBTQ+ young people's experiences of discrimination and harassment in the home, educational settings and in public spaces have well-documented impacts on their mental health and well-being (Hill et al. 2021, Strauss et al. 2020). According to the Australian *Writing Themselves In 4* report, 81 per cent of LGBTQ+ young people have reported high or very high levels of psychological distress (Hill et al. 2021). As many as 63 per cent have reported they had been diagnosed with a mental illness in their lifetime and had received professional treatment, most commonly for depression and generalized anxiety disorder, while 58 per cent of those surveyed had seriously considered suicide in the previous twelve months. These effects are compounded for trans and gender diverse (TGD) young people: almost half of all respondents to an Australian survey of 859 TGD people aged 14–25 had attempted suicide. As many as 79 per cent of this group had self-harmed, and 82 per cent had had suicidal thoughts (Strauss et al. 2020). This survey also found an association between poor mental health outcomes and trans and gender-diverse young people's experiences of educational settings and precarious accommodation (Strauss et al. 2020).

Intersectional factors and their associated experiences of marginalization and discrimination are now also recognized as having an impact on the mental well-being of LGBTQ+ young people, with 39 per cent of LGBTQ+ young people with disability reporting having attempting suicide in their lifetime, over twice the rate of those without disability. Seventy-nine per cent of participants from a multicultural background had experienced suicidal ideation in their lifetime (Hill et al. 2021). Geographic location has also had a significant impact on mental health for LGBTQ+ young people in Australia. Rates of psychological distress are higher for LGBTQ+ young people in regional and remote areas, who also experience higher rates of homelessness. The situation for young Australian LGBTQ+ people is exacerbated for those who experience barriers to accessing health services due to discriminatory or inappropriate treatment from clinicians (Albury et al. 2024) and/or financial constraints (Cronin et al. 2021).

Social connectivity and a sense of affirmation have been found to be significant remedies for poor mental health (Hill et al. 2021). Important to recognize, then, is that social connectivity is not always limited to face-to-face engagement with family, friends and peers, but also involves an affirmative relationship with the wider discourse of LGBTQ+ subjectivity and culture through screen media (Cover 2012a).

The power of positive representations

Participants in the *AusQueerScreen* study often emphasized the importance of the visibility of queer characters in screen media for mental well-being during the years they were growing up. Many participants connected their experience of growing up feeling abnormal or wrong, or being unable to recognize their gender or sexuality until later in life to negative representations in screen texts. Many viewed queer visibility on-screen as both validating their experiences and enabling them to recognize their identity. One participant, Marie, explained:

> I think visibility in any media gives people the courage to articulate things . . .
> and when they articulate things, other people hear those things and go, 'Oh, also
> . . .'. Like it's, 'Is it safe to come out to you? Oh, you've given me a cue?' Like it
> gives a reference point that's common. And I think that was missing for a while.

In these examples, participants linked visibility to identification with LGBTQ+ characters that allowed for self-recognition, validation and a shared point of reference or prompt for coming out. Andrew, who born in the 1980s, described seeing the film *Love and Other Catastrophes* (1996) as a teenager:

> That was actually a huge film for me. I went and saw it with a girlfriend when it
> came out. And I walked out of that show and said, 'I'm a lesbian.' I walked out of
> the movie and said it out loud. And I think before that, I would have said that I
> was bisexual or felt like I didn't really know who I was. And I saw that film and I
> was like – It made me feel very good to be gay.

Importantly, this self-identification is described not as static or singular but rather as an unfolding process: Andrew later saw the film *Boys Don't Cry* (1999) and was then able to recognize himself as transgender.

Rachel, a bisexual cis woman, noted the challenge of coming to recognize one's identity before the proliferation of LGBTQ+ media, and the gradual process of recognizing aspects of one's gender and sexuality diversity in this context:

> I can't even describe how important [representation] should be. Like, people want to be seen; people want to see themselves, and people want to know that who they are is a valid person. And one of the main ways that we get that is through visibility, through representation. I feel like if I'd had more stories that were validating of bisexuality at the time, or more outreach – like, I think now it's a lot easier for kids with YouTube, and they have YouTubers who are out and they have various different streams of, like, places they can get representation. I think for me, you know, going into the library, even, there wasn't a section where I could explore that. There wasn't a way for me to kind of know that I, that I could be anything else because I didn't see myself represented. And I saw, like, one aspect of me represented, so I kind of went, okay, well, I guess that's how it is then.

Visibility was also valued in terms of its impact on heterosexual audiences and helping participants' families to understand queer lives as viable and joyful, rather than tragic or shameful. For example, Sam said that when they were growing up in the 1980s, their parents' knowledge of LGBTQ+ lives based on screen representations was limited to 'HIV and Mardi Gras'.

The attitudes of heterosexual family members were noted for their effect on the mental well-being of LGBTQ+ young people, and queer visibility was articulated as important for helping their families understand LGBTQ+ identities, and in turn becoming better sources of support, as participant Col observed:

> not to have validating, strong, accepting media representation for that journey is, I think, really detrimental to their health, like their mental health . . . and for their navigating stuff with their family who are otherwise only going to be experiencing, yeah, really mainstream, heteronormative examples of sexuality and relationships.

Participants referenced films they grew up with like *Priscilla* (1994) and *The Sum of Us* (1994) as having popular appeal and facilitating broader awareness of LGBTQ+ issues among mainstream audiences. A participant perceived *Please Like Me* (2013–16) as positively impacting the outcome of the marriage equality plebiscite, and another was heartened when the show was made available for streaming globally on Netflix, alongside Hannah Gadsby's comedy special *Nanette* (2017).

Many participants noted the importance of LGBTQ+ characters who are not portrayed in gimmicky or tokenistic ways, citing examples such as the TV series *Janet King* (2014–17) for its portrayal of a complex character. Sometimes tokenism was linked to the brevity of the character's appearance, for example a character 'who comes in for two episodes or, you know, the best friend who stands behind the protagonist on the cover', as participant Jeremy put it. Sarah commented that, in meaningful queer representation, characters are more than their sexuality or gender:

> Their queerness isn't there as decoration. It's something that affects the way that they move within the space. But it's not their only defining feature, which is what you want, because otherwise people are going to see queer people as only queer as opposed to a person that you should care about and think about.

Participants also spoke about the importance of screen texts that directly addressed mental health among LGBTQ+ characters. The series *Please Like Me* was praised by many participants for its portrayal of fallible, flawed queer characters who experience mental health challenges alongside relationships and other ordinary life events, and 'queerness being a bit chaotic at times', as Col put it.

Participants strongly valued narratives featuring characters with intersectional identities, with several praising the nuanced portrayal of queer and trans second-generation Greek migrants in the film *Head On* (1998). For interviewees from migrant backgrounds, the centrality of the 'coming out' narrative for LGBTQ+ screen characters since the 1990s was viewed as particularly limiting, insofar as it foregrounded disclosure over an internal process of self-recognition: 'that kind of like linear, really heartfelt type communication that I feel like you see in narratives about Anglos', as Wei put it. Abigail spoke about her appreciation for films like *Head On* where 'coming out' was not synonymous with disclosure to families, and characters negotiated intersecting forms of 'otherness'. Wei observed that 'there's no map for you, you know, being a second generation or 1.5 generation, migrant queer person', and valued the way *Head On* depicted 'their community having different levels of knowledge, I guess, about who they are and their queerness'.

Some participants noted that meaningful LGBTQ+ representation did not need to involve a straightforward identification with the character or setting in order to 'see themselves' in a text, but was more related to its complexity and lack of tokenism. For example, Abigail spoke about her teenage love of the Australian films *Walking on Water* (2002) and *Head On,* which centred on gay male and trans characters. Indeed, several queer women and non-binary participants commented on identifying with gay male screen characters while growing up, not only because these were more available, but because of a sense that gay male characters were offered more complex, resonant and interesting storylines. By contrast, representations of LBQ women were imagined temporally as a 'passing phase' or brief rupture within the narrative (Monaghan 2016: 151) and a cause of distress. For example Stevie, a lesbian/gay cis woman, praised the representation of a male character coming out on *The Secret Life of Us* (2001–5) in contrast with the same series' depiction of a bisexual woman:

> There was someone in the friendship group who had a very, very tortured coming out and that wasn't handled so well. Um, I just remember that it was all about her turmoil. You know, it was like, 'Oh, it's so hard.' And 'Oh, I don't know who I am.' And it was like, oh, for fuck's sake, you just made out with a woman. Like, who cares? Like we care, but it doesn't change your ability to live in the world, actually. And I found that handwringing really frustrating when I was younger.

At the same time, a few participants recognized the negative side to increased queer visibility as the potential to inflame homophobic and transphobic attitudes among the community and draw unwanted attention to LGBTQ+ people, especially in regional areas or in contexts of online trolling. As Sam noted, 'There is definitely a freedom that comes with not having representation.'

Participants characterized 'positive' portrayals of LGBTQ+ life variously. All agreed that screen texts played a role in attitudes of the broader population, as well as queer people's own self-perception: many spoke about 'normalizing' or 'everyday' representations, and queer characters threaded into straight/ mainstream films and series, as being helpful for their families' understanding. Some who grew up in the 1990s praised the film *Priscilla* as representing strength in adversity, celebrating flamboyance, and foregrounding chosen family and community. They also noted the portrayal of strong queer relationships, and characters who were open and unashamed of their identities, as being helpful for their mental well-being while growing up. Others spoke about the importance of narratives featuring LGBTQ+ young people as finding acceptance from their family and community. Jane noted the power of positive representations even in depictions of challenging circumstances: 'Positive representation is always needed. And it can be positive representation, even for negative situations. It doesn't need to be that everything is all rainbows all of the time.'

Participants reflected on the importance of 'positive' screen representations for young LGBTQ+ people in terms of imagining a future for themselves, or as Beth put it, 'giving you hope', extending a vision of a queer future that 'allows us to see and feel beyond the quagmire of the present' (Muñoz 2009). A number of participants connected the difficulty of being openly queer as a young person with screen representations of gay life prior to the 2000s, 'reinforced by what I saw in the media and around: like, it was just not good to be gay', as Josie put it. Participant Andrew explained that the TV series *Prisoner* (1979–86) made him feel that as a queer person, 'you weren't gonna live a nice life. And that definitely, I think, impacted me in my teenage years.' Nevertheless, some participants said that seeing queer characters and storylines as a young person was 'aspirational' and 'reassuring'.

In reflecting on the significance of social engagement for improved mental health among LGBTQ+ young people, for some, LGBTQ+ characters in TV series such as *The Secret Life of Us* and in films such as *Priscilla* were said to have stood in for potential future friendships and communities. This was particularly important for those who came of age before the proliferation of screen content addressing queer adolescence or childhood.

At the same time, the notion of 'positive' representation was engaged with critically by some participants as an unnecessary burden on queer screen texts. In keeping with their concerns about gimmicks and tokenism, participants favoured three-dimensional characters over 'upstanding and righteous' ones, as James put it. Jarad pointed to the increase in representations of the 'palatable, cisnormative, middle-class, sort of aspirational gay couple' during the marriage equality debates in Australia. Wei characterized 'positive representation as a frame as a bit frustrating and limiting', and mentioned *The Family Law* (2016–19) and *Please Like Me* as examples of TV series with 'complex and not-always-likeable characters' that were more impactful than homonormative representations.

While participants engaged critically with the concept of 'positive' representations, they noted the impact of negative portrayals of queer livability when they were growing up. As Bec put it:

there's also that other dynamic to consider, of like only seeing negative representation and loss and death and sickness and that sort of thing . . . I think when there's representation of like, being healthy and happy and proud, that's important, too.

Many audience interviewees felt that 'negative' portrayals of LGBTQ+ characters were more damaging to young people's mental well-being during a period of limited access to queer screen texts. As James commented, 'despite, you know, the openness of "It gets better" and kids are coming out younger than ever, but we still need these kind of positive representation or even just honest representation, good and bad'. Some other participants reflected on the well-being of future generations of young LGBTQ+ people, and viewed the current proliferation of queer screen representations in hopeful terms. As Josie observed:

I do think it's going to have a massive impact on 'generation now' . . . in 10–15 years, when you've grown up seeing that there's lots of different people on TV, it's not going to be such a big deal as it was when you didn't see it. And so, who's the freak in the family that's come out as different. It won't be as different if you've grown up on a diet of television and movies with characters that are portrayed in a positive light, which, you know, yeah, as I said wasn't the case with me growing up.

In this respect, there was a broad tendency among Australian audience interviewees to think in terms of future generations of LGBTQ+ young people, and a view that Australian screen cultures had a role to play in protecting against representations that may contribute to negative well-being outcomes.

Queer death

One framework through which the increased representation of gender- and sexually-diverse characters and stories over the past two decades may be considered problematic or harmful for LGBTQ+ audiences is the prevalence of stories that end in death. This broadly takes two forms: stories that include LGBTQ+ suicides and stories that fall into the television trope known as 'Bury Your Gays', being the consummation of a non-heteronormative relationship involving a supporting cast member that quickly ends in the character's death. Although research has been conducted into the positive effects of minority inclusion in media, there is a considerable scholarly gap in studies about the potential negative impact of the *repetition* of death of queer characters, or those deaths in light of the identifications forged with those characters through para-social relationships, which describes the way in which audience members form attachments and a perception of 'knowability' of on-screen figures (Horton and Wohl 1956). There is also little to account for the kinds of engagement formed between young audiences and queer and trans on-screen characters through the *pleasure* of representation, recognition and stories for which one may wish to see a happy long-term.

Suicidality in queer screen representation is actually quite an old trope. Between 1961 and 1976, thirteen of thirty-one English-language international films with major homosexual characters featured suicide, which is about forty percent (Gross 1991). There is little statistical listing of suicides in screen media since the mid-1970s onwards, but it has remained common enough in international cinema that it is broadly unsurprising when a queer or trans characters self-harms (Cover 2012a). In the Australian context, suicide attempts and completions by a queer character are actually much more common in recent queer films and television miniseries than in North American or British queer films: *Monster Pies* (2013), *Boys in the Trees* (2016), *The Slap* (2011), *Drown* (2015) and *Cut Snake* (2015). The four-part miniseries *Deep Water* (2016) is among these, although also depicts investigations into real-world past suicide cases that turned out to be hate crimes. Queer youth suicide was a significant media talking-point in the 1990s in Australia, subsequent to the very public story of fourteen-year-old Christopher Tsakalos who had taken the NSW Department of School Education to court for failure to protect him against vilification and violence, and in which there was notable coverage of the specifics of Tsakalos' suicide attempts: 'he has tried to commit suicide three times and says this was a plea for help' (Passey 1997). This became a node in the cultural knowledge of 1990s Australia LGBTQ+ experience, and for some years suicidality was repeated regularly in journalism that mentioned any LGBTQ+ young people, regardless of the extent to which suicide was relevant to the article (Cover 2012b).

As noted by one participant, Andrew, in the *AusQueerScreen* study, suicidality in queer screen media is deeply problematic for the mental well-being of young queer Australians:

> If people can't see themselves getting older and they can't see positive representations of themselves, it's a key contributor to suicide. Like if you just can't see a life, you know how you can be in the world in a positive way, in a future way, it's, it's a major problem.

What Andrew alludes to is the way in which the repetition of suicidality as an 'expected outcome' of LGBTQ+ growing up operates as a stereotype that reinforces the idea that queer and trans people do not get to grow old in a normative way. Stereotypes link an identity (such as LGBTQ+) with a set of attributes (such as self-harm or suicidality) and preserve that association over time through repetition (Rosello 1998). Richard Dyer (1993) identified older film stereotypes of gay men from the 1950s that linked male homosexuality with melancholy, producing the repetitive figure he called the 'sad young man' (73–92). Along with stereotypes of equally suicidal lesbians as psychopathic and self-destructive, the sad young man persisted through subsequent decades in international film and television, dominating the screen representation of gender/sexual minorities until approximately the mid-1990s when a more positive set of gay men and lesbians began to make it into North American film. Why suicidality remains so dominant in Australian film and television texts is difficult to understand, although we can speculate a kind of conformity to 1990s thinking and discourse, and an inability of some creative producers to tap the contemporary conditions of queer and trans liveability, is at least partly responsible.

Repeating this unfortunate stereotype arguably establishes negative health and mental well-being outcomes for young people because it role models a dangerous 'logic' for what to do when times are tough. Indeed, a number of international studies have suggested a correlation between the deaths of mainstream actors/characters and copycat suicides after their death (Stack 2005, Sudak and Sudak 2005, Gould and Shaffer 1986). To pay attention to links made between suicide and gender- and sexuality-diverse people is not, of course, to suggest that there is a *linear causality* between media representation of suicide and suicide itself. Warwick Blood and Jane Pirkis' (2001) extensive analysis of this belief revealed that fiction media portrayal of suicide does *not* have a linear causal relationship with actual suicide attempts or completions, and is likely to have less of a causal relationship than media reporting of suicides of real-life persons and celebrities. Media depictions of queer death may, however, create the conditions for a what Michael Kral (2019) identified as the *social logic* in which suicide becomes a normative practice for some identities and is *available* to be imitated because other stories or ways of coping with difficult times are not as dominant. Significant, then, is the fact that a repeated trope in contemporary popular culture circulated by popular film and television has the potential to operate as a discourse that operates as a normative identity resource, with a negative well-being impact on those who may have fewer other resources available to them.

The 'bury your gays' trope is, alongside suicidality, considered by many to be equally harmful to young queer audience members' mental health and well-being. Bury your gays is a trope that is repeated in popular culture across television series; the fact it has a specific label indicates not only its instant recognizability but the presence of a global trend in much screen depiction of queer and trans characters, despite ongoing calls for greater diversity in queer characterization and storyline (GLAAD 2017). We note here that the Bury Your Gays trope has a potentially significant negative effect on minority audiences, especially bisexual and lesbian women, some of whom have drawn attention to the importance of fictional characters in the formulation of their identity and as a resource for navigating their own minority sexuality (Gomillion and Giuliano 2011). Healthy media depictions of characters identified as minority gender and sexuality (fictional or otherwise) support the self-esteem of audiences identifying similarly and can often be read as resources for the production of healthy identities and as information can assist audience members to empathize with character situations (Cover 2000).

There are no existing contemporary statistics for LGBTQ+ death in film and television, although several online authors have compiled lists noting more than 200 cases of bury your gays (e.g. Rude 2022, Riese 2023) The fact that it is so common in international screen media could be said to indicate that many stories are not only drawing on a tired trope of queer and trans unliveability, but that they overwhelm the stories that are more reflective of real-world resilience, self-esteem, relationships and belonging experienced by gender- and sexuality-diverse persons in a contemporary era. Instead, they depict what are sometimes referred to as 'deficit' assumptions about gender- and sexuality-diverse subjects.

While there is no legitimate argument that the representation of queer death on-screen is actually harmful, it remains the case that the audience response that actively identified the Bury your Gays trope in contemporary television points to the deeply-felt meaningfulness of the representation of queer characters and the desire to see successful relationships, liveable lives, ongoing storylines and character longevity. Popular culture remains a significant site for adolescent pedagogy in relation to sexual identities (Ashcraft 2003) due in part to the visual resource and repetition of narratives directed towards teenaged audiences (Clarke 2013).

Several interviewees in the *AusQueerScreen* study noted the negative impact of becoming attached to queer and trans characters who were killed off. Peter, for example, objected to the prominence given to *Holding the Man* (2015), the Australian film based on Timothy Conigrave's memoir of his relationship and the AIDS death of his partner. Peter's concern was that while it was an important historical story depicting the HIV experience in 1980s and 1990s Australia, the release of the film twenty years after the book misrepresented queer Australian life as one of tragedy.

> Today, surely, we can have representations where it's not about it all being a bloody tragedy, like tragic representations of gays is kind of done to death, literally. Yeah, kill your gays trope. Exactly. I'm kind of over it. So I don't know if that's on balance, a good thing just because they didn't represent it and then being killed or whatever. Yeah. Holding the Man was of its time, of a particular era. So not also have movies of this, like, now.

Peter has rightly pointed to not only the difficulty of putting an outdated experience on-screen, but the fact that the film did not do enough to present itself as a historical drama in the way, perhaps, Russell T. Davies' *It's a Sin* (2021) managed in representing the advent of HIV in the United Kingdom. By appearing as a queer screen text of the 2010s, *Holding the Man* (2015) arguably adds to the significant corpus of Australian queer screen texts that depict death of characters with whom an audience identifies and becomes attached – because they are queer characters – depicted living a very truncated life.

Participant Mark made a more explicit reference to the harms of exposure to this negative trope in Australian and international texts:

> Seeing myself as expendable in the 'bury your gays trope', which is more prominent to women than it is for gay men. So while it's more prominent to women still, it existed for the male characters. Even though the characters died, having the characters appear in the first place was a positive. Seeing them constantly die wasn't.

What Mark points to is not merely that the characters die, but that exposure to that particular story – told multiple times and in only marginally different ways – gives a sense of expendability, a sense of worthlessness, of not being a full subject. Ultimately, this translates to a sense of hopelessness for livability.

Discourses of hope have been known to be significant for vulnerable and at-risk queer and trans youth to maintain a sense of futurity, of the possibility of a liveable life during times when it appears unliveable, and thereby not fall into despair or hopelessness that exacerbates risks to mental health. Where, for example, bullying, violence and harassment have been substantial parts of the ongoing lived experience of a queer or trans young person at a particular point in time, a sense of hope for a future is recognized as a mechanism for resilience and maintenance of liveability (Kalliotis 2000, Kim and Leventhal 2008) and managing psychological distress (Espelage and Swearer 2008).

Stories of hopelessness are not, in themselves, problematic. As Terry Eagleton (2015) has explained, bleakness, hopelessness and negativity can serve political ends by arguing for a more radical posture. We can see this, perhaps, in the 2010 film *Amphetamine*, which although set in Hong Kong might fall under the bracket of Australian queer screen media given its Australian-trained main actor, Thomas Price, and the character he plays (Daniel) being an ex-pat Australian working in finance in Hong Kong. *Amphetamine* is very much a story of hopelessness as Daniel begins a relationship with the troubled Kafka, who has suffered childhood poverty, and violence and sexual assault, all contributing to his amphetamine addiction and erratic behaviour. As the relationship crumbles and Daniel eventually returns to Australia, Kafka self-harms and then ultimately dies by suicide. Throughout the narrative, the lack of hope of a happy, romantic coupled relationship is persistently shattered by the conditions of Kafka's trauma. To read the film through a lens of hopelessness, then, is to read it as a call not for LGBTQ+ rights or mechanisms to address a sense of endemic queer vulnerability or a fight against the abuse of recreational drugs; rather it is a statement calling for socio-economic equality and an end to gang violence as necessary components for liveable lives regardless of genders, sexualities or relationships. However, to read the film from the perspective of mental health and well-being attuned to audience needs is, alternatively, to see that it *also* contributes to the wider cultural myth of queer expendability and the perception that queer futurity may be unachievable. Read, then, in the context of all the other texts which depict a queer death, Mark's response of feeling 'expendable' is more easily understood.

Discussing queer screen media with others

In the *AusQueerScreen* interviews, many participants reflected on their experiences of discussing TV and films with LGBTQ+ content with friends –

and sometimes family – when they were younger. Tom spoke about the discourse surrounding the TV series *Prisoner* (1979–86) when he was growing up in the 1980s:

> I just think because it was so different. And it was a big thing at the time, as well. Everyone at school was watching it, so it was very much a peer thing. And people I knew, that's what they were talking about at school, you know, or down the shops.

Similarly, James recalled schoolyard discussions of an episode of *Heartbreak High* (1994–9) in which a character was possibly a lesbian: 'and by the end of the episodes, they'd kind of wrapped up that – "oh, no, she's not. So it's okay", – and it was never touched upon again. And so it was always these very fleeting moments.' Similarly, Clea described conversations with high school friends about Sharon Stone's role in *Basic Instinct* (1992), and speculating on her bisexuality while they were working out their own identities. Jeremy spoke about introducing films and TV series with LGBTQ+ narratives or characters to his heterosexual friends as a teenager, but only after having vetted the texts first:

> I feel like if it was charted territory, if it was something I'd watched before, and I kind of knew what to expect, I did feel comfortable with, with watching that with friends . . . And when I did share those kind of, and consume stories with other people, that was a positive experience . . . if I was choosing what we were watching, then they were experiencing storylines that weren't just the same ones that they would ordinarily be picking out. For example, if I was with straight friends, they would normally go for something like . . . your typical 10 different boy-loves-girl stories on at once, where everyone's white and cis. And then I guess if I was picking something slightly different but I knew that they were actually widening their view, their understanding, their experience.

In this example, Jeremy invited discussion with his friends after carefully considering the content of the screen text. However, many participants said they did not have opportunities to discuss queer film and TV with friends as teenagers. For some participants who were teenagers in the late 1990s and early 2000s, in the absence of LGBTQ+ peers, internet forums were an important space for connecting with other queer fans of TV series like *Buffy: The Vampire Slayer* (1997–2003) internationally.

Some of the participants described 'catching up' on queer film later in life that had been difficult to access in the era of broadcast television, and prior to widespread internet access. Liza, who was born in the 1970s, spoke about watching 1980s lesbian films such as *Desert Hearts* (1985) and *Personal Best* (1982) with groups of university friends, and finding these both 'amazing' and 'cringey'. Indeed, many participants discussed LGBTQ+ screen content with others only after entering their twenties and connecting with queer community. For example, James recalled his first share house, where he was able to watch queer films and TV in the lounge room without secrecy and discuss these texts critically with friends and housemates. Abigail described watching queer films at an independent cinema and having lively discussions with university friends afterward, alongside difficult evenings with LGBTQ+ friends at tram stops and bus shelters who had been rejected by their family.

In these peer discussions, the quality of the film or series was not always judged as synonymous with good LGBTQ+ representation: Sienna spoke about gathering with a group of LGBTQ+ friends to watch TV and film with queer content and discuss 'whether they did it well or not, whether the show was good, whether the show was not good but the representation was really good', mentioning a series she considered to be 'bad, but the relationship is amazing. So everybody watches it for that.' Stevie talked about watching *The L Word* (2004–9) every week with friends, and loudly criticizing the warnings of sexual content displayed at the start of each episode. Jarad said that as a teen in the 1990s he and friends would gather to watch and discuss *Queer as Folk* (1999–2000) and interpret queer codes in camp films such as *Sister Act* (1992) or *Bram Stoker's Dracula* (1992). Indeed, many participants spoke about queer-coded characters in Australian film and television as prompting discussion between peers: as Peter observed, 'it's never been the explicit characters in Australian media that have stood out, as written into queer storylines. It's always been the ones I've read that way.'

Discussions with family were less common. As we discussed in Chapter 10, many participants had awkward and painful experiences of commentary from family members about LGBTQ+ screen content when growing up in the context of the shared viewing space of the family living room. Josie described homophobic comments from her parents about gay TV personalities as compounding her sense that her sexuality should remain a secret: 'I was . . . very aware that I could not tell that to anyone around me, um, not at school or anywhere.' Karen described watching *The Hunger* (1983) on SBS one night with her mother and feeling uncomfortable with the feelings it prompted in her, leaving the room without speaking: 'I did not have any role models growing up at all. You know, I thought I was the only one in the world, which is what I'm so grateful to see now, the kids that, you know, it's out there and spoken about.'

Depictions of family acceptance on-screen could emphasise the lack of support participants felt from their own family: Marie commented, 'I remember seeing *The Sum of Us* and thinking about coming out to my family and thinking that my family were in no way as nice as Jack Thompson.' At the same time, she noted that depictions of homophobic characters on-screen can provide opportunities to educate heterosexual family members or recognize them as potential allies, or at least gauge their attitudes.

In contrast, Josie discussed her experiences as a queer parent watching and discussing LGBTQ+ TV and film with children, and the ways this set them apart from other parents. Josie said that her children 'grew up on *Will and Grace*' and the family travelled regularly across Melbourne to visit a queer video shop. Josie spoke about her son's love of the film *Brokeback Mountain* (2005):

> He's a very sensitive kid. And he really got it. He must have been in late primary school, something like that. And he brought the DVD with him on the sleepover because he thought it was a really good movie. And when I went to pick him up, the parents sort of made this kind of comment that they had this movie and I went, 'Oh right, okay, you know, yet it's a good, good movie.' And they were really kind of not approving. But what was really funny years later, their son came out as gay. So, I was like, that wouldn't have gone down so well.

Josie's story points to both the next generations of queer household viewing practices and discussions, as well as the ongoing challenges faced by queer young people in interacting with their families about LGBTQ+ screen representation.

Conclusion

Judging by the responses received in the *AusQueerScreen* study, Australian LGBTQ+ audiences are indeed concerned about the mental health and well-being of younger gender- and sexuality-diverse people, and for a few reasons. First, many related the expectations of the plight of young people to their own experiences growing up, although they often occurred decades earlier. This is a common framework in queer studies in which older generations sometimes re-frame the experiences, vulnerabilities and resiliences of younger people through their own understanding, regardless of changed socio-cultural and political conditions, and shifts in screen representation and digital connectivity (Cover 2023). However, secondly, there was a profound reflection on the significance of positive representations as not only serving as a barrier to poor well-being, but as actively bolstering positive mental health among younger audiences. Nevertheless, thirdly, the over-preponderance in Australian queer screen texts of suicidality and poor mental health was deemed broadly problematic and felt to be likely to affect audiences substantially by reinforcing myths of queer youth 'vulnerability'. Since queer screen texts are not necessarily engaged with in isolation, the role of discussion with others emerged as a key factor in the extent to which both positive and negative representations had an effect on audience members, with a range of ways in which discussion both ameliorated negative depictions and encouraged more critical views, including particularly in multi-generational social engagement.

12

Queer Screens and Social Change

Introduction

There is no doubt that the various emergences of screen media over the past century – cinema, televisions in the private home, time-shifting recording devices, streaming – have substantially shaped society on a global scale. However, the extent to which screen representation, storytelling and the depiction of queer and trans identities and communities themselves have shaped the wider community, whether positively or negatively, is something we need to be very careful about. It is important to avoid falling into the trap of what is sometimes called the 'media effects' model, which in some versions claims that exposure to screen content somehow 'automatically' changes behaviours, attitudes or practices both individually and socially. Certainly, there is enough of that kind of false thinking behind the problematic claims of the anti-trans lobby and those opposed to 'gender theory', as they put it. In many instances, they use such ideas of media exposure to lobby legislatures and local councils to ban books and other information on gender-diverse persons for fear it will 'automatically' cause too much public acceptance, or will 'automatically' turn children into trans-kids, or other kinds of outcomes feared by ultra-conservatives. Just as words and representations about gender can never be transformative in such a simplistic way (Butler 2024), we also need to understand that there is nothing 'automatic' about positive social changes resulting from queer on-screen representation. That does not mean that they do not *contribute* to social change in very general terms, only that they do not cause change. Rather, such representation may be one small but very important ingredient contributing to the positive shifts towards queer acceptance we have seen in the past, and to the current and future needs for greater acceptance of trans people in Australia.

One way to make sense of how much queer screen representation contributes to social change is to analyse, through media and cultural theories, how people themselves actually talk about the transformation, increased acceptance and enhanced belonging they themselves have witnessed, and how they relate these to the presence of queer stories, characters and themes on Australian screens. In the *AusQueerScreen* study, participants were asked the extent to which they thought queer representation in Australian film and television had shaped – or had the potential to further shape – social change. They were asked if screen representation was likely to increase acceptance of LGBTQ+ subjects, and if it was felt to contribute to advances in belonging among gender- and sexuality-diverse Australians, such as marriage equality. Overwhelmingly, our participants felt that media played a significant role in the increasing acceptance of gender and sexuality diversity they had seen over their lives. But, importantly, they had very nuanced views about what kinds of screen representation contributed to social change, where representations had also held it back, and what forms such representations need to take to bring about further positive change. In other words, simply making queer and trans people visible was, for the most part, not seen to be enough; rather, they spoke of what counted as positive representation and how they had seen that change the views of family and friends, and some even talked of audience engagement such as the importance of post-screening conversations.

This final chapter begins with a brief analysis of some of the theoretical considerations of the relationship between screen media and social change, returning again to our critique of perspectives that see visibility per se as a key ingredient of transformation, and investigating ways in which we can think of certain kinds of representation as pedagogical. We then consider some of the audience participants' perceptions of social change in terms of their own lived experience: the tendency again to reiterate visibility's importance, but also their views on how 'palatable' queer and trans characters might be both beneficial and problematic, their ideas on how audiences engage in para-social contexts with queer and trans characters on-screen, and their views on how media fosters discussion that changes attitudes. As a book about Australian queer screen media, it is important of course that we think about how the 'Australianness' of Australian queer screen media performs a special role in shaping local attitudes and forms of acceptance. Finally, we discuss some of the ways in which participants have described the utility of queer and trans characters in media whose presence in stories is unrelated to their gender or sexual identity.

Screen media and social change

A number of different approaches, theories and discourses have attempted to unpack the role of screen media in producing social change, looking to determine if it has any role in shaping attitudes, practices, behaviours and societies. Some approaches suggest there is little impact of media and over-determines audience members' agency, while others see screen media as powerfully influential and sometimes controlling. We have long recognized that the development of cultural *technologies* of communication both respond to and sustain socio-cultural changes (Williams 1975), but we need to be more careful in talking about specific representations, since it is important not to suggest that 'exposure' to individual or repeated media representations itself is wholly and exclusively causal of social or behavioural changes, either for individuals or broad communities. Often, the extent to which media is perceived to play such a role depends on the theoretical grounding of the assertion. Psychoanalytic film theory, for example, is pessimistic about the role of screen media in producing social change because it understands instinctual drives of human subjects as themselves being unchanging (Ryan 1988). Other twentieth-century theories, such as those of the Frankfurt School, saw screen media as having the potential for revolutionary social change but found that the ideological underpinnings of media more generally blocked such changes from coming about (Adorno 2003).

On the other hand, theories such as the 'media effects' model made exaggerated assumptions about the role of screen representation and content in affecting individual attitudes and behaviour. Media effects models continue to dominate much public discourse and journalism about screen representation, certain brands of psychology and hysteria or moral panic about media. Typically, such models present very narrow, linear understandings of media by assuming that audiences are actively 'duped' into performing or copying types of behaviour – whether positive or problematic – that are presented to us on-screen, without accounting for the complexity of reading practices, capacity to interpret critically, ability to be active in making identifications and recognitions with a text or any element of agency of the self. Media effects models are often related to discussions of violent television and pornographic representation in mainstream screen texts, whereby exposure to the first is seen to produce violent personalities and violent behaviours, while exposure to the second is seen to encourage problematic sexual behaviour, assault or promiscuous behaviour.

Here, social change is perceived as the sum total of *individuals* who have been altered by exposure to media content.

Theories that assume a causal effect of screen content position audiences as wholly passive. Emerging from predominantly North American communications research of the 1940s, media effects theories are based on a linear understanding of communication; that is, messages sent and received in a particularly 'unmediated' and fashion and in which the message or meaning itself is understood as unproblematic and easily comprehended (Shannon and Weaver 1949). Looking for a purely 'scientific' model of influence, those who worked on and developed the effects approach ignored the role of interpretation, more complex understandings of reception and diverse meanings (what we often refer to as textual polysemy). Effects theories suggest that behavioural and belief changes occur through persuasion, propaganda, manipulation, brainwashing and the encouragement of 'copycat' behaviour. Naturally, ultra-conservative commentators have worried that representation of LGBTQ+ and, particularly, trans persons will be, or indeed has been, causal of young people becoming queer or considering gender affirmative healthcare.

While we would ordinarily acknowledge that media stories *can* influence behaviour, attitudes and change, the ways in which that influence occurs is complex and always contingent. In dismissing such effects and persuasion approaches, we need to remain aware that screen media does indeed contribute strongly to how audiences make sense of the world, of ourselves, and of our relationships with others, including sexuality and gender minorities. As media theorist James Curran (2002: 158) has argued, '[T]he conviction . . . that the media are important agencies of influence is broadly correct. However, the ways in which the media exert influence are complex and contingent.' To put this another way, we might say that while there is influence through the dominant role media practices play in everyday and working life, how we respond to our media encounters with stories and diverse characters, and how they are *incorporated* into attitudes and behaviours and the change and development of broader social norms, is wildly dependent on a constellation of conditions.

Some of those conditions include (a) the *matrix* of different screen media – alongside other communication – that is accessed, used, deployed and engaged with in cross-influential or conflicting ways; (b) the increasing *ubiquity* of access to sources of information in which an answer (whether right, wrong or indifferent) to any question can be found very quickly; (c) the capacity of ostensible or unconscious *memory* to incorporate alternative stories and to keep them available to the self to reflect upon critically; (d) the *intersection* of different texts as a corpus or body of information – such as multiple queer television and film characters at around approximately the same time – that help in adjusting social normativities; and (e) the *context* of such characterizations and diversities in media, for example, the ways in which other characters react to a trans character.

All of this is to say that queer and trans representation on Australian screens may well play a role in social change, or may well underpin and confirm social changes that are already happening so they become sustained into the longer term, and may indeed change the attitudes and behaviours of those who encounter such stories individually, but the *fact* of their representation does not guarantee change in itself.

An alternative way of theorising the role that queer screen representation may play in terms of social change and increased tolerance or acceptance, and inclusivity, is through perspectives attentive to the *media experience as educational*; that is, as cultural pedagogy (Giroux 2004). A cultural pedagogy acknowledges that experiences and opportunities of 'education' are dispersed across both institutional and noninstitutional settings, through audience members' everyday engagement with the environment, via nonauthorized and noninformational sources and, today, through practices of engagement and spectatorship of screen entertainment media. A cultural pedagogy not only argues that other cultural settings such as screen entertainment may be more educational than school teaching because it is more engaging, but that the two are substantially interrelated to the extent that the school curriculum on gender and sexuality inclusion may only make sense in terms of what is 'learned' from queer storytelling in film and television.

Screen entertainment has an advantage over other kinds of learning, we argue, because it engages in storytelling. Indeed, film and television are among the most powerful settings for the telling of stories through narrative that give meaning to otherwise disjunct and disconnected events and phenomena in everyday life (Plummer 1995). In this respect, when screen entertainment is pedagogical, it acts not because it is providing a content-based resource that is then at scale 'taken on' by audiences in ways that bring about social change or shifts in public attitude, but because the social conditions are right for screen media's knowledge frameworks themselves to become contagious, or 'catch on' (Berger 2013). The key to understanding the relationship between queer screen representation in Australia and the transformation of Australian society to one ostensibly more accepting of gender and sexuality diversity than it was half-a-century ago is that media is an important force in prompting the kind of shifts in attitude, behaviour and engagement, but only alongside other forces of change.

Visibility and positivity considerations

Theorising media's role in producing social change is useful because it allows us to give a critical nuance that overcomes both the pessimism of approaches that see media only as reflective, and the oversimplifications of approaches that see media as determining behaviour and attitude. However, if we want to understand this fully, theoretical accounts are only a portion of the picture, and it is helpful to deepen this by analysing how people with lived experience of changing social circumstances and shifts in inclusivity and belonging perceive their peers, families and wider society as transformed in the context of queer screen representation. Audience participants in the *AusQueerScreen* project were asked about the extent to which they felt queer representation in Australian film and television had had a positive impact on mainstream, cisgender and straight audiences, and if it had encouraged a greater sense of acceptance of queer and trans people in Australian society. Most felt very strongly that exposure to quality storylines had helped make mainstream audiences, whether peers or strangers, more accepting of gender and sexuality diversity in Australia. Interviewees in that project described screen media's role in social change through a range of themes.

We have mentioned several times across this book the continuing public fixation on concepts of visibility and invisibility, whether that is journalists over-emphasising past absences of LGBTQ+ characters on-screen, screen producers motivated by a desire to make queer stories visible, or narrow scholarly assumptions that visibility per se is still considered an achievement or that instances of characters and texts can still be collated (Cover and Dau 2021). This is not to suggest that visibility itself is necessarily a problem, since it is well-recognized that LGBTQ+ identities, communities and cultures came to the notice of a widespread public through shifts in popular cultural representation (Barber 2010). Rather, it is to say that visibility itself is not necessarily productive of social change, and that what is needed is a nuanced understanding of what kind of visibility is helpful in changing social attitudes and increasing acceptance among the wider population.

Some participants in the *AusQueerScreen* project drew on discourses of visibility to associate queer representation with social change, and these ranged from those which broadly repeated the visibility imperative to those which discussed what makes a more positive form of visibility to those which recognized the potential for backlash. Among participants who were born later, however, there was a more nuanced approach to representation whereby the emphasis was not on making queer characters and stories visible on-screen, but on how such representations had moved from negative stereotypes towards 'positive' depictions. For some, positive depictions were a necessary component of on-screen queer presence that had actively changed views among mainstream audiences by encouraging those with outdated views that relied on stereotypes to correct them through exposure to more genuine or more nuanced stories – particularly, as one participant put it, 'more positive depictions of queer relationships' in place of assumptions about casual sexual behaviour. James felt this went quite a way back in Australia's television history to *A Country Practice* (1981–94), a rural medical drama which dealt with weekly issues, and on a few occasions included LGBTQ+ stories and characters as 'issue'. For James, these stories were helpful in shaping public attitudes during an era in which HIV had resulted in increased anti-gay hostility. He spoke of the

> open-minded things presented by *A Country Practice* that were introducing that idea into these straight, broad Australian consciousness, because it was a very popular show in its heyday. And you know, they'd have characters that were, you know, closeted . . . [but] always seem very sympathetic. And you look back now, probably they were a bit, quite, preachy, but at the time that was really revolutionary in my opinion, yeah. And really probably changed attitudes.

This perspective demonstrates some of the ways in which queer audiences had witnessed social change through positive perspectives that, in John D'Emilio's (1992) terms, served to lessen prejudice by presenting opportunities for audience knowledge to correct the misinformation that had circulated through stereotypes and limited encounters with gender- and sexuality-diverse communities and individuals at that time. That is, by presenting queer characters with depth, histories, meaningful relationships and complex issues to navigate, such television series and film generated sympathy, engagement and greater understanding, leading to broad adjustments in public opinion.

Others felt that positive depictions were nevertheless too few for changing public attitudes both in the past and present, suggesting that no matter how positive some examples were, they were otherwise swamped by problematic or negative representation. For example, Jay felt that 'a lot of Australian film and TV that exists with queer representation at the moment still falls into the trap of, um, either representing the characters in a poor light or having them sort of end up not having that classic happy ending'. It certainly remains the case that a significant portion of LGBTQ+ representation continues to depict an unhappy end for queer and trans characters, relationship or life, both internationally with what is known as the 'bury your gays' trope in which both supporting and central queer characters are killed off in television series (Cover and Milne 2023) or in the Australian setting where an over-abundance of suicidality of queer characters in film persists (Cover 2021). In that respect, while depictions of less-vulnerable are typically those that viewers deem as positive and therefore more likely to foster greater acceptance of gender- and sexuality-diverse people, as well as dispel myths and stereotypes, there is a continuing need to balance the range of stories and characterizations to affect social change more broadly.

Palatability and tolerance

Despite the significance of a more critical engagement with the kinds of media representations that were available, some of the *AusQueerScreen* interviewees expressed concerns about too much emphasis on positivity, suggesting this is sometimes felt to be a cynical production and network attempt to present queer and trans characters and stories that were palatable for mainstream, cisgender and straight audiences, while ignoring the realities, depth, complexity and hardship of some queer and trans lives, and the broad diversity among gender- and sexuality-diverse people.

Such views speak to what Evan Cooper (2003) outlined two decades ago in his analysis of the social impact of *Will & Grace* (1998–2006, 2017–20). For Cooper, shows like *Will & Grace* encouraged social acceptance of non-heteronormative identities and cultures by deliberately focusing on a queer character represented as the antithesis of spectacle and by marginalising 'outrageous, fun characters' (531). Indeed, its use of a more outrageous (and sexually active) character in Jack actively centred the normativity and therefore palatability of Will in the terms of mainstream audience desires, narrowing possibilities of what might constitute a 'positive' representation. Cooper's view was that the juxtaposition of the two characters allowed heterosexual audiences to see Will's behaviour, outlook and queerness as acceptable on the basis that a secondary character was framed as potentially problematic.

This is where we can understand some of our participants' responses in terms of the distinction between 'tolerance' and 'acceptance': respectable, 'positive' characterizations may increase tolerance of gender- and sexuality-diverse people, but is does this not fall short of the goal of genuine acceptance and inclusivity? Jarad, who identifies as queer cisgender and was born in the 1980s, noted the sort of respectability across Australian queer screen content that served social change for a time but was broadly narrow and, to himself, unappealing:

> I think we've kind of come out of it now, but we spent a few years during the same sex marriage debates, really sort of labouring under this campaign of like, positive images of gay people in love. And I think often that was really shaped by this kind of palatable, cisnormative, middle class, sort of aspirational gay couple, that would be like, two men or two women who wanted to have a family and a house and have their relationship recognized. And, you know, I think that that was very much held up as positive image *de jour* of our kind of epoch. And thank god we kind of had the plebiscite and moved on . . . I think now there's less of this kind of official political agenda, or requisite to paint images of queer people as family friendly.

What Jarad, like many others who were critical of the dominance of safe and non-threatening queer and trans depictions, points to are the key questions of *what sort of social change* and whether or not *tolerance is enough*. Here, we argue, such depictions may foster only the sort of social change that tolerates a narrow set of behaviours, depictions and representations that do not challenge established norms.

Tolerance is often defined as the capacity to endure that which is difficult or painful to encounter – that is, the capacity of straight, cisgender and mainstream audiences to endure exposure to gender- and sexuality-diverse themes, characters and narratives in the screen entertainment they choose to watch. In its most colloquial form, tolerance means 'to put up with'. For 1970s Gay Liberation, the notion of tolerance was itself just another form of oppression. Writing in the very early years of Gay Liberation, Dennis Altman (1971) argued that tolerance was one of three types of oppression encountered by early non-heterosexual persons, alongside persecution (e.g. criminality of homosexuality) and discrimination (e.g. prejudicial treatment queer people). In Altman's framework, tolerance is an emotional disposition that internalizes a prevailing ideological perspective

– he pointed out that 'most intelligent heterosexuals reject, intellectually, their hostility to homosexuals while unable to conquer their emotional repugnance. The outward result is tolerance' (63). Tolerance in this sense represses because it does not fully accept non-heterosexual and gender-diverse persons *on our terms* as equally welcome in society as straight and cisgender persons. Indeed, as Wendy Brown (2006) has noted, tolerance has persistently moved from a framework for managing *some* minority participation towards serving as an instrument for consolidating the norm by limiting minority, alternative and critical perspectives through marginal incorporation.

Social change is more than simply an attitude shift from hatred or wilful exclusion to tolerance and 'putting up with', but accepts that a whole-of-society will indeed be changed by the inclusion of those who have been marginalized. And here is where our participants rightly point to the difficult, tight cultural shifts that must take place in screen media to depict queer and trans characters that are both appealing without being only a gesture towards tolerance.

Where *Priscilla* (1994), for example, depicted queerness as spectacle that may be tolerable for its spectacularity, the narrative of *Holding the Man* (2015) presents the tolerable as the 'rightness' of properly coupled relationships and the failure of promiscuous sexuality. Or where *Prisoner* (1979–86) presented lesbian women who were lower-class, criminal, malevolent, violent or sometimes pathetic, *Janet King* (2014–17) depicts lesbianism through stable relationships, child-rearing and the professional life of a prosecutor upholding the normative law. It is no surprise, of course, that the late twentieth-century texts depicted more queer disestablishmentarian than the twenty-first century texts in which what some would call beneficially 'positive' can also be read as the limits of tolerance. In that respect, what is celebrated as visible and positive is not necessarily itself a text fostering social change towards acceptance and social transformation.

One 1970s-born interviewee, Maisy, who was active in both liberal and radical politics, noted that one aspect of the tolerable at play was the common failure to generate intersectional characters in Australian queer screen media; that is, to disrupt the norm by representing characters who were not 'safe' by virtue of their gayness in combination with whiteness or middle-class sensibility. Maisy put it this way:

> And the characters that do exist suck, so, and obviously, I'm biased, because those are the things that I identify as. I think, like, definitely the intersections of LGBTI, like [there are] enough white, gay and lesbian people. Like, yeah,

more people of colour, more Indigenous people. I've had conversations recently, where, um, people actually struggled to get their heads around the idea that you can be Indigenous and queer at the same time.

Although there have, of course been examples in recent Australian queer screen depictions of intersectional characters, including particularly in the newer iteration of *Heartbreak High* (2022–5). However, the fact that most queer characterizations are normative, white, cisgender and ostensibly middle-class is, as Maisy noted, not conducive to the kind of radical social change in which a culture is transformed to treat all subjects with equal hospitality regardless of identity demarcations. A greater focus on intersectionality, then, helps undo the limited tolerance by generating more critical insight into the complexity of identity and belonging, with queer screens thereby advancing that pedagogical role of destabilising the norm.

Audience engagement

One of the ways in which *AusQueerScreen* interviewees described that kind of pedagogy towards more meaningful social change was not in terms of the content they viewed, but the viewing practices they recognized among their cisgender and straight peers that encouraged a sense of *engagement* and *relationality* with queer and trans characters and stories. For some, this was noted most readily among their friends. Jeremy, who was born in the 1990s and grew up in a rural town, spoke of how the opportunity to choose films with queer themes among straight friends was helpful for expanding their knowledge and understanding of diversity: 'If I was choosing what we were watching, they heteronomy were experiencing storylines that weren't just the same ones that they would ordinarily be picking out.' Jeremy felt that this exposure leads to, in his words 'desensitization' and is important for social acceptance because in many cases screen representation is 'the closest they will actually get to an experience with somebody who is outwardly or openly trans or openly gay or lesbian or bisexual'.

However, this was not, for him, a matter of exposure or positive representation, but had a great deal to do with the form of viewership that he felt encouraged a sense of inclusivity:

it is actually a very, it's intimate, when you're in your lounge room with the lights off, it's an intimate experience; you are actually in a position where you might absorb, that you might actually be positioned to come around to it, if that makes sense.

Here, Jeremy aligns the practice of viewing as encouraging what is sometimes referred to as 'para-social' relationships with on-screen characters. Para-social relationality is a concept developed in the 1950s by David Horton and Richard Wohl (1956), and taken up again in the 1990s by Joshua Meyrowitz (1997). It describes the psychological perception by audience members that media characters are knowable, and in which one develops attachments of intimacy, perceived friendship and identification.

This framing of audiencehood is significant as it moves the perspective on social change away from ideas grounded in screen media providing 'role models' for social and behavioural change (e.g. Gomillion and Giuliano 2011, Bond and Miller 2017) which often assume a passive, inactive audience who bring little themselves to the act of media engagement. It also helps move away from unfortunate perceptions that problematic social attitudes towards LBGTQ+ people and communities is the result of a lack of exposure that is sometimes read uncritically as 'ignorance' (Gilbert 2014). Rather, what Jeremy alludes to is that mainstream audiences are better positioned to form a sense of relationship with diverse on-screen characters through the setting of media spectatorship in ways which, arguably, may open a framework of mutuality, understanding and care that may, then, lead to wider social change through shifts towards a more empathic attitude.

Such relatability was echoed by other participants in terms of queer television's potential in generating a sense of 'comfort' with queer and trans characters not because they are depicted but because they are viewed in the comfortable setting of the domestic home. These comments resonated with some of our analysis in Chapter 11 where we discussed the spatiality of viewing. Karen, for example, noted that viewing queer content on televisions and smart phones may help mainstream audiences to connect with characters in ways that may be more difficult in the public setting of a cinema. In her perspective, bringing such characters into home screens not only made them 'more normalized' but gave an opportunity for cross-generational exposure through family television viewing:

> I've got a niece and nephew, my niece is five, my nephew's four, and I just think they're going to be hopefully exposed to things more than I ever was.

This reiterates the kind of social changes identified in the 1970s by Raymond Williams (1975) who argued that the development of television was not an accident of invention but a well-developed response to changing cultural practices that was already moving sociality and entertainment away from public settings and into the domestic home, itself becoming more significant with the rise of nuclear families. The development of television responded to the need to bring visual information and entertainment across the threshold into that private domestic sphere. Here, the potential for relating to on-screen queer characters is because they have come into the 'safe space' of the normative family home, rather than being something represented as radically distinct from domesticity, nuclear families and everyday spaces. This created what Karen felt was a greater acceptance of a 'plethora of ways of desiring' that seemed more natural because it is seen 'at home' rather than 'out there'.

For a subject to be recognized as a subject is to be entered into a relationship with, and even a negative or disapproving perspective of a queer on-screen character is a para-social relationship. Here, a secondary benefit of audience engagement and the forms para-social relationship in which recognition has been produced through conversation is activated: a potential for a queer or trans ally to correct misunderstandings and open new horizons for critical engagement. As participant Sienna poignantly noted:

> this sense of humanization takes people out of that, . . . and even just out of echo rooms, echo chambers, where they are only hearing the same opinion over and over again. It's a slow process, but it's one that helps people figure out themselves and . . . instead of just being like, 'yep, I've seen two things about this and that's the impression I have and that doesn't fit in with what I lie, so that's it.'

By thinking about the fact that audience engagement and interpretation are central to the screen media experience we can see how texts which invoke para-social recognition with non-normative characters due to the space in which these texts are viewed or the conversation with others they invoke encourages forms of recognition. It is always pertinent to keep in mind that audiences are not atomized individuals pondering alone what they see on screen, but part of what Etienne Wenger (1998) suggests are communities of audiences or readers who may not have a close relationship themselves but always provide an imagined audience other – the potential of conversation and the obligation of critical assessment about whether one's own thoughts are shared by that community. Recognition *among a group* is key to making sense of queer media's contribution to social change and greater community acceptance. And it is through relationships between audiences and characters and between audience members themselves, whether in agreement or discord, that queer screen media operates most effectively as a cultural pedagogy that educations towards acceptance.

Representing allyship and belonging

Another way in which we can consider queer screen media's contribution to social change is in role-modelling on screen some practices of belonging, acceptance and allyship. Allies broadly describe those straight and cisgender people who not only form friendships with queer and trans individuals, but are willing to combat homophobia, biphobia and transphobia, engage in LGBTQ+ activism and demonstrate genuine knowledge and understanding of queer and trans lives (Cumming-Potvin 2024). The concept of allies can be a marker of increasing acceptance and social belonging for LGBTQ+ individuals, although the very terminology of allegiance retains the concept of a societal 'enemy' preventing the universality of queer and trans acceptance, and the ongoingness of political, social and cultural struggle. Whether the coalitional allegiances among organizations aligned with LGBTQ+ politics in the 1990s (Vaid 1995), presidential candidate Hilary Clinton noting that LGBTQ+ people living in oppressive countries have an 'ally' in the United States (Altman and Symons 2016), the formation of gay/straight alliance clubs to support minority students in schools (Muller 2011) or the perceived well-being benefits for young LGBTQ+ people to feel they have allies supporting LGBTQ+ causes (Rostosky et al. 2015), the idea of allyship saturates public discourse overcoming the idea of queer and trans people as alone, isolated and vulnerable, as having an existence in 'apartness' from wider society. Rather, it marks zones of inclusivity within the context of the unfinished project to achieve universal acceptance. In that sense, allyship has ongoing potential to fulfil the project of social change because, unlike liberal multiculturalism that regulates difference in way to prevent blurring, spillage and diffusion of a white, heteronormative and cisgender national core (Gunew 2000), it presents a sense of belonging that places inclusion 'here' among others, rather than 'over there' as tolerated but separate communities and cultural practices.

Certainly, the era is now mostly over in which 'positive' narratives of LGBTQ+ stories were framed by an idea that queer characters must overcome the obstacle of non-belonging in a small town or suburb by finding their true place of inclusion by joining a ghettoized, inner-urban queer community 'over there' (Cover 2000). This trope was common in much North American queer film and television representation, and is perhaps most marked in the Australian experience in *Priscilla*: fruition for the queer characters is found in the return to queer community in the safety of Sydney and away from the small towns and the outback. On the other hand, these narratives have dissipated in favour of stories that do away with queer and trans communities altogether: again, many North American queer screen texts now depict queer characters primarily in their suburban homes, schools and friendship groups, with their principal connection to other queer people being a coupled, domestic relationship. That is, on the one hand, such texts present queer characters as atomized and separate from the less-tolerable queer community, but on the other hand permit them to remain in straight and cisgender spaces. Allyship, however, presents something different: acknowledging that leaving the space as an unwanted individual is neither feasible nor desirable, and also acknowledging that such non-queer and non-trans spaces and cultures must adapt towards more genuine inclusivity. When we see this on Australian screens, what we see is another pedagogical action that presents role models of individuals who demonstrate to mainstream audiences that queer and trans people are not a threat, can be made to feel welcome in their communities and that interdependencies between straight and queer and cisgender and trans subjects are not only possible but fruitful.

One interviewee, Michael, in the *AusQueerScreen* study noted that this allyship was most visible in Australian soap series with queer characters, and he referred to this as a form of 'mainstreaming':

> You know, having it mainstream, for example recently, like *Home and Away*, they actually had one of the characters who was gay-emerging, coming out of the closet, and, you know, there was actually the support, as corny . . . as it was, there was actually the support.

Likewise, Mark noted that supportive characters provide a roadmap for the wider community by 'showing us, like, a positive way of handling the concept of a "trans-cis relationship"'. Finally, for participant Beth, this is most powerful when queer characters are doing 'normal everyday stuff' with their straight and cisgender peers on-screen which demonstrates the success of belonging, affiliation and allyship rather than focusing the narrative on how to achieve it. Representing allyship through role-modelling straight and cisgender characters who are supportive or active in defending those queer and trans characters in the on-screen imagined community provides a framework that breaks older stereotypes of exclusion and the need to move away from straight and cisgender spaces.

Australian scenes and sounds

Australian audiences experience both international and local film and television production in what Alan McKee (2001) has described as two very distinct faces of the media experience. The distinction is one often made by audiences, although not necessarily in relation to a cultural patriotism supporting local production or media industries; rather, it often relates to the recognizability of 'Australianness' on screens in both visual and auditory terms. Vinodh Venkatesh (2016) describes such representation as part of the 'milieu of techniques, images, sounds, textures, and surfaces that engender a polysensorial, haptic interaction with the moving image' (6). Here, audiences are positioned by that schema to draw that distinction between international queer texts (which may be in familiar but 'foreign' setting such as New York, London or San Francisco) and Australian texts marked by a viewer's relationship with the images (internationally recognizable images of Australianness such as beaches, deserts, major city landmarks), surfaces (water, desert sands, suburban and semi-rural visualities, urban environments), sounds (Australian natural soundscapes, accents, idiomatic ways of speaking), that place the viewer's body in the context of that which is made familiar through national myth. In this sense, queer characters are spectatorially recognized not just as located *on* Australian land, but *within* the Australian national mythos, thereby positioning mainstream audiences to make an awkward choice: reject that screen presence as improper to Australianness or accept that screen presence as part of the context of Australian belonging. Arguably, a progression towards the latter among the wider viewership has occurred, in part through the four factors of social change described above. This context adds a fifth.

AusQueerScreen participants were asked questions about their thoughts on Australian screen media's representation of LGBTQ+ and gender-diverse subjects in relation to the more regular influx of North American and European queer film and television. Almost all felt that the recognizable backdrop of Australian space, landscapes and recognizable cities, alongside Australia accents, were important for locating queerness as a reality in Australia in ways which they felt contributed to greater acceptance in this country. That is, the visual and audio framing of queerness *in* Australia was seen to have shifted public attitudes away from *queerness as otherness* by reducing the ostensible or unconscious view that queer and trans people are something 'foreign' in the way depicted in foreign screen media.

As with the para-social relations that develop because viewing queer depictions on television occurs in the private, domestic space of the home, Robyn felt that Australian settings help produce more widespread acceptance because it 'gets a lot of Australians where they live. I think we do respond to media that's Australian'. In this sense, the intersection between national/residential identity and LGBTQ+ subjectivity is perceived as possible in ways that European or North American queer and trans depictions do not quite facilitate, allowing diversity to be something that is incorporated into an 'Australianness' rather than as something that may be tolerated elsewhere but is 'less thinkable' for some in their own identity context.

Others found that the metaphor of landscape has shifted in ways that help place queerness into the spatiality of Australia. In his interview, Jay spoke about the change from the era of *Priscilla* in which the Australian natural landscape (the desert) was presented as hostile and dangerous, and queer characters were seen to be 'at odds' with Australian as a place, while more recent queer film texts were notably different. He referred to two films, *Downriver* (2015) and *Newcastle* (2008), both of which presented queerness alongside and in a positive relationship with Australian water. Beaches and rivers are, of course, an Australian self-reflective national myth or icon (Evers 2008), which suggests that what Jay is pointing to is an inclusion of queerness within that national myth rather than as characters who are only 'at home' in the built environment or urban setting where *Priscilla* begins and ends, or the suburban domesticity of *Home & Away, Neighbours* or *The Secret Life of Us*.

Others drew specific attention to the audio component of film and television. Lavinia, for example, noted that it had been important that Australian productions and on-screen settings represented LGBTQ+ characters and stories in increasing public acceptance, because it represented queer and trans people with distinctly Australian voices:

> you can relate more to people who seem more like you, to people who speak with the same accent that you do and people who are more culturally similar to you . . . to assist non-queer Australians to maybe be more accepting of queerness if they're seeing a portrayal of queerness in a context that feels more local to them.

McKee (1999) has drawn attention to the ways in which Australian-made gay pornography often over-emphasized Australian semi-rural nature sounds, accents and idiomatic ways of speaking to better represent an 'Australianness' with which porn consumers could identify. Although marketing to an Australian audience is less ostensibly the intention of Australian film and television producers, arguably the distinctiveness of Australian language, expression, accents and other sounds appropriate to Australia are part of what positions audiences to distinguish between offshore and Australian screen texts, gains the appreciation of queer and trans viewers – including many of the project participants – and, as they suggest, creates identifications and recognitions that enhance the possibility of promoting social change towards acceptance.

On the whole, participants spoke of the Australian setting in terms of what is seen and heard in engaging with queer characters or stories on-screen, and it was notable that their reflections were far more often oriented towards past, present and future social change among mainstream audiences towards acceptance and hospitality than concerns about the pleasure they derived themselves, or the benefits to media industries in Australia.

Just because queer . . .

Finally, we would like to turn to some of the ways in which queer screen representation can be understood as a normativizing force, that is, making queer and trans people part of the Australian cultural scene through screen media. Although normativization is a problematic term because it is sometimes mistaken for assimilation or invisibilization of specificity and different, changing 'the norm' such that queer and trans people are incorporated within rather than at its margins is a key component of genuine social acceptance. This is to consider the ways in which screen media plays a role in *relaxing the norm's* functions for social exclusion, by representing a more ethical, inclusive and interdependent norm or set of norms. One of the ways in which queer screen representation does so is by depicting queer and trans characters as unremarkable and without spectacle: that is, by allowing characters where queer or trans identity is not the 'issue' of their story, where the obstacle of forging belonging is not part their narrative, and where queer-specific or trans-specific vulnerability is immaterial to the text.

Although, as we have shown in Chapters 2 and 3, and elsewhere in this book, there are some distant historical examples of unremarkable queer sexualities in Australian film and television, for the most part there has long been a tendency of following the international norm of depicting an LGBTQ+ character's story as 'special' because their sexuality or gender is the 'issue' or 'stumbling block' of their narrative. Facing obstacles such as homophobia or transphobia, coming out, finding a genuine same-sex relationship or achieving an understanding with a hostile family or peers in order to reach identity and narrative fruition, and thereby conclude their story, is so remarkably common in the representation of queer and trans characters that is now a cliché (Roof 1996). This is alongside the tendency in Australian stories of queer boys and men represented as inherently vulnerable and tragic, with a very high rate of on-screen queer male suicidality in Australia (Cover 2021).

Real social change sponsored by screen media needs, we argue, a form of representation that actually alters the norm which, in this case, is the norm of Australian heteromasculinity and cis-masculinity that is exclusive of its 'others' and so often remains the core 'go to' in Australian self-perception. In other words, something beyond the limited cultural liberalism that makes only the mildest gesture towards tolerance through spectacular inclusivity without upsetting the more conservative norm (Eagleton 1968). We are therefore arguing here that disrupting the norm requires presenting queerness and trans subjectivity *as the norm*. That is, to produce social change not by screen texts which argue for inclusion or tolerance but which represent queer and trans characters as part of the everyday landscape of ordinary Australian life without issue – as unremarkable. This calls for storytelling which eschews queer vulnerability, and stories based on something other than queer and trans people seeking belonging or non-violence or self-dignity by overcoming a set of narrative obstacles towards a screen-based sense of an ending.

There are, of course, many instances in international queer screen media where a character's sexuality is submerged. Hart (2016), for example, notes the significance of *Six Feet Under* (2001–5) in representing a non-threatening queer character (David Fisher) whose sexuality is only sometimes an issue. What is notable about a long-form series like *Six Feet Under* is that, like many series emerging on cable in the 1990s and 2000s, it was able to have three narrative forms: an episodic story (in which David's sexuality may be unmentioned, immaterial, gestural or mentioned in passing without issue); an episodic story (which may sometimes focus explicitly on David's sexuality, returning to the 'immaterial' norm by the next episode), and the long duration narrative over the course of a season or the entire series (such as David's slow, quiet development into a confident gay man). Such multiple narratives were made possible through the growth of cable television that did not rely on episodic 'reset' because such series did not need to seek a high network ratings share by serving casual and inconsistent viewers. Rather, as Reeves and colleagues (1996) noted, were able to serve different kinds of audiences, including those regular viewers enjoying the long narrative while not confusing those who only encounter the show casually. As a result, David's sexuality can be represented as 'just because he is gay' in most episodes, because the 'issue' of his sexuality (belonging, encountering homophobia, navigating queer relationships, etc.) can be packaged in occasional episodes and the submerged long narrative. *Six Feet Under*, in this sense, enables a queer character without becoming a queer series, exposing a wider mainstream audience to queerness as backdrop rather than queer focus, and prompting a representation of normativity of queerness in the everyday setting of ordinary family life, drama and entertainment.

There are, indeed, some Australian queer screen texts that represent queerness as ordinary, unremarkable and unchallenging in ways which make queerness part of the everyday picture of Australian life, and such texts are perhaps the most radical in their potential for social change. One notable example is Grant Scicluna's 2015 film, *Downriver*. This mystery drama tells the story of a young man, James, recently released from juvenile detention having been falsely accused years earlier of deliberately drowning a toddler near a caravan park alongside the Yarra river in Victoria. James has returned to the small town to solve the mystery, encountering both people he knew there as a child and new families holidaying at the park. There are multiple, cisgender same-sex relationships in the town, including James' emerging relationship with Damian, a young visitor. And, with the exception of James' mother and her new lover, no different-sex relationships or attractions depicted. What is notable is that although there is some violence, the town in general does not express homophobia, the relationships and sexual encounters are depicted as unremarkable and broadly normative. We see this is an excellent example that shifts queerness into the norm by hiding its normativity within the action of a mystery or thriller – characters are queer just because they happen to be queer, and no aspect of the story presents queerness as obstacle, spectacle or gestural. And it may well be that such representations are precisely what is needed to shift attitudes among a broader public to perceiving queerness as unremarkable, as *acceptable.* Indeed, it could be said that such a utopic depiction is the fruition of the early, post-tolerance Gay Liberation framework that sought an end to homosexuality's distinctiveness, transcending the normativity of straight/other in favour of new ways of perceiving human relationships (Altman 1971).

There has been little scholarship on queer screen entertainment about the possibility of non-spectatorial queer representation. It has, however, been noted in literary studies. Bittner (2016), for example, has studied the representation of what he refers to as 'just happens to be gay' representations in young adult literature that avoid coming out storytelling, albeit arguing against the utility of such normativization in favour of the suggestion that queerness is such a significant and sometimes difficult part of identity that such distinctiveness should be foregrounded through narratives of coming out, characterizations based in self-evident 'otherness' and the difficulties gaining recognition. We would disagree with such an approach in the context of film and television representation, and so too did many of the participants in the *AusQueerScreen* study when asked about social change.

A considerable number of interviewees emphasized the importance of queer and trans characters whose on-screen presence is not about struggles of queerness and trans identity. For example, although participant Jeremy enjoyed Ana Kokkinos' 1998 film *Head On*, he contrasted its focus on the struggle Ari experienced across his Greek heritage and queer identity with more recent American television series in which queerness was barely apparent, and how that would serve his desires for Australian television:

> sexuality . . . wasn't mentioned until maybe the second, third episode. And when it was, it was neither skirting around it, so it wasn't trying to just make vague references to it, but it also wasn't being like, Oh my God, you're gay. It was kind of just a part of that person . . . it wasn't the only part of why they were. So I think that my perception of a . . . typical positive perception and depiction of an LGBTQ person on Australian television is [that they are] just like any other character, but they're also queer in whatever way they might be. And it's not that it is nothing about them, but it's also not that this is everything about them. It is a normal amount of some things about them.

Rebecca, likewise, felt that stronger acceptance would emerge from a stronger set of stories that are not 'about someone's transition, or about someone struggling to be accepted by their family because of their sexuality, or, you know, being oppressed for this sexuality or whatever'. What Jeremy and Rebecca point to could perhaps be described as a radical separation of *queer story* from *queer character*, emphasizing increased representation of the latter as not only entertaining but serving social change and acceptance among wider audiences.

One participant, Col, suggested that the current, pallid forms of positive representation focused on vulnerable queers and their narratives have produced but also limited social change:

> we've met a standard of queer acceptance in media. Instead, they wanted to see more examples that just normalize it . . . or just like I being a thing is similar to, I think, other groups, like people with disabilities, just to have them as characters, even on the sidelines of shows. Like, to have, I don't know, a trans woman making the coffee for the person who's like buying coffee who's the main character . . . being the boss at the office . . . . If I was to ever start seeing that on my TV, I feel like we were actually moving to a space of inclusion in film industry and television industry.

The normativization of queer and trans characters as part of the everyday backdrop of Australian represented on screen would, then, simultaneously produce acceptance and serve as a proof that social change was working.

Notably, the call for more queer and trans on-screen characters whose narratives are not related to their gender or sexuality but, as Joanne defined it, 'just are', was something described most regularly by the youngest participants in the *AusQueerScreen* study, usually those born in the mid- to late-1990s. This is significant, partly because they were in a position to draw on international examples from Netflix and Amazon series which they found more advanced than Australian queer and trans representation, and partly because as a generation they grew up with the stronger and more regular kinds of representations we have described across his book emerging from the mid-1990s. They not only were more used to international texts in which queer characters whose role in series and film narratives were, as Beth put it, to do 'normal everyday stuff' and not be, as Sienna agreed, having 'their whole problem to be "Oh, woe is me, I've just discovered I'm gay and I have to hide it from everybody" and then internal conflict'. Rather, they were also drawing on discourses that seek further diversification of screen representation and a viewpoint that the next phase of social change is to sustain everyday normativization of queer and trans people. What is called for, then, is a strong re-balancing with 2020s Australian texts in which stories of vulnerability, struggle, difficulty, spectacle or other clichés are not connected queer and trans characters who, instead, are simply unremarkably queer or trans.

Conclusion

As we have noted, no media event, media inclusivity or shift in screen representation 'causes' social change towards acceptance of gender- and sexuality-diverse people on their own. Rather, as with every movement for change, multiple social sectors are at play, whether that is the key political actors lobbying for protections, legitimacy from governments or legislative protections, the many thousands who agitate through resistance and social activism over long periods of time, or the individuals who unwittingly spread attitude change among their peers (Clarke 2000). However, screen entertainment has indeed played a palpable role in changing social attitudes towards LGBTQ+ people in Australia and elsewhere. As many of the research participants noted, this is across increased visibility, strong representation of 'positive' queer characters, the frameworks in which these are watched in ways that generate engagement and a sense of affiliation, the significance of Australian settings in making queer people 'more like us', and in the sense of belonging and allyship that is promoted in the depiction of friendship groups on film and television that unproblematically include queer and trans characters. Most of all, we argue, the representation of gender- and sexuality-diverse people in film and television without reference to gender and sexuality as 'issue' was argued by younger, everyday audiences as most likely to have the greatest impact on normativization of queer people by depicting queerness as part of everyday, Australian life rather than as spectacle.

13

Queer Australian Screen Futures and Affordances

There is no doubt that Australia has an incredibly rich history of on-screen representation of gender and sexuality diversity, and right now its future looks bright, with new series and films each depicting queer characters, themes or stories. In this book, we have worked through some of those histories, a range of issues in the creative production of texts, some of the ways in which we can read and interpret screen texts including how critics help condition meanings, and the views and experiences of queer audiences. There are, sometimes, grounds for worrying whether or not the ever-increasing depiction of screen queer stories is because they have a ready-made market and if this is more the effect of a neoliberal, profit-driven screen media system today than it is the result of activism and creative endeavour among queer communities. Nevertheless, as we know from our audience analyses, representation is important and meaningful; and from our discussion of creative producers, critics, festivals and local communities, queer on-screen depiction is a key part of the everyday lived experience of a wide array of people.

The task of inclusivity, as we have shown, is by no means complete. While lesbians, gay men, bisexuals and, most recently, non-binary characters are fairly well represented on Australian screens, trans people are much more of a rarity, despite a few high-profile examples of the kind we discussed in Chapter 8. This is concerning, particularly at a time in which a global alliance of institutions and public figures claiming to be opposed to 'gender ideology' seeks more marginalization, exclusion and denial of the reality of trans lives in everyday culture (Cover and Newman 2025).

Working across the broad set of histories, contexts, production, textuality and audience spectatorship in this book is to draw attention not merely to the presence of queer screen culture in Australia, but to understand how it is useful to people and communities. Pointing to utility is not to take a wholly utilitatarian perspective, such as suggesting queer screen culture only has value if it is good for mental wellbeing or helps generate greater tolerance and acceptance in society. Rather, it is to imagine queer screen culture as very much beyond the text itself, integrated into a broad cycle of imagination, creativity, dissemination, spectatorship and meaning-making that has *affordances* for everyday life. Affordances, as a concept underlying our approach to Australian queer screen culture in this book, provides a powerful framework for extending the study of screen media from texts to the broad and diverse uses made of those texts by people at all stages of their production and engagement. It is to be attentive to media culture's continued development and change within a matrix of user engagement and the participation of all parties, pointing most of all to the participatory nature of creative screen cultures. That Australian queer screen culture has generated such participation across production, audiencehood, festivals and events, critique and scholarship is to see it as a model for how to approach screen media's futures in the 2020s – as that which remains at the core of interdependency, cohabitation and belonging for everyone.

References

Adorno, T. (2003), *The Jargon of Authenticity*, trans. K. Tarnowski and F. Will, London and New York: Routledge.

Aguayo, A. J. (2019), *Documentary Resistance: Social Change and Participatory Media*, New York: Oxford University Press.

Ahmed, S. (2004), *The Cultural Politics of Emotion*, Edinburgh: Edinburgh University Press.

Albury, K., C. Dietzel, T. Pym, S. Vivienne, and T. Cook (2024), 'Not Your Unicorn: Trans Dating App Users' Negotiation of Personal Safety and Sexual Health', in C. E. Newman, A. K. J. Smith, E. Duck-Chong, S. Vivienne, C. Davies, K. H. Robinson, and P. Aggleton (eds), *Social Perspectives on Trans Health*, 72–86, London: Routledge.

Allen, J. (2013), Interview by Scott McKinnon for the Pride History Group, 26 January.

Altman, D. (1971), *Homosexual Oppression and Liberation*, New York: New York University Press.

Altman, D. (1978), 'Gay Film Festivals: The Importance of Images', *Campaign*, 32: 19–20.

Altman, D. (2013), *The End of the Homosexual?* Brisbane: University of Queensland Press.

Altman, D. and J. Symons (2016), *Queer Wars*, Cambridge: Polity.

Anderson, D. (1972), 'Coming Out', *The Bulletin*, 11 (November): 39.

Ang, I. (1991), *Desperately Seeking the Audience*, London: Routledge.

Ashcraft, C. (2003), 'Adolescent Ambiguities in *American Pie*: Popular Culture as a Resource for Sex Education', *Youth & Society*, 35 (1): 37–70.

Atay, A. (2019), 'Defining Transnational Queer Media and Popular Culture', *Queer Studies in Media and Popular Culture*, 4 (3): 233–9.

Baltruschat, D. (2010), *Global Media Ecologies: Networked Production in Film and Television*, New York: Routledge.

Barber, T. (2010), 'Stephanie is Wired: Who Shall Turn Him On?', in C. Pullen and M. Cooper (eds), *LGBT Identity and Online New Media*, 245–57, London and New York: Routledge.

Barker, C. (1999), *Television, Globalization and Cultural Identities*, Buckingham: Open University Press.

Beirne, R. (2009), 'Screening the Dykes of Oz: Lesbian Representation on Australian Television', *Journal of Lesbian Studies*, 13 (1): 25–34.

Benson, C. (2020), 'Out in the Regions: Queer Film Festivals, Community-Building and the Cultivation of Creative Talent in Regional Victoria', in A. Campbell, M. Duffy, and B. Edmondson (eds), *Located Research: Regional Places, Transitions and Challenges*, 351–68, Singapore: Palgrave Macmillan.

Bereson, R. (2005), 'Advance Australia: Air or Foul? Observing Australian Arts Policies', *Journal of Arts Management, Law and Society*, 35 (1): 49–59.

Berger, J. (2013), *Contagious: Why Things Catch On*, New York: Simon & Schuster.

Bittner, R. (2016), '(Im)Possibility and (In)Visibility: Arguing Against "Just Happens to Be" in Young Adult Literature', *Queer Studies in Media & Popular Culture*, 1 (2): 199–214.

Blood, R. W. and J. Pirkis (2001), 'Suicide and the Media, Part III: Theoretical Issues', *Crisis*, 22 (4): 163–9.

Bond, B. J. and B. Miller (2017), 'From Screen to Self: The Relationship Between Television Exposure and Self-Complexity Among Lesbian, Gay, and Bisexual Youth', *International Journal of Communication*, 11 (1): 94–112.

Boucher, L. and R. Reynolds (2018), 'Decriminalisation, Apology and Expungement: Sexual Citizenship and the Problem of Public Sex in Victoria', *Australian Historical Studies*, 49 (4): 457–74.

Bridges, T. (2014), 'A Very "Gay" Straight?: Hybrid Masculinities, Sexual Aesthetics, and the Changing Relationship between Masculinity and Homophobia', *Gender & Society*, 28 (1): 58–82.

Brophy, P. (2008), *The Adventures of Priscilla, Queen of the Desert*, Sydney, NSW: Currency Press.

Brown, W. (2006), *Regulating Aversion: Tolerance in the Age of Identity and Empire*, Princeton, NJ: Princeton University Press.

Bryan, S. (2012), 'Silent Movie Finds New Voice', *ABC*, 30 January. Available online: https://www.abc.net.au/news/2012-01-30/silent-movie-finds-new-voice/3799934?section=entertainment (accessed 3 July 2024).

Bull, M., S. Pinto, and P. Wilson (1991), 'Homosexual Law Reform in Australia', *Australian Institute of Criminology Trends & Issues in Crime and Criminal Justice*, 29. Available online: https://eprints.qut.edu.au/128198/1/7c5c1e7daf802d9c49c6f2e259991d3d0ca8.pdf (accessed 15 September 2024).

Butler, J. (1993), *Bodies That Matter: On the Discursive Limits of 'Sex'*, London and New York: Routledge.

Butler, J. (2020), *The Force of NonViolence: An Ethico-Political Bind*, London: Verso.

Butler, J. (2022), *What World Is This? A Pandemic Phenomenology*, New York: Columbia University Press.

Butler, J. (2024), *Who's Afraid of Gender?* London: Allen Lane.

Calder, B. (2016a), 'Feminist Collectives or Private Owners: Both Used Media to Advance Lesbian Goals', *Feminist Media Studies*, 16 (3): 413–28.

Calder, B. (2016b), *Pink Ink: The Golden Era for Gay and Lesbian Magazines*, Newcastle upon Tyne: Cambridge Scholars Publishing.

Camp Ink (1970), 'Saving One's Neck…', *CAMP Ink*, 1 (2): 2.

Campbell, R. (1966), 'From Frank to Fearless', *The Bulletin*, 21 (May): 29.

Capsuto, S. (2000), *Alternate Channels: The Uncensored Story of Gay and Lesbian Images on Radio and Television, 1930s to the Present*, New York: Ballantine Books.

Caputo, R. (2009), '*Wake in Fright*: An Interview with Ted Kotcheff', *Senses of Cinema* 51. Available online: https://www.sensesofcinema.com/2009/feature-articles/ted -kotcheff-interview/ (accessed 7 July 2024).

Carswell, P. (1980), 'Clones: The New Gay Image?', *Gay Community News*, 2 (9): 24–6.

Cee, D. (1978), 'Gay Film Retrospect', *Campaign*, 34: 20.

Cettl, R. (2014), *Offensive to a Reasonable Adult: Film Censorship and Classification in Australia*, Adelaide, SA: Wider Screenings TM.

Chaples, E. (1985), 'Wran in Government: 1976–1981', in E. Chaples, H. Nelson, and Ken Turner (eds), *The Wran Model: Electoral Politics in New South Wales 1981 and 1984*, 38–49, Melbourne: Oxford University Press.

Charles, B. (2022), Interviewed by Scott McKinnon, State Library NSW. Available online: https://collection.sl.nsw.gov.au/record/nvgp7Q01 (accessed 13 September 2024).

Chasin, A. (2000), *Selling Out: The Gay and Lesbian Movement Goes to Market*, New York: Palgrave.

Ciamparella, A. (2016), 'From Good to Bad Stories: Examining the Narrative of Pregnancy in *The L Word* as a Means to Teach and Destabilize Queerness', in K.-P. R. Hart (ed.), *Queer TV in the 21st Century: Essays on Broadcasting from Taboo to Acceptance*, 77–92, Jefferson, NC: McFarland & Company.

Ciasullo, A. M. (2001), 'Making Her (in)Visible: Cultural Representations of Lesbianism and the Lesbian Body in the 1990s', *Feminist Studies*, 27 (3): 577–608.

Clark, D. (1993), 'Commodity Lesbianism', in H. Abelove, M. A. Barale, and D. M. Halperin (eds), *The Lesbian and Gay Studies Reader*, 186–201, London and New York: Routledge.

Clarke, K. (2013), 'Pedagogical Moments: Affective Sexual Literacies in Film', *Sex Education*, 13 (3): 263–75.

Clarke, K., R. Cover, and P. Aggleton (2018), 'Sex, Sexuality and Ambivalence: LGBTQ Youth Negotiating Sexual Feelings, Desires and Attractions', *Journal of LGBT Youth*, 15 (3): 227–42.

Clarke, M. (2000), 'Rosa Parks' Performativity, Habitus, and Ability to Play the Game', *Philosophy Today*, 44 (supplement): 160–8.

Cooper, A. (2023), 'Barry Humphries, Known for His Drag Persona Dame Edna Everage, Dead at 89', *The Advocate*, 22 April. Available online: https://www.advocate .com/obituaries/drag-dame-edna-everage-dead (accessed 19 September 2024).

Cooper, E. (2003), 'Decoding *Will and Grace:* Mass Audience Reception of a Popular Network Situation Comedy', *Sociological Perspectives,* 46 (4): 513–33.

Cordoba, S. (2023), *Non-Binary Gender Identities: The Language of Becoming,* London and New York: Routledge.

Couldry, N. and T. Dreher (2007), 'Globalization and the Public Sphere: Exploring the Space of Community Media in Sydney', *Global Media and Communication,* 3 (1): 79–100.

Cover, R. (1999), 'Queer with Class: Absence of the Third World Sweatshop in Lesbian/Gay Discourse and a Rearticulation of Materialist Queer Theory', *Ariel: A Review of International English Literature,* 30 (2): 29–48.

Cover, R. (2000), 'First Contact: Queer Theory, Sexual Identity, and "Mainstream" Film', *International Journal of Gender and Sexuality,* 5 (1): 71–89.

Cover, R. (2002), 'Re-Sourcing Queer Subjectivities: Sexual Identity and Lesbian/Gay Print Media', *Media International Australia,* 103 (1): 109–23.

Cover, R. (2005), 'Changing Channels: Scheduling, Temporality, New Technologies (and the Future of "Television" In Media Studies)', *Australian Journal of Communication,* 32 (2): 9–24.

Cover, R. (2012a), *Queer Youth Suicide, Culture & Identity: Unliveable Lives?* London and New York: Routledge.

Cover, R. (2012b), 'Mediating Suicide: Print Journalism and the Categorisation of Queer Youth Suicide Discourses', *Archives of Sexual Behavior,* 41 (5): 1173–83.

Cover, R. (2019), *Emergent Identities: New Sexualities, Gender and Relationships in a Digital Era,* London and New York: Routledge.

Cover, R. (2021), 'Gender and Sexual Diversity and Suicide on Australian Screens: Popular Culture, Representation and Health Pedagogies', *The Journal of Popular Culture,* 54 (2): 365–87.

Cover, R. (2023a), 'Queer Screen Pedagogies: Australian Queer Audiences and the Educational Value of LGBTQ Film and Television Stories', in N. Rodriguez, L. Allen, R. Mizzi, and R. Cover (eds), *Queer Studies and Education: An International Reader,* 234–53, Oxford: Oxford University Press.

Cover, R. (2023b), 'Straight and Cisgender Actors Playing Queer and Trans Characters: The Views of Australian Screen Stakeholders', *Media, Culture & Society,* 45 (1): 57–73.

Cover, R. (2024a), 'LGBTQ+ Collecting Institutions: The Culture of Strategic Management, Motivation and Professionalisation', *Continuum: Journal of Media & Cultural Studies,* 38 (1): 111–23.

Cover, R. (2024b), 'The Violence of Contesting Non-Binary, Trans and Diverse Gender Identities: Emergent Cultural Formations, Adversities, and Ethics', *Humanities Research Journal,* 20 (1): 243–59.

Cover, R. and D. Dau (2021), 'Placing the Queer Audience: Literature on Gender and Sexual Diversity in Film and Television and Reception', *MAI Feminism & Visual*

Culture 7. Available online: https://maifeminism.com/literature-on-gender-and -sexual-diversity-in-film-and-television-reception/ (accessed 12 February 2024).

Cover, R. and C. Milne (2023), 'The "Bury your Gays" Trope in Contemporary Television: Generational Shifts in Production Responses to Audience Dissent', *Journal of Popular Culture*, 56 (5–6): 810–23.

Cover, R. and C. E. Newman (2025), 'Introduction to the Elgar Encyclopedia of Queer Studies', in R. Cover and C. E. Newman (eds), *Elgar Encyclopedia of Queer Studies*, 1–8, Cheltenham: Edward Elgar Publishing.

Cover, R. and R. Prosser (2024), *Queer Memory and Storytelling: Gender and Sexually-Diverse Identities and Trans-Media Narrative*, London and New York: Routledge.

Cover, R., P. Aggleton, M. L. Rasmussen, and D. Marshall (2020), 'The Myth of LGBTQ Mobilities: Framing the Lives of Gender and Sexually-Diverse Australians between Regional and Urban Contexts', *Culture, Health & Sexuality*, 22 (3): 321–35.

Cover, R., R. Prosser, and D. Dau (2022), 'The Corporeality of Sound: Drag Performance, Lip-Synching and the Popular Critique of Gendered Theatrics in Australian Film and Television', *Media International Australia*, 182 (1): 81–94.

Cover, R., M. L. Rasmussen, P. Aggleton, and D. Marshall (2017), 'Progress in Question: Temporalities of Politics, Support and Belonging in Sexual- and Gender-Diverse Pedagogies', *Continuum: Journal of Media and Cultural Studies*, 31 (6): 767–79.

Creed, B. (2014), 'Political Activism and Radical Change: *Homosexuality: A Film for Discussion* (1975)', in C. D'Cruz and M. Pendleton (eds), *After Homosexual*, 75–83, Crawley, WA: University of Western Australia Publishing.

Cronin, T. J., C. A. Pepping, W. K. Halford, and A. Lyons (2021), 'Mental Health Help-Seeking and Barriers to Service Access Among Lesbian, Gay, and Bisexual Australians', *Australian Psychologist*, 56 (1): 46–60.

'Cruising' (1980), *Campaign*, June: 1.

Cubitt, S. (1991), *Timeshift: On Video Culture*, London & New York: Routledge.

Cumming-Potvin, W. (2024), 'LGBTQA+ Allies and Activism: Past, Present and Future Perspectives', *Continuum: Journal of Media & Cultural Studies*, 38 (3): 338–52.

Curran, J. (2002), *Media and Power*, London: Routledge.

D'Emilio, J. (1992), *Making Trouble: Essays on Gay History, Politics and the University*, New York & London: Routledge.

Davis, K. (1980), '*Witches and Faggots, Dykes and Poofters*: A Review', *Gay Community News*, 2 (5): 34.

Davis, M. (1997), *Gangland: Cultural Elites and the New Generationalism*, St. Leonards, NSW: Allen & Unwin.

de Boise, S. (2015), 'I'm Not Homophobic, "I've Got Gay Friends": Evaluating the Validity of Inclusive Masculinity', *Men and Masculinities*, 18 (3): 318–39.

de Lauretis, T. (1989), 'Queer Theory: Lesbian and Gay Sexualities: An Introduction', *Differences*, 3 (2): iii–xvii.

De Valck, M. (2007), *Film Festivals: From European Geopolitics to Global Cinephilia*, Amsterdam: Amsterdam University Press.

De Valck, M. (2016), 'Introduction: What Is a Film Festival? How to Study Festivals and Why You Should', in M. de Valck, B Kredell, and S. Loist (eds), *Film Festivals*, 1–2, London: Routledge.

Debord, G. (1967), *Society of the Spectacle*, Detroit, MI: Black & Red.

Delamoir, J. (2012), '*Jewelled Nights*: "Can Good Movies Be Made in Australia?"' *Senses of Cinema* 65. Available online: https://www.sensesofcinema.com/2012/tasmania -and-the-cinema/jewelled-nights-can-good-movies-be-made-in-australia-1 (accessed 28 June 2024).

Dennison, G. (1972), 'The R Certificate and Camp Themes', *CAMP Ink*, 2 (7): 4–6.

Dickson, L.-A. (2015), '"Ah! Other Bodies!": Embodied Spaces, Pleasures and Practices at Glasgow Film Festival', *Participations: Journal of Audience & Reception Studies*, 12 (1): 703–24.

DiPiero, T. and P. Gill (eds) (1997), *Illicit Sex: Identity Politics in Early Modern Culture*, Athens, GA: University of Georgia Press.

Dooley, M. and B. McKay (2004), 'Imagining Queer', *Feast: Australian Lesbian and Gay Cultural Festival Guide*, November 2024. Available online: https://feast.org.au/wp -content/uploads/2023/09/2004_Full-Program.pdf (accessed 2 August 2024).

Doty, A. (1993), *Making Things Perfectly Queer: Interpreting Mass Culture*, Minneapolis, MN: University of Minnesota Press.

Dow, S. (2001), 'In Case You've Been on Mars, the Woman in the Bunny Ears Is About to Get Lots of Green Stuff', *The Sunday Age*, 15 July: 4.

Dowsett, G. (2003), 'Johnnie Comes Marching . . . Where? Australian Gay Men, Masculinity, HIV/AIDS and Sex', *Culture, Health & Sexuality*, 5 (3): 237–47.

Driver, S. (2008), 'Introducing Queer Youth Cultures', in S. Driver (ed.), *Queer Youth Cultures*, 1–18, Albany, NY: SUNY Press.

Duggan, L. (2003), *The Twilight of Equality? Neoliberalism, Cultural Politics and the Attack on Democracy*, Boston, MA: Beacon Press.

Dyer, R. (1993), *The Matter of Images: Essays on Representations*, London & New York: Routledge.

Eagleton, T. (1968), 'The Idea of a Common Culture', in T. Eagleton and B. Wicker (eds), *From Culture to Revolution*, 35–57, London: Sheed and Ward.

Eagleton, T. (2015), *Hope Without Optimism*, New Haven, CN: Yale University Press.

Edward, M. and S. Farrier (eds) (2020), *Contemporary Drag Practices and Performers. Vol 1: Drag in a Changing Scene*, London: Bloomsbury.

Edwards, M. (2010), 'Transconversations: New Media, Community, and Identity', in C. Pullen and M. Cooper (eds), *LGBT Identity and Online New Media*, 159–72, London and New York: Routledge.

Edwards, T. (2005), 'Queering the Pitch? Gay Masculinities', in M. S. Kimmel, J. R. Hearn, and R. W. Connell (eds), *Handbook of Studies on Men and Masculinities*, 51–68, London: Sage Publications.

Elsaesser, T. (2005), *European Cinema: Face to Face with Hollywood*, Amsterdam: Amsterdam University Press.

Epstein, S. (1996), 'A Queer Encounter: Sociology and the Study of Sexuality', in S. Seidman (ed.), *Queer Theory/Sociology*, 145–67, Cambridge, MA: Blackwell.

Espelage, D. L. and S. M. Swearer (2008), 'Addressing Research Gaps in the Intersection Between Homophobia and Bullying', *School Psychology Review*, 37 (2): 155–9.

Evers, C. (2008), 'The Cronulla Race Riots; Safety Maps on an Australian Beach', *South Atlantic Quarterly*, 107 (2): 411–29.

Falassi, A. (1987), 'Festival: Definition and Morphology', in A. Falassi (ed.), *Time Out of Time: Essays on the Festival*, 1–10, Albuquerque, NM: University of New Mexico Press.

Farmer, B. (2000), *Spectacular Passions: Cinema, Fantasy, Gay Male Spectatorships*, Durham, NC: Duke University Press.

Film Censorship Board (1961), *Report for Period 1st January 1960 to 30th June 1961*, Canberra, ACT: Commonwealth of Australia Department of Customs and Excise.

Fiske, J. (1989a), *Understanding Popular Culture*, London: Unwin Hyman.

Fiske, J. (1989b), *Reading the Popular*, Boston: Unwin Hyman.

Fiske, J. (1996), *Media Matters: Everyday Culture and Political Change*, Minneapolis: University of Minnesota Press.

Ford, A. (2014), 'Curating a Regional, Queer Film Festival', *Fusion Journal*, 4. Available online: https://fusion-journal.com/issue/004-fusion-the-town-and-the-city/curating -a-regional-queer-film-festival/ (accessed 12 September 2024).

Ford, A. (2017), 'Regional & Queer: Refusing to Be Invisible, Creating Queer Space in a Non-Queer World', *Cybergeo: European Journal of Geography*. Available online: https://journals.openedition.org/cybergeo/27962 (accessed 12 September 2024).

Foss, P. (1972), 'A Haven for Homosexuals', *Sydney Gay Liberation Newsletter*, 1 (4): 8–11.

Foucault, M. (1977), *The Politics of Truth*, S. Lotringer (ed.), L. Hochroth and C. Porter (trans.), New York: Semiotext(e).

Foucault, M. (1990), *The History of Sexuality: An Introduction*, R. Hurley (trans.), London: Penguin.

Franklyn, L. (1978), 'Word Is Out – Now', *Campaign*, 33: 3.

Free, E. (2018), 'The Making of *the Sum of Us*', *Film Ink*, 23 August. Available online: https://www.filmink.com.au/not-typical-father-son-story-making-sum-us/ (accessed 12 August 2024).

Freeman, M. and E. Ross (2022), 'The Larrikin Girl: Challenging Archetypes in Australian Cinema', *Senses of Cinema*, 103 (October). Available online: https://www

.sensesofcinema.com/2022/feature-articles/the-larrikin-girl-challenging-archetypes
-in-australian-cinema/ (accessed 3 July 2024).

Frow, J. (1995), *Cultural Studies and Cultural Value*, Oxford: Oxford University Press.

Fuss, D. (1995), 'Homospectatorial Fashion Photography', in K. A. Appiah and H. L.
Gates Jr (eds), *Identities*, 90–114, Chicago: University of Chicago Press.

Galloway, S. and S. Dunlop (2007), 'A Critique of Definitions of the Cultural and
Creative Industries in Public Policy', *International Journal of Cultural Policy*, 13 (1):
17–31.

Gay Liberation Front (1970), *Come Out! A Liberation Forum for the Gay Community*, 1
(4). Available online: https://outhistory.org/files/original/f6d46c5d90761e3a66edcd4
fe32a6785.pdf (accessed 12 April 2024).

Gerbner, G. and L. Gross (1976), 'Living with Television: The Violence Profile', *Journal
of Communication*, 26 (2): 172–99.

Gibson, C., B. Gallan, and A. Warran (2012), 'Engaging Creative Communities in
an Industrial City Setting', *International Journal of Community Research and
Engagement*, 5 (1): 1–15.

Gilbert, J. (2014), *Sexuality in School: The Limits of Education*, Minneapolis, MN:
University of Minnesota Press.

Giles, N. (2017), *Number 96: Australian TV's Most Notorious Address*, Melbourne:
Melbourne Books.

Gill, R. (2012), 'Media, Empowerment and the "Sexualization of Culture" Debates', *Sex
Roles: A Journal of Research*, 66 (11–12): 736–45.

Gilson, E. (2011), 'Vulnerability, Ignorance, and Oppression', *Hypatia*, 26 (2): 308–32.

Giroux, H. A. (2003), 'Public Pedagogy and the Politics of Resistance: Notes on a
Critical Theory of Educational Struggle', *Educational Philosophy and Theory*, 35 (1):
5–16.

Giroux, H. A. (2004), 'Cultural Studies, Public Pedagogy, and the Responsibility of
Intellectuals', *Communication and Critical/Cultural Studies*, 1 (1): 59–79.

Giroux, H. A. (2010), 'Bare Pedagogy and the Scourge of Neoliberalism: Rethinking
Higher Education as a Democratic Public Sphere', *The Educational Forum*, 74 (3):
184–96.

GLAAD (2017), *Where We Are On TV '16-'17*. Available online: http://glaad.org/files/
WWAT/WWAT_GLAAD_2016-2017.pdf (accessed 12 January 2019).

Gluyas, S. D. (2013), 'Missing the Lesbian and the Missing Lesbian: A Study of the
Forgotten Lesbian in 1970s Australian Cinema', in G. Willett and Y. Smaal (eds),
*Intimacy, Violence and Activism: Gay and Lesbian Perspectives on Australian History
and Society*, 90–104, Melbourne: Monash University Publishing.

Glynn, M. (1995), Interviewed by Larry Galbraith, *Pride History Group*, 3 December
1995.

Goldberg, G. (2018), *Antisocial Media: Anxious Labor in the Digital Economy*, New
York: New York University Press.

Gomillion, S. C. and T. A. Giuliano (2011), 'The Influence of Media Role Models on Gay, Lesbian, and Bisexual Identity', *Journal of Homosexuality,* 58 (3): 330–54.

Gould, M. S. and D. Shaffer (1986), 'The Impact of Suicide in Television Movies', *The New England Journal of Medicine,* 315 (11): 690–4.

Grant, B. K. (1991), 'Science Fiction Double Feature: Ideology in the Cult Film', in J. P. Telotte (ed.), *The Cult Film Experience: Beyond All Reason,* 122–37, Austin, TX: University of Texas Press.

Griffin, F. H. (2016), *Feeling Normal: Sexuality and Media Criticism in the Digital Age,* Bloomington, IN: Indiana University Press.

Griffiths, R. (ed.) (2006), *British Queer Cinema,* London: Routledge.

Gross, L. (1991), 'Out of the Mainstream: Sexual Minorities and the Mass Media', in M. A. Wolf and A. P. Kielwasser (eds), *Gay People, Sex, and the Media,* 19–46, New York & London: Harrington Park Press.

Gross, L. (2001), *Up from Invisibility: Lesbians, Gay Men, and the Media in America,* New York: Columbia University Press.

Groves, D. (2012), *Out of the Ordinary: Popular Art, Architecture and Design,* Newcastle upon Tyne: Cambridge Scholars Publishing.

Guiffre, L. and S. Attfield (2022), 'Finding the "Perfect Blend" in an Undervalued Genre: Considering the Importance of "Ordinariness" in Australian Soap Opera *Neighbours',* *Journal of Popular Television,* 10 (2): 199–211.

Gunew, S. (2000), 'Introduction: Multicultural Translations of Food, Bodies, Language', *Journal of Intercultural Studies,* 21 (3): 227–37.

Halberstam, J. (2005), *In a Queer Time and Place: Transgender Bodies, Subcultural Lives,* New York: NYU Press.

Hall, S. (1980a), 'Encoding/Decoding', in Centre for Contemporary Cultural Studies (ed.), *Culture, Media, Language: Working Papers,* 128–38, London: Routledge.

Hall, S. (1980b), 'Cultural Studies: Two Paradigms', *Media, Culture and Society,* 2 (1): 57–72.

Hall, S. (1988), 'The Toad in the Garden: Thatcherism among the Theorists', in C. Nelson and L. Grossberg (eds), *Marxism and the Interpretation of Culture,* 35–73, Urbana and Chicago: University of Illinois Press.

Harbord, J. (2009), 'Film Festivals – Time Event', in R. Rhyne and D. Iordanova (eds), *Film Festival Yearbook: The Festival Circuit,* 40–6, St Andrews: College Gate Press.

Harris, G. (1995), 'Perving on Perversity: A Nice Night in Front of the Tele', *Media International Australia,* 78 (1): 20–32.

Hart, K.-P. R. (2016), 'Introduction: Media Representation and Sensitive Subjects', in K.-P. R. Hart (ed.), *Queer TV in the 21st Century: Essays on Broadcasting from Taboo to Acceptance,* 1–7, Jefferson, NC: McFarland & Company.

Harvey, R. (2012), 'Young People, Sexual Orientation, and Resilience', in M. Unger (ed.), *The Social Ecology of Resilience: A Handbook of Theory and Practice,* 325–35, New York: Springer.

Hawkins, G. (1993), *From Nimbin to Mardi Gras: Constructing Community Arts*, St. Leonards, NSW: Allen & Unwin.

Hegna, K. and L. Wichstrøm (2007), 'Suicide Attempts among Norwegian Gay, Lesbian and Bisexual Youths: General and Specific Risk Factors', *Acta Sociologica*, 50 (1): 21–37.

Heller-Nicholas, A. (2017), 'Alvin Purple', *Metro Magazine*, 191: 108–16.

Hill, A. O., A. Lyons, J. Jones, I. McGowan, M. Carman, M. Parsons, J. Power, and A. Bourne (2021), *Writing Themselves In 4: The Health and Wellbeing of LGBTQA+ Young People in Australia*, Melbourne: Australian Research Centre in Sex, Health and Society, La Trobe University.

Hills, M. (2007), 'From the Box in the Corner to the Box Set on the Shelf: "TVIII" and the Cultural/Textual Valorisations of DVD', *New Review of Film and Television Studies*, 5 (1): 41–60.

Hillier, L., T. Jones, M. Monagle, N. Overton, L. Gahan, J. Blackman, and A. Mitchell (2010), *Writing Themselves In 3: The Third National Study on the Sexual Health and Wellbeing of Same Sex Attracted and Gender Questioning Young People*, Melbourne: Australian Research Centre in Sex, Health & Society. Available online: https://www.acon.org.au/wp-content/uploads/2015/04/Writing-Themselves-In-3-2010.pdf (accessed 12 August 2024).

Ho, C. (2012), 'Western Sydney Is Hot! Community Arts is Changing Perceptions of the West', *Gateways: International Journal of Community Research and Engagement*, 5 (1): 35–55.

Hoberman, J. and J. Rosenbaum (1991), *Midnight Movies*, Boston, MA: Da Capo Press.

Hooks, B. (1982), 'Colourful, Sympathetic Picture of Gay Life', *The Age*, 2 September: 7.

Horley, J. and J. Clarke (2016), *Experience, Meaning, and Identity in Sexuality: A Psychosocial Theory of Sexual Stability and Change*, London: Palgrave Macmillan UK.

Horton, D. and R. Wohl (1956), 'Mass Communication and Para-Social Interaction: Observation on Intimacy at a Distance', *Psychiatry*, 19 (3): 215–29.

Horvat, A. (2021), *Screening Queer Memory: LGBTQ Pasts in Contemporary Film and Television*, London: Bloomsbury.

Howes, K. (1993), *Broadcasting It: An Encyclopaedia of Homosexuality in Film, Radio and TV in the UK, 1923–1993*, London: Cassell.

Howes, K. (1998), 'Gays of Our Lives: 30 Years of Gay Australian TV', *OutRage*, 177: 38–49.

Howes, K. (2002), 'Australian Television', *GLBTQ Archive*. Available online: http://www.glbtqarchive.com/arts/aus_tv_A.pdf (accessed 19 June 2024).

Hughes, J. (2015), 'A Work in Progress: The Rise and Fall of Australian Filmmakers Co-operatives', *Senses of Cinema*, 77. Available online: https://www.sensesofcinema.com/2015/australian-film-history/australian-filmmakers-co-operatives/ (accessed 9 August 2024).

Hughes, J. (2015), 'A Work in Progress: The Rise and Fall of Australian Filmmakers Co-operatives, 1966–86', *Senses of Cinema, 77*. Available online: https://www .sensesofcinema.com/2015/australian-film-history/australian-filmmakers-co -operatives/ (accessed 12 September 2024).

Human Rights Campaign (2023), *Human Rights Campaign Working to Defeat 340 Anti-LGBTQ+ Bills at State Level Already, 150 of Which Target Transgender People – Highest Number on Record.* Available online: https://www.hrc.org/press-releases /human-rights-campaign-working-to-defeat-340-anti-lgbtq-bills-at-state-level -already-150-of-which-target-transgender-people-highest-number-on-record (accessed 9 June 2024).

Irigaray, L. (1985), *This Sex Which Is Not One*, trans. C. Porter with C. Burke, Ithaca, NY: Cornell University Press.

Jagose, A. (1996), *Queer Theory*, Carlton South: Melbourne University Press.

Johnson, D. (2007), 'Inviting Audiences In: The Spatial Reorganisation of Production and Consumption in "TVIII"', *New Review of Film and Television Studies*, 5 (1): 61–80.

Kalliotis, P. (2000), 'Bullying as a Special Case of Aggression: Procedures for Cross-Cultural Assessment', *School Psychology International*, 21 (1): 47–64.

Kay, R. (1981), 'Out! in Australia', *Klick!*, 36: 46.

Kellaway, M. (2014), 'OKCupid Unveils New Options for Gender, Sexuality', *The Advocate*, 18 November. Available online: http://www.advocate.com/business/ technology/2014/11/18/okcupid-unveils-new-options-gender-sexuality (accessed 12 June 2019).

Kelly, C. (2023), 'Councils Call Off Drag Storytime and LGBTQ+ Events in Victoria After Far-Right Threats', *The Guardian*, 13 May. Available online: https://www .theguardian.com/world/2023/may/13/councils-call-off-drag-storytime-and-lgbtq -events-in-victoria-after-far-right-threats#:~:text=At%20least%20nine%20queer %20events,from%20far%2Dright%20fringe%20groups (accessed 19 September 2024).

Keltie, E. (2017), *The Culture Industry and Participatory Audiences*, Cham: Palgrave Macmillan.

Kennerly, K. (1983), Interview with L. Watson and R. French, *Good Morning Australia*. Available online: https://youtu.be/J32DoVYL1tw?si=xs5H5_a2UCJcj31S (accessed 13 September 2024).

Kim, Y. S. and B. Leventhal (2008), 'Bullying and Suicide: A Review', *International Journal of Adolescent Medical Health*, 20 (2): 133–54.

Kral, M. (2019), *The Idea of Suicide*, London and New York: Routledge.

Lacan, J. (1968), *The Language of the Self: The Function of Language in Psychoanalysis*, trans. A. Wilden, Baltimore, MD: Johns Hopkins University Press.

Lahr J. (1992), *Dame Edna Everage and the Rise of Western Civilization: Backstage with Barry Humphries*, Hammersmith: Flamingo.

Leder, M. (2021), 'The Web Series: Empowering Diversity on the Australian Screen', *Continuum: Journal of Media & Cultural Studies*, 35 (4): 585–99.

Lee, J. (1972), 'Leafletting', *Sydney Gay Liberation Newsletter*, 1 (4): 2.

Lipton, M. (2008), 'Queer Readings of Popular Culture: Searching [to] Out the Subtext', in S. Driver (ed.), *Queer Youth Cultures*, 163–79, Albany, NY: SUNY Press.

Loist, S. (2013), 'The Queer Film Festival Phenomenon in a Global Historical Perspective (The 1970s–2000s)', in A. Fléchet, P. Gœtschel, P. Hidiroglou, S. Jacotot, C. Moine, and J. Verlaine (eds), *Une Histoire des Festivals: XXe–XXIe Siècle*, 109–21, Paris: Publications de la Sorbonne.

Lotz, A. D. (2022), *Netflix and Streaming Video: The Business of Subscriber-Funded Video on Demand*, Cambridge: Polity.

Lovett, K. (1980), 'Sydney and *Cruising*', *Gay Community News*, 2 (6): 7.

Lowe, B. (1984), 'Editorial', *Campaign*, January: 97.

Luby, B. (1993), 'So What Is Queer Cinema?', *Film News*, 1 September: 5–8.

Lumby, C. (1991), 'Stereotypes: Taking Control', *Lesbians on the Loose*, November: 12–13.

Lumby, C. (2008), *Alvin Purple*, Sydney, NSW: Currency Press.

Mackay, B. and K. Dooley (2004), *Imagining Queer: Historical Views from Australian Film and Television in the National Screen and Sound Archives*, Notes, Research and Academic Outreach Program of Screensound Australia, Canberra, ACT: The National Film and Sound Archive.

Macleod, A. (2018), *Irish Queer Cinema*, Edinburgh: Edinburgh University Press.

Marcuse, H. (1969), *Eros and Civilization: A Philosophical Inquiry into Freud*, London: Sphere.

Mardell, A. (2016), *The ABC's of LGBT+*, Coral Gables, FL: Mango Media.

Marshall, D., P. Aggleton, R. Cover, M. L. Rasmussen, and B. Hegarty (2019), 'Queer Generations: Theorizing a Concept', *International Journal of Cultural Studies*, 22 (4): 558–76.

Marshall, V. (1966), 'Anne Calls a Spade a Spade', *The Sun-Herald*, 20 February: 82.

Maslin, J. (1989), 'An Australian Tale of Sex and the Power it Confers', *The New York Times*, 17 November. Available online: https://www.nytimes.com/1989/11/17/movies /reviews-film-an-australian-tale-of-sex-and-the-power-it-confers.html (accessed 19 August 2024).

Matheson, J. (2019), '"About Gays by Gays": The Politics of Representation in Early Australian Gay Film Culture, 1971–1982', *Studies in Australasian Cinema*, 13 (1): 16–29.

McIntyre, J. (2011), 'Before Priscilla: Male-to-Female Transgender in Australian Cinema until the 1990s', *Refractory*, 18. Available online: https://research.usc.edu.au/ esploro/outputs/99448957002621#file-0 (accessed 17 August 2024).

McIntyre, J. (2015), 'Mass Communication, Minority Representation, and National Identity: Transgender in Mainstream Australian Television and Film', *Refereed*

Proceedings of the 2015 ANZCA Conference: Rethinking Communication, Space and Identity, 1–12, Australia and New Zealand Communication Association.

McIntyre, J. (2017), 'Transgender Idol: Queer Subjectivities and Australian Reality TV', *European Journal of Cultural Studies*, 20 (1): 87–103.

McIntyre, J., D. W. Riggs, and C. Bartholomaeus (2023), 'Jazz Jennings and Evie Macdonald: Trans Child Celebrities, Transnormativity, and Childhood "Innocence"', *Celebrity Studies*, 14 (2): 214–26.

McKee, A. (1999), 'Suck on that Mate: Australian Gay Porn Videos', in D. Verhoeven (ed.), *Twin Peaks: Australian and New Zealand Feature Films*, 119–28, Melbourne: Damned Publishing.

McKee, A. (2001), *Australian Television: A Genealogy of Great Moments*, Oxford: Oxford University Press.

McKee, A. (2016), *Fun! What Entertainment Tells Us About Living a Good Life*, London: Palgrave Macmillan.

McKinnon, S. (2012), 'Witches, Faggots, Dykes and Poofters', in J. E. Bennett and R. Beirne (eds), *Making Film and Television Histories: Australia and New Zealand*, 225–30. New York: I. B. Tauris.

McKinnon, S. (2013), 'The Activist Cinema-Goer: Gay Liberation at the Movies', *History Australia*, 10 (1): 125–43.

McKinnon, S. (2014), 'The Curious Case of Cruising: Debating Gay Male Identity and Visibility via the Movies', in L. Featherstone, R. Jennings, and R. Reynolds (eds), *Acts of Love and Lust: Sexuality in Australia from 1945–2010*, Newcastle upon Tyne: Cambridge Scholars Publishing.

McKinnon, S. (2016), *Gay Men at the Movies: Cinema, Memory and the History of a Gay Male Community*, Bristol: Intellect Books.

McKinnon, S. (2020), 'Restricted to Adults Only: Homosexuality and Film Censorship Reform in 1970s Australia', *Journal of Popular Film and Television*, 48 (3): 134–44.

McManus, B. (2019), 'Neighbours Set to Introduce First-Ever Transgender Character', *Sydney Morning Herald*, 25 August. Available online: https://www.smh.com.au/ culture/tv-and-radio/neighbours-set-to-introduce-first-ever-transgender-character -20190814-p52h4e.html (accessed 15 October 2024).

McNab, D. (2017), *Getting away with Murder*, North Sydney, NSW: Vintage Books.

McNeil, I. (1998), 'Tellin' Ya', *Metro Magazine*, 115: 69–72.

Mercado, A. (1998), 'From the Closet to the Shelf: Seven's Big Lesbian Coverup', *Sydney Star Observer*, 403: 9.

Mercado, A. (2004), *Super Aussie Soaps: Behind the Scenes of Australia's Best Loved TV Shows*, North Melbourne: Pluto Press.

Meyrowitz, J. (1997), 'The Separation of Social Space from Physical Place', in T. O'Sullivan and Y. Jewkes (eds), *The Media Studies Reader*, 41–52, London: Edward Arnold.

Millar, A. (2022), 'James Majoos on the Duality of Darren, Rewriting Queer Stereotypes & the Runaway Success of "Heartbreak High"', *GQ*, 1 December. Available online: https://www.gq.com.au/culture/entertainment/james-majoos-heartbreak-high -interview/image-gallery/c5080ea7c60f61890040b46605e8c993 (accessed 19 September 2024).

Miller, D. A. (2007), 'Cruising', *Film Quarterly*, 61 (2): 70–3.

Miller, Q. (2019), *Camp TV: Trans Gender Queer Sitcom History*, Durham, NC: Duke University Press.

Molloy, P. M. (2014), 'Facebook Expands Gender Options for Trans and Gender-Nonconforming Users', *The Advocate*, 13 February. Available online: http://www .advocate.com/politics/transgender/2014/02/13/facebook-announces-expanded -gender-options-transgender-and-gender (accessed 16 February 2014).

Monaghan, W. (2016), *Queer Girls, Temporality and Screen Media: Not 'Just a Phase'*, Cham: Springer.

Monaghan, W. (2017), 'Starting From.. . . . Now and the Web Series to Television Crossover: An Online Revolution?', *Media International Australia*, 164 (1): 82–91.

Monaghan, W. (2020), 'Lesbian, Gay and Bisexual Representation on Australian Entertainment Television: 1970–2000', *Media International Australia*, 174 (1): 49–58.

Monaghan, W. (2024), 'Streaming Queer Content: LGBTQ Media on BVOD and SVOD Services in Australia', *Television & New Media*, 25 (7): 656–72.

Moorehouse, F. (1988), *The Everlasting Secret Family*, Sydney: Press Kit.

Moran, R. (2018), '"Shut Up and Retire": Barry Humphries Slammed for Transphobic Comments', *Sydney Morning Herald*, 23 July. Available online: https://www.smh .com.au/entertainment/celebrity/shut-up-and-retire-barry-humphries-slammed-for -transphobic-comments-20180723-p4zt0h.html (accessed 26 July 2018).

Morley, D. (1980), *The 'Nationwide' Audience*, London: British Film Institute.

Muller, A. (2011), 'Virtual Communities and Translation into Physical Reality in the "It Gets Better" Project', *Journal of Media Practice*, 12 (3): 269–77.

Mulligan, M. and P. Smith (2011), 'Art, Governance and the Turn to Community: Lessons from a National Action Research Project on Community Art and Local Government in Australia', *Journal of Arts and Communities*, 2 (1): 27–40.

Muñoz, J. E. (2009), *Cruising Utopia: The Then and There of Queer Futurity*, New York: New York University Press.

Munt, S. (2007), *Queer Attachments: The Cultural Politics of Shame*, Aldershot: Ashgate.

Murphy, T. F. (1997), *Gay Science: The Ethics of Sexual Orientation Research*, New York: Columbia University Press.

Murray, J. B. (2006), 'The Genesis of *The Naked Bunyip*', *Senses of Cinema*, 38. Available online: http://www.sensesofcinema.com/2006/australian-cinema-38/naked_bunyip/ (accessed 17 August 2024).

Nestingen, A. (2011), *Crime and Fantasy in Scandinavia: Fiction, Film and Social Change*, Seattle, WA: University of Washington Press.

Netflix (2023), 'What Was Watched: A Netflix Engagement Report', *Netflix*, 12 December. Available online: https://about.netflix.com/en/news/what-we-watched-a-netflix-engagement-report (accessed 28 January 2024).

Nichols, B. (1994), 'Global Image Consumption in the Age of Late Capitalism', *East-West Film Journal*, 8 (1): 68–85.

O'Brien, G. (2019), 'Witches, Faggots, Dykes and Poofters', *Metro*, 20. Available online: https://metromagazine.com.au/witches-and-faggots-dykes-and-poofters/ (accessed 12 August 2024).

O'Connor, J. (2024), *Culture Is Not an Industry*, Manchester: Manchester University Press.

O'Grady, J. D. (2013), *Preaching to the Perverted: The Life and Times of Michael Glynn*, PhD thesis, The University of Sydney. Available online: https://ses.library.usyd.edu.au/handle/2123/13997 (accessed 14 September 2024).

O'Meara, D. J. and W. Monaghan (2024), 'Lesbian, Gay, Bisexual, Transgender, and Nonbinary Representation on Australian Scripted Television in the 2000s and 2010s', *Media International Australia*. Available online: https://journals.sagepub.com/doi/10.1177/1329878X241236990 (accessed 12 August 2024).

O'Regan, T. (1991), 'From Piracy to Sovereignty: International Video Cassette Recorder Trends', *Continuum: Journal of Media & Cultural Studies*, 4 (2): 112–35.

Oswald, R. F., J. M. Routon, J. K. McGuire, and E. G. Holman (2018), 'Tolerance Versus Support: Perceptions of Residential Community Climate Among LGB Parents', *Family Relations*, 67 (1): 41–54.

Padva, G. (2000), '*Priscilla* Fights Back: The Politicization of Camp Subculture', *Journal of Communication Inquiry*, 24 (2): 216–43.

Padva, G. (2004), 'Edge of Seventeen: Melodramatic Coming-Out in New Queer Adolescence Films', *Communication and Critical/Cultural Studies*, 1 (4): 355–72.

Page, P. (1978), 'Word Is Out', *Gay Changes*, 2 (2): 23.

Papanikolaou, D. (2008), 'New Queer Greece: Thinking Identity through Constantine Giannaris's From the Edge of the City and Ana Kokkinos's Head On', *New Cinemas*, 6 (3): 183–96.

Passey, D. (1997), 'Schoolyard Victims', *Sydney Morning Herald*, 4 April, 38.

Peach, R. (2005), *Queer Cinema as a Fifth Cinema in South Africa and Australia*, PhD Thesis, University of Technology, Sydney.

Peele, T. (2007), 'Introduction: Popular Culture, Queer Culture', in T. Peele (ed.), *Queer Popular Culture: Literature, Media, Film and Television*, 1–8, London: Palgrave Macmillan.

Petrychyn, J. (2022), 'A Gay Killer on the Police Force: Cruising and Queer Police Abolition', *Public*, 33 (65): 327–8.

Pfeiffer, O. (2016), 'Queer Controversy: Roger Ward and Sean Myers on *The Set*', *Metro: Media & Education Magazine*, 187: 110–12.

Pinedo, I. and W. D. Phillips (eds) (2023), *Camp TV of the 1960s: Reassessing the Vast Wasteland*, Oxford: Oxford University Press.

Plummer, K. (1995), *Telling Sexual Stories: Power, Change and Social Worlds*, London & New York: Routledge.

Poll, C. and J. Ware (1970), 'Editorial: What's in It for Me?', *CAMP Ink*, 1 (1): 2.

Probyn, E. (1996), *Outside Belongings*, New York & London: Routledge.

Queer Screen (2018), 'Pat Fiske, Digby Duncan and Melanie Rodriga in Q&A at the Screening of Witches, Faggots, Dykes and Poofters', *Queer Screen Film Festival*. Available online: https://www.facebook.com/queerscreen/videos/pat-fiske -digby-duncan-and-melanie-rodriga-in-qa-at-the-screening-of-witches-and /10155624362868495/ (accessed 12 August 2024).

Radbourne, J. (1996), 'Creative Nation: A Policy for Leaders or Followers? An Evaluation of Australia's 1994 Cultural Policy Statement', *Journal of Arts, Management Law & Society*, 26 (4): 271–83.

Radway, J. (1984), *Reading the Romance*, Chapel Hill, NC: The University of North Carolina Press.

Rand, E. J. (2013), 'An Appetite for Activism: The Lesbian Avengers and the Queer Politics of Visibility', *Women's Studies in Communication*, 36 (2): 121–41.

Rand, F. (1998), 'LOTL Hits a Century', *Lesbians on the Loose*, April: 3.

Rand, F. and J. Scherer (1990), 'Welcome!', *Lesbians on the Loose*, January: 1.

Rasmussen, M. L., R. Cover, D. Marshall, and P. Aggleton (2016), 'Sexuality, Gender, Citizenship and Social Justice: Education's Queer Relations', in A. Peterson (ed.), *Handbook of Education for Citizenship and Social Justice*, 73–96, London: Palgrave.

Rastegar, R. (2012), 'Difference, Aesthetics and the Curatorial Crisis of Film Festivals', *Screen*, 53 (3): 310–17.

Reece, A. (2020), 'The Art of Festival', in J. Lillie, K. Larsen, C. Kirkwood, and J. J. Brown (eds), *The Relationship Is the Project: A Guide to Working with Communities*, 103–10, Sydney, NSW: UNSW Press.

Reeves, J. L., M. C. Rodgers, and M. Epstein (1996), 'Rewriting Popularity: The Cult Files', in D. Lavery, A. Hague, and M. Cartwright (eds), *Deny All Knowledge: Reading the X-Files*, 22–35, London: Faber and Faber.

Reynolds, R. (2002), *From Camp to Queer: Remaking the Australian Homosexual*, Carlton: Melbourne University Press.

Rhyne, R. (2007), *Pink Dollars: Gay and Lesbian Film Festivals and the Economy of Visibility*, PhD Thesis, Department of Cinema Studies, New York University.

Rich, B. R. (1992), 'New Queer Cinema', *Sight and Sound*, 2 (5): 30–5.

Rich, B. R. (2013), *New Queer Cinema: The Director's Cut*, Durham, NC: Duke University Press.

Richards, S. (2016), *The Queer Film Festival: Popcorn & Politics*, London: Palgrave.

Richards, S. (2018), 'Swapping Goats for Snakes: *Australian Survivor*, Narrative Complexity and Audience Expectations', *Metro*, 29 January. Available online: https:// metromagazine.com.au/swapping-goats-for-snakes/ (accessed 7 April 2025).

Richards, S. (2019), 'More Than Just a Gay Pun: The Changing Nature of Australian Queer Film Criticism', *Studies in Australasian Cinema*, 13 (2–3): 51–66.

Richardson, D. (2005), 'Desiring Sameness? The Rise of a Neoliberal Politics of Normalisation', *Antipode*, 37 (3): 515–35.

Riese (2023), 'All 235 Dead Lesbian and Bisexual Characters On TV, And How They Died', *Autostraddle*, 27 February. Available online: https://www.autostraddle.com /all-65-dead-lesbian-and-bisexual-characters-on-tv-and-how-they-died-312315/ (accessed 16 September 2024).

Riggs, D. (2006), *Priscilla, (White) Queen of the Desert: Queer Rights/Race Privilege*, Bern: Peter Lang.

Roberts, F. (1966), 'Love Is What?', *The Bulletin*, 26 (February): 45.

Roof, J. (1996), *Come as You Are: Sexuality and Narrative*, New York, NY: Columbia University Press.

Rosello, M. (1998), *Declining the Stereotype: Ethnicity and Representation in French Cultures*, Hanover, NH: University Press of New England.

Rostosky, S. S., W. W. Black, E. D. B. Riggle, and D. Rosenkrantz (2015), 'Positive Aspects of being a Heterosexual Ally to Lesbian, Gay, Bisexual and Transgender (LGBT) People', *American Journal of Orthopsychiatry*, 85 (4): 331–8.

Rude, M. (2022), '15 Recent, Especially Brutal, Examples of the Bury Your Gays Trope', *Out*, 19 September. Available online: https://www.out.com/television/2022/9/19/ most-brutal-examples-of-bury-your-gays-trope-in-television-movies#rebelltitem1 (accessed 16 September 2024).

Russo, V. (1981), *The Celluloid Closet: Homosexuality in the Movies*, New York: Harper & Row.

Rustin, E. (2001), 'Romance and Sensation in the "Glitter Cycle"', in I. Craven (ed.), *Australian Cinema in the 1990s*, 131–48, New York: Frank Cass Publishers.

Ryan, M. (1988), 'The Politics of Film: Discourse, Psychoanalysis, Ideology', in C. Nelson and L. Grossberg (eds), *Marxism and the Interpretation of Culture*, 477–86, Urbana and Chicago, IL: University of Illinois Press.

Sackar, J. (2023), *Special Commission of Inquiry into LGBTIQ Hate Crimes: Volume 1*, Sydney, NSW: State Government of New South Wales. Available online: https:// www.nsw.gov.au/sites/default/files/noindex/2023-12/SCOI-LGBTIQ-Hate-Crimes -Volume-1-181223.pdf (accessed 14 September 2024).

Sanders, D. (2008), 'Don't Let Them Drag You Down: *The Adventures of Priscilla, Queen of the Desert* by Philip Brophy', *Senses of Cinema*, 48. Available online: http:// sensesofcinema.com/2008/book-reviews/adventures- priscilla-queen-desert/ (accessed 19 July 2024).

Sargent, D. P. (1980), 'Witches and Faggots, Dykes and Poofters', *Campaign*, 54: 30.

Savage, J. (2012), 'The Lost Cult of Wake in Fright', *Intensities: Cult Media*, 4. Available online: https://intensitiescultmedia.com/wp-content/uploads/2012/12/savage-lost -cult-of-wake-in-fright.pdf (accessed 19 August 2024).

Schaefer, E. (1999), *'Bold! Daring! Shocking! True!': A History of Exploitation Films, 1919–1959*, Durham, NC: Duke University Press.

Schmith, M. (1982), 'Refreshing, Heartening', *The Age*, 6 September: 2.

Screen Australia (2016), *Seeing Ourselves: Reflections on Diversity in Australian TV Drama*. Available online: https://www.screenaustralia.gov.au/getmedia/157b05b4 -255a-47b4-bd8b-9f715555fb44/TV-Drama-Diversity.pdf (accessed 12 August 2024).

Screen Australia (2023), *Seeing Ourselves 2: Diversity, Equity and Inclusion in Australian TV Drama*. Available online: https://www.screenaustralia.gov.au/fact-finders/reports -and-key-issues/reports-and-discussion-papers/seeing-ourselves-2 (accessed 12 August 2024).

Searle, S. (1995), '"Our" ABC?: The 1994 Gay and Lesbian Mardi Gras Parade Broadcast', *Media International Australia*, 78 (1): 13–19.

Searle, S. (1997), *Queer-ing the Screen: Sexuality and Australian Film and Television*, St Kilda: Australian Teachers of Media.

Sedgwick, E. K. (1990), *Epistemology of the Closet*, London: Penguin.

Sedgwick, E. K. (1993), *Tendencies*, Durham, NC: Duke University Press.

Sender, K. (2004), *Business, Not Politics: The Making of a Queer Market*, New York: Columbia University Press.

Severiche, G. (2020), 'Embodied Nations: Masculinities, Nationhood and (Homo) sexual Desire: From *Borstal Boy* (2000) to *God's Own Country* (2017)', *Queer Studies in Media and Popular Culture*, 5 (1): 7–25.

Shannon, C. E. and W. Weaver (1949), *The Mathematical Theory of Communication*, Urbana, IL: University of Illinois Press.

Snickars, P. and P. Vonderau (2009), *The YouTube Reader*, Stockholm: National Library of Sweden.

Snider, Z. (2016), 'Gay It Forward: How *Will & Grace* Made Gay Male Couples Okay on Television', in K.-P. R. Hart (ed.), *Queer TV in the 21st Century: Essays on Broadcasting from Taboo to Acceptance*, 9–25, Jefferson, NC: McFarland & Company.

Stack, S. (2005), 'Suicide in the Media: A Quantitative Review of Studies based on Nonfictional Stories', *Suicide & Life-Threatening Behavior*, 35 (2): 121–33.

Staiger, J. (2000), *Perverse Spectators: The Practices of Film Reception*, New York: NYU Press.

Stein, A. and K. Plummer (1994), '"I Can't Even Think Straight": "Queer" Theory and the Missing Sexual Revolution in Sociology', *Sociological Theory*, 12 (2): 178–87.

Stein, E. (1989), 'The Everlasting Secret Family', *The Village Voice*, 21 November: 96.

Stewart, A. (1980), 'Homosexuals Angered by Violent US Film', *Sydney Morning Herald*, 15 June: 15.

Stewart, W. (1995), *Cassell's Queer Companion: A Dictionary of Lesbian and Gay Life and Culture*, London: Cassell.

Stokes, T. (1980), 'Stone the Clones', *Gay Community News*, 2 (10): 4.

Stone, G. (2019), 'I Wrote into *Neighbours* and Asked Them to Put a Trans Character on my Screen', *Metro*, 31 August. Available online: https://metro.co.uk/2019/08/31/i-wrote-into-neighbours-and-asked-them-to-put-a-trans-character-on-my-screen-10651301/ (accessed 15 October 2024).

Storey, J. (1993), *An Introduction to Cultural Theory and Popular Culture*, New York: Harvester Wheatsheaf.

Straayer, C. (1996), *Deviant Eyes, Deviant Bodies: Sexual Re-Orientation in Film and Video*, New York: Columbia University Press.

Strauss, P., A. Cook, S. Winter, V. Watson, W. T. Dani, and A. Lin (2020), 'Associations Between Negative Life Experiences and the Mental Health of Trans and Gender Diverse Young People in Australia: Findings from Trans Pathways', *Psychological Medicine*, 50 (5): 808–17.

Streitmatter, R. (1998), 'Vice Versa: America' s First Lesbian Magazine', *American Periodicals*, 8 (1): 78–95.

Sudak, H. S. and D. M. Sudak (2005), 'The Media and Suicide', *Academic Psychiatry*, 29 (5): 495–9.

Sydney Star Observer (1998), 'Ellen Protest', *Sydney Star Observer*, 404: 13.

Tamagne, F. (2007), *A History of Homosexuality in Europe: Berlin, London, Paris 1919–1939*, ed. A. Seberry, New York: Algora Publishing.

Thomas, K. (1988), 'The Everlasting Secret Family', *Los Angeles Times*, 18 July.

Tresca, D. (2016), 'Skeletons in the Closet: The Contradictory Views of the Queer in the Works of Joss Whedon', in K.-P. R. Hart (ed.), *Queer TV in the 21st Century: Essays on Broadcasting from Taboo to Acceptance*, 26–40, Jefferson, NC: McFarland & Company.

Tropiano, S. (2002), *The Prime Time Closet: A History of Gays and Lesbians on TV*, New York: Applause Theatre & Cinema Books.

Tudor, D. (2014), 'Cultural Intersections in Early Australian Sound Films: Rangle River (1936)', *Democratic Communiqué*, 19 (1): 3.

Turner, G. (2009), 'Catching the Wave: Britain's Lesbian Publishing Goes Commercial', *Journalism Studies*, 10 (6): 769–88.

Vaid, U. (1995), *Virtual Equality: The Mainstreaming of Gay and Lesbian Liberation*, New York: Anchor.

van der Naald, J. (2015), 'The Mission as Master Signifier: Documentary Film, Social Change and Discourse Analysis', *Psychoanalysis, Culture & Society*, 20 (2): 207–16.

Veenstra, A. and R. Byatt (1974), 'Art and Culture', *Campink*, 4 (1): 19–20.

Venkatesh, V. (2016), *New Maricón Cinema: Outing Latin American Film*, Austin, TX: University of Texas Press.

Verhoeven, D. (1997), 'The Sexual Terrain of the Australian Feature Film: Putting the Out: back into the Ocker', in C. Jackson and P. Tapp (eds), *The Bent Lens: A World Guide to Gay and Lesbian Film*, 25–32, St Kilda: Australian Catalogue Company.

Villarejo, A. (2014), *Ethereal Queer: Television, Historicity, Desire*, Durham, NC: Duke University Press.

Walls, N. E., S. Freedenthal, and H. Wisneski (2008), 'Suicidal Ideation and Attempts Among Sexual Minority Youths Receiving Social Services', *Social Work*, 53 (1): 21–9.

Ward, S., T. O'Regan, and B. Goldsmith (2010), 'From *Neighbours* to *Packed to the Rafters*: Accounting for Longevity in the Evolution of Aussie Soaps', *Media International Australia*, 136 (1): 162–76.

Wenger, E. (1998), *Communities of Practice: Learning, Meaning, and Identity*, Cambridge: Cambridge University Press.

West Campaigner (1973), 'Fists up, Teeth Bared: SA Camps Come out Fighting', *West Campaigner*, September.

White, P. (1999), *Uninvited: Classical Hollywood Cinema and Lesbian Representability*, Indianapolis, IN: Indiana University Press.

White, R. (1981), *Inventing Australia*, St. Leonards, NSW: Allen & Unwin .

Willett, G. (2000), *Living Out Loud: A History of Gay and Lesbian Activism in Australia*, St Leonards, NSW: Allen & Unwin.

William & John (1972), 'Editorial', *William & John*, January: 4.

Williams, K. (2018), 'Eulogies for the Video Store: Remembering the Practices and Objects of the Rental Era', in M. D. Ryan and B. Goldsmith (eds), *Australian Screen in the 2000s*, 321–40, Cham: Springer.

Williams, R. (1975), *Television: Technology and Cultural Form*, New York: Schocken.

Wilson, J. (2007), 'Setting the Record Straight', *The Age*, 23 March. Available online: https://www.theage.com.au/entertainment/movies/setting-the-record-straight -20070323-ge4hh3.html (accessed 12 July 2024).

Wolf, M. A. and A. P. Kielwasser (eds) (1991), *Gay People, Sex, and the Media*, New York & London: Harrington Park Press.

Wong, C. M. (2014), 'OKCupid begins Rolling Out New Gender, Sexuality Options', *Huffington Post*, 18 November. Available online: http://www.huffingtonpost.com.au/ entry/okcupid-new-gender-options_n_6172434.html?section=australia (accessed 12 June 2018).

Wood, R. (1978), 'Responsibilities of a Gay Film Critic', *Film Comment*, 12–17.

Wotherspoon, G. (1991), *'City of the Plain': History of a Gay Sub-Culture*, Sydney, NSW: Hale and Iremonger.

Wyn, J. and D. Woodman (2006), 'Generation, Youth and Social Change in Australia', *Journal of Youth Studies*, 9 (5): 495–514.

Young, D. R. (2018), *Making Sex Public and Other Cinematic Fantasies*, Durham, NC: Duke University Press.

Zhao, Jamie J. (2023), *Queer TV China: Televisual and Fannish Imaginaries of Gender, Sexuality, and Chineseness*, Hong Kong: Hong Kong University Press.

Filmography

52 Tuesdays (2014), [Film] Dir. Sophie Hyde, Australia: Closer Productions.

A Comedy in Six Unnatural Acts (1979), [Film] Dir. Jan Oxenberg, USA: Good Taste Productions.

A Country Practice (1981–93), [TV programme] Australia: Seven Network.

A Farewell to Charms (1979), [Film] Dir. Carla Pontiac, Australia: Swinburne Institute of Technology, Film and Television School.

A Place to Call Home (2013–18), [TV programme] Australia: Seven Network.

Above the Law (2000–1), [TV programme] Australia: Network Ten.

Adam (1975), [Film] Dir. Paul Budgen, Australia: Quest Films.

Adventure Island (1967–72), [TV programme] Australia: Australian Broadcasting Corporation.

Advise and Consent (1962), [Film] Dir. Otto Preminger, USA: Columbia Pictures.

After the Beep (1996), [TV programme] Australia: Australian Broadcasting Corporation.

All Men Are Liars (1995), [Film] Dir. Gerard Lee, Australia: Arenafilm.

Ally McBeal (1997–2002), [TV programme] USA: Fox.

Alvin Purple (1973), [Film] Dir. Tim Burstall, Australia: Hexagon Productions.

Always Greener (2001–3), [TV programme] Australia: Seven Network.

Amphetamine (2010), [Film] Dir. Scud, Hong Kong: Artwalker.

Arcade (1980), [TV programme] Australia: Network Ten.

Are You Being Served? (1972–85), [TV programme] UK: British Broadcasting Corporation (BBC).

Are You Being Served? (1980–1), [TV programme] Australia: Network Ten.

Australia's Next Top Model (2005–16), [TV programme] Australia: Granada Media Australia and Shine Australia.

Australian Idol (2003–24), [TV programme] Australia: Network Ten.

Barracuda (2016), [TV programme] Australia: Australian Broadcasting Corporation.

Barry McKenzie Holds His Own (1974), [Film] Dir. Bruce Beresford, Australia: Reg Grundy Productions.

Basic Instinct (1992), [Film] Dir. Paul Verhoeven, USA: Carolco Pictures and Le Studio Canal+.

Beauty and the Beast (1964–73), [TV programme] Australia: Network Ten.

Beverly Hills, 90210 (1990–2000), [TV programme] USA: Fox.

Beyond the Valley of the Dolls (1970), [Film] Dir. Russ Meyer, USA: Twentieth Century Fox.

Big Brother Australia (2001–23), [TV programme] Australia: Seven Network.

Bitter Springs (1950), [Film] Dir. Ralph Smart, Australia: Ealing Studios.

Blessed Are Those Who Thirst (1997), [Film] Dir. Carl Jørgen Kiønig, Norway: Nordic Screen Production AS.

Blue Heelers (1994–2006), [TV programme] Australia: Seven Network.

Bound (1996), [Film] Dir. Lana Wachowski and Lilly Wachowski, USA: Spelling Films.

Boys Don't Cry (1999), [Film] Dir. Kimberly Peirce, USA: Searchlight Pictures.

Boys in the Band, The (1970), [Film] Dir. William Friedkin, USA: Cinema Center Films.

Boys in the Trees (2016), [Film] Dir. Nicholas Verso, Australia: Mushroom Pictures.

Bram Stoker's Dracula (1992), [Film] Dir. Francis Ford Coppola, USA: American Zoetrope and Osiris Films.

Breakers (1997–9), [TV programme] Australia: Network Ten.

Buffy: The Vampire Slayer (1997–2003), [TV programme] The WB and UPN, 10 March 1997–20 May 2003.

But I'm a Cheerleader (1999), [Film] Dir. Jamie Babbit, USA: Ignite Entertainment.

Butterfly Kiss (1995), [Film] Dir. Michael Winterbottom, UK: British Screen Productions.

Carlotta (2014), [Film] Dir. Samantha Lang, Australia: Australian Broadcasting Corporation.

Carson's Law (1983–4), [TV programme] Australia: Network Ten.

Chasing Amy (1997), [Film] Dir. Kevin Smith, USA: View Askew Productions.

Chequerboard (1969–75), [TV programme] Australia: Australian Broadcasting Corporation.

Children of Hiroshima (1952), [Film] Dir. Kaneto Shindô, Japan: Japan Teacher Union.

Coming Out (1972), [Film] Dir. Arthur J. Bressan Jr, USA: Independent Production.

Cop Shop (1977–84), [TV programme] Australia: Seven Network.

Cruising (1980), [Film] Dir. William Friedkin, USA: Lorimar.

Cut Snake (2014), [Film] Dir. Tony Ayres, Australia: Matchbox Pictures.

Dad and Dave Come to Town (1938), [Film] Dir. Ken G. Hall, Australia: Cinesound Productions Limited.

Dad Rudd MP (1940), [Film] Dir. Ken G. Hall, Australia: Cinesound Productions Limited.

Daily at Dawn (1981), [TV programme] Australia: Seven Network.

Dance Academy (2010–13), [TV programme] Australia: Australian Broadcasting Corporation.

Dangerous Women (1991), [TV programme] USA: USA Network.

Deathtrap (1981), [Film] Dir. Sidney Lumet, USA: Warner Bros.

Deep Water (2016), [TV programme] Australia: Special Broadcasting Service.

Degrassi Junior High (1987–9), [TV programme] Canada: CBC.

Desert Hearts (1985), [Film] Dir. Donna Deitch, USA: Desert Hearts Productions.

Division 4 (1969–76), [TV programme] Australia: Nine Network Australia.

Downriver (2015), [Film] Dir. Grant Scicluna, Australia: Screen Australia.

Drown (2015), [Film] Dir. Dean Francis, Australia: JJ Splice Films.

Eat Carpet (1989–2005), [TV programme] Australia: Special Broadcasting Service.

Eliza Fraser (1976), [Film] Dir. Tim Burstall, Australia: Hexagon Productions.

Ellen (1994–8), [TV programme] USA: ABC Network.

Ellie and Abbie (and Ellie's Dead Aunt) (2020), [Film] Dir. Monica Zanetti, Australia: Cobbstar Productions.

ER (1994–2009), [TV programme] USA: NBC.

Everything Will Be Fine (1998), [Film] Dir. Angelina Maccarone, Germany: Norddeutscher Rundfunk (NDR).

Fame (1980), [Film] Dir. Alan Parker, USA: MGM.

Fast Forward (1989–92), [TV programme] Australia: Seven Network.

Feed Them to the Cannibals (1993), [Film] Dir. Fiona Cunningham Reid, Australia: Baobab Productions.

Fire (1995–6), [TV programme] Australia: Seven Network.

Fireworks (1947), [Film] Dir. Kenneth Anger, USA: Cinema 16.

First Day (2020–2), [TV programme] Australia: Australian Broadcasting Corporation.

Flaming Creatures (1963), [Film] Dir. Jack Smith, USA: Independent production.

Flesh (1969), [Film] Dir. Paul Morrissey, USA: Sherpix.

Flying Doctors (1986–92), [TV programme] Australia: Nine Network.

Foolish Things (1981), [Film] Dir. Peter Wells, Australia: Independent production.

Fortune and Men's Eyes (1971), [Film] Dir. Harvey Hart and Jules Schwerin, Canada: Cinemax.

Friends (1994–2004), [TV programme] USA: NBC.

Gallipoli (1981), [Film] Dir. Peter Weir, Australia: R&R Films.

Gay Deceivers, The (1969), [Film] Dir. Bruce Kessler, USA: Fanfare Films.

Gentlemen Prefer Blondes (1953), [Film] Dir. Howard Hawks, USA: Twentieth Century Fox.

GP (1989–96), [TV programme] Australia: Australian Broadcasting Corporation.

Hannah Gadsby: Nanette (2018), [TV programme] USA: Netflix, June.

Head On (1998), [Film] Dir. Ana Kokkinos, Australia: Great Scott Productions Pty. Ltd.

Heartbreak High (1994–9), [TV programme] Australia: Network Ten.

Heartbreak High (2022–5), [TV programme] Australia: Netflix.

Heartstopper (2022–), [TV programme] UK: Netflix.

High Art (1998), [Film] Dir. Lisa Cholodenko, USA: October Films.

High Rolling (1977), [Film] Dir. Igor Auzins, Australia: Hexagon Productions.

Hinter Gittern – Der Fraukenast (1997–2007), [TV programme] Germany: RTL.

Holding (1970), [Film] Dir. Coni Beeson, Australia: Multi-Media Resource Centre.

Holding the Man (2015), [Film] Dir. Neil Armfield, Australia: Screen Australia.

Home and Away (1988–), [TV programme] Australia: Seven Network.

Homecoming Queens (2018), [TV programme] Australia: Generator Pictures.

Homicide (1964–77), [TV programme] Australia: Seven Network.

Homosexuality: A Film for Discussion (1975), [Film] Dir. Barbara Creed, Australia: Melbourne Filmmakers Co-operative.

Hotel Story (1977–8), [TV programme] Australia: Seven Network.

Housekeeping for Beginners (2023), [Film] Dir. Goran Stolevski, North Macedonia: List Production.

In Melbourne Tonight (1957–70), [TV programme] Australia: Nine Network Australia.

Internal Affairs (1990), [Film] Dir. Mike Figgis, USA: Paramount Pictures.

It's a Sin (2021), [TV programme] UK: Channel 4.

Janet King (2014–17), [TV programme] Australia: Australian Broadcasting Corporation.

Jewelled Nights (1925), [Film] Dir. Louise Lovely and Wilton Welch, Australia: Louise Lovely Productions.

Killing of Sister George, The (1968), [Film] Dir. Robert Aldrich, UK: Palomar Pictures.

La Dolce Vita (1960), [Film] Dir. Federico Fellini, Italy: Société Nouvelle Pathé Cinéma.

LA Law (1986–94), [TV programme] USA: NBC.

Les Biches (1968), [Film] Dir. Claude Chabrol, France: Les Films de la Boétie.

Lonesome (2022), [Film] Dir. Craig Boreham, Australia: JJ Splice Films.

Lonesome Cowboys (1968), [Film] Dir. Andy Warhol and Paul Morrissey, USA: Sherpix.

Love and Other Catastrophes (1996), [Film] Dir. Emma-Kate Croghan, Australia: Beyond Films.

Love Lies Bleeding (2024), [Film] Dir. Rose Glass, UK: A24.

Lovers and Luggers (1937), [Film] Dir. Ken G. Hall, Australia: Cinesound Productions Limited.

Mad About You (1992–9), [TV programme] USA: NBC.

Mad Max (1979), [Film] Dir. George Miller, Australia: Kennedy Miller Productions.

Mad Max 2 (1981), [Film] Dir. George Miller, Australia: Kennedy Miller Productions.

Maidens (1978), [Film] Dir. Jeni Thornley, Australia: Anandi Films.

Making Love (1982), [Film] Dir. Arthur Hiller, USA: Twentieth Century Fox.

Monster Pies (2013), [Film] Dir. Lee Galea, Australia: Babaloo Studios.

Muriel's Wedding (1994), [Film] Dir. P. J. Hogan, Australia: CiBy 2000.

My First Summer (2020), [Film] Dir. Katie Found, Australia: Noise & Light.

Mysterious Skin (2004), [Film] Dir. Gregg Araki, USA: Fortissimo Films.

Neighbours (1985–), [TV programme] Australia: Network Ten.

Neighbours: Erinsborough High (2019), [TV programme] Australia: Network Ten.

Newcastle (2008), [Film] Dir. Dan Castle, Australia: Dragonfly Pictures.

Night Out (1990), [Film] Dir. Stratos Tzitzis, Germany: GiGi Pictures.

Number 96 (1972–7), [TV programme] Australia: Network Ten.

Of an Age (2022), [Film] Dir. Goran Stolevski, Australia: Causeway Films.

Outland (2012), [TV programme] Australia: Australian Broadcasting Corporation.

Pacific Drive (1996–7), [TV programme] Australia: Nine Network.

Partners (1982), [Film] Dir. James Burrows, USA: Paramount Pictures.

Performance (1970), [Film] Dir. Donald Cammel and Nicolas Roeg, UK: Goodtime Enterprises.

Personal Best (1982), [Film] Dir. Robert Towne, USA: The Geffen Company.

Peterson (1974), [Film] Dir. Tim Burstall, Australia: Hexagon Productions.

Philadelphia (1994), [Film] Dir. Jonathan Demme, USA: TriStar Pictures.

Picket Fences (1992–6), [TV programme] USA: CBS.

Picnic (1948), [Film] Dir. Curtis Harrington, USA: Independent Production.

Picnic at Hanging Rock (1975), [Film] Dir. Peter Weir, Australia: British Empire Films Australia.

Pink Narcissus (1971), [Film] Dir. James Bidgood, USA: Strand Releasing.

Please Like Me (2013–16), [TV programme] Australia: Australian Broadcasting.

Point of Departure (1975), [Film] Dir. Don McLennan, Australia: Experimental Film and Television Fund.

Predestination (2014), [Film] Dir. Michael Spierig and Peter Spierig, Australia: Screen Australia.

Prisoner (1979–86), [TV programme] Australia: Network Ten.

Queer as Folk (1999–2000), [TV programme] UK: Channel 4.

Querelle (1982), [Film] Dir. Rainer Werner Fassbinder, Germany/France: Gaumont S.A. Paris.

Rangle River (1936), [Film] Dir. Clarence G. Badger, Australia: Clarence Badger Productions.

Raw FM (1997–8), [TV programme] Australia: Australian Broadcasting Corporation.

Relax... It's Just Sex (1998), [Film] Dir. P. J. Castellaneta, USA: Forefront Films.

Satdee Night (1973), [Film] Dir. Gillian Armstrong, Australia: Film Australia.

Scobie Malone (1975), [Film] Dir. Terry Ohlsson, Australia: Kingcroft Australia.

Scorpio Rising (1963), [Film] Dir. Kenneth Anger, USA: Puck Film Productions.

SeaChange (1998–2000), [TV programme] Australia: Australian Broadcasting Corporation.

Sequin in a Blue Room (2019), [Film] Dir. Samuel Van Grinsven, Australia: Australian Film. Television and Radio School.

Shannon's Mob (1975–6), [TV programme] Australia: Nine Network.

Should a Girl Propose? (1926), [Film] Dir. P. J. Ramster, Australia: P.J. Ramster Photoplays.

Showtime (1978), [Film] Dir. Jan Chapman, Australia: Sydney Filmmakers Co-operative.

Silent Number (1974), [TV programme] Australia: Network Ten.

Silks and Saddles (1921), [Film] Dir. Robert F. Hill, USA: Victory Pictures Corporation.

Single White Female (1992), [Film] Dir. Barbet Schroeder, USA: Columbia Pictures.

Sister Act (1992), [Film] Dir. Emile Ardolino, USA: Touchstone Pictures and Touchwood Pacific Partners 1.

Six Feet Under (2001–5), [TV programme] USA: HBO.

Skyways (1979–81), [TV programme] Australia: Seven Network.

Some of My Best Friends Are... (1971), [Film] Dir. Mervyn Nelson, USA: Bluebird Productions.

Sons and Daughters (1982–7), [TV programme] Australia: Seven Network.

Starting From Now (2014–16), [Web series] Australia: Common Language Films. Available at https://www.youtube.com/c/StartingFromNow

Strange World (2022), [Film] Dir. Don Hall, USA: Walt Disney Animation Studios.

Strictly Ballroom (1992), [Film] Dir. Baz Luhrmann, Australia: Beyond Films.

Submerge (2012), [Film] Dir. Sophie O'Connor, Australia: Independent Production.

Summer Heights High (2007), [TV programme] Australia: Australian Broadcasting Corporation.

Sunday, Bloody Sunday (1971), [Film] Dir. John Schlesinger, UK: Vic Films Productions.

Sunflower (2023), [Film] Dir. Gabriel Carrubba, Australia: Pancake Originals.

Sunshine Sally (1922), [Film] Dir. Lawson Harris, Australia: Austral Super Films.

Sweat (1996), [TV programme] Australia: Network Ten.

Sylvania Waters (1992), [TV programme] Australia: Australian Broadcasting Corporation.

Taxi zum Klo (1980), [Film] Dir. Frank Ripploh, Germany: Promovision.

Television and Radio School (AFTRS)

The Adventures of Barry McKenzie (1972), [Film] Dir. Bruce Beresford, Australia: Longford Productions.

The Adventures of Priscilla, Queen of the Desert (1994), [Film] Dir. Stephan Elliott, Australia: PolyGram Filmed Entertainment.

The Aunty Jack Show (1972–3), [TV programme] Australia: Australian Broadcasting Corporation.

The Birdcage (1996), [Film] Dir. Mike Nichols, USA: United Artists.

The Block (2003–), [TV programme] Australia: Nine Network.

The Box (1974–7), [TV programme] Australia: Network Ten.

The Breaking of the Drought (1920), [Film] Dir. Franklyn Barrett, Australia: Golden Wattle Films.

The Cars That Ate Paris (1974), [Film] Dir. Peter Weir, Australia: Royce Smeal Film Productions.

The Devil's Playground (1976), [Film] Dir. Fred Schepisi, Australia: The Film House.

The Dingo Principle (1988), [TV programme] Australia: Australian Broadcasting Corporation.

The Dreamlife of Georgie Stone (2022), [TV programme] USA: Netflix.

The Everlasting Secret Family (1988), [Film] Dir. Michael Thornhill, Australia: FGH.

The Family Law (2016–19), [TV programme] Australia: Special Broadcasting Service.

The Getting of Wisdom (1977), [Film] Dir. Bruce Beresford, Australia: Nine Network Australia.

The Horizon (2009–17), [Web series] Australia: Cobbstar Productions. Available at https://www.youtube.com/@WeArePride.

The Incredibly True Adventure of Two Girls in Love (1995), [Film] Dir. Maria Maggenti, USA: Fine Line Features.

The L Word (2004–9), [TV programme] Showtime: USA and Canada, 18 January 2004–8 March 2009.

The Last of the Australians (1975–6), [TV programme] Australia: Nine Network.

The Last Wave (1977), [Film] Dir. Peter Weir, Australia: McElroy & McElroy.

The Laugh on Dad (1918), [Film] Dir. A. C. Tinsdale, Australia: Austral Photoplay Company.

The Mad King of Bavaria (1972), [Film] Dir. Luchino Visconti, Italy: Mega Film.

The Mavis Bramston Show (1964–8), [TV programme] Australia: Seven Network.

The Naked Bunyip (1970), [Film] Dir. John B. Murray, Australia: Southern Cross Films Pty. Ltd.

The Pirate Movie (1982), [Film] Dir. Ken Annakin and Richard Franklin, Australia: Joseph Hamilton International Productions.

The Power of the Dog (2021), [Film] Dir. Jane Campion, New Zealand: BBC Film.

The Secret Life of Us (2001–5), [TV programme] Australia: Network Ten.

The Set (1970), [Film] Dir. Frank Brittain, Australia: David Hannay Productions.

The Silence of the Lambs (1991), [Film] Dir. Jonathan Demme, USA: Orion Pictures.

The Slap (2011), [TV programme] Australia: Australian Broadcasting Corporation.

The Squatter's Daughter (1933), [Film] Dir. Ken G. Hall, Australia, Cinesound Productions Limited.

The Sum of Us (1994), [Film] Dir. Geoff Burton and Kevin Dowling, Australia: Southern Star Entertainment.

The Well (1997), [Film] Dir. Samantha Lang, Australia: Southern Star Xanadu.

The Year My Voice Broke (1987), [Film] Dir. John Duigan, Australia: Kennedy Miller Productions.

Thelma and Louise (1991), [Film] Dir. Ridley Scott, USA: Pathé Entertainment.

Tootsie (1982), [Film] Dir. Sydney Pollack, USA: Columbia Pictures.

Transparent (2014–19), [TV programme] USA: Amazon Studios.

Trash (1970), [Film] Dir. Paul Morrissey, USA: Filmfactory.

Triple Oh! (2024), [TV programme] Australia: Sirius Pictures.

Turkish Baths (1975), [Film] Dir. Maya Frankel, Australia: Sydney Filmmakers Co-operative.

Victim (1961), [Film] Dir. Basil Dearden, UK: Michael Relph and Basil Dearden Production.

Victor/Victoria (1982), [Film] Dir. Blake Edwards, USA: MGM.

Wake in Fright (1971), [Film] Dir. Ted Kotcheff, Australia: NLT Productions.

Walking on Water (2002), [Film] Dir. Tony Ayres, Australia: SBS Independent.

Water Rats (1996–2001), [TV programme] Australia: Nine Network Australia.

Wentworth (2013–21), [TV programme] Australia: SoHo.

Wild Things (1998), [Film] Dir. John McNaughton, Mandalay Entertainment.

Will & Grace (1998–2006; 2017–20), [TV programme] USA: NBC.

Winners & Losers (2011–16), [TV programme] Australia: Seven Network.

Witches and Faggots, Dykes and Poofters (1980), [Film] Dir. Digby Duncan, Australia: One-in-Seven Collection.

Word Is Out: Stories of Some of Our Lives (1977), [Film] Dir. Mariposa Film Group, USA: Mariposa Film Group.

Young Royals (2021–4), [TV programme] Sweden: Nexiko.

Index

52 Tuesdays (2014), [Film]   15, 125
1978 Mardi Gras   143

Aboriginal land rights and women's rights
        movements   93
Academy Twin Cinemas   99
activism, of LGBTQ+   58–60, 69
Adair, Peter   65
Adam (1975), [Film]   93
Adelaide Queer Film Festival   96
adolescent sexual identities   81
Adventure Island (1967–72), [TV
        programme]   42
The Adventures of Barry McKenzie (1972),
        [Film]   33
*The Adventures of Priscilla, Queen of the
        Desert* (1994), [Film]   3, 31, 35,
        96, 122, 171
affordances   210
    of digital and networked
        platforms   130
    screen affordances   17
Allen, Johnny   66
Allen, Karen   138
allies, concept of   198–9
All Men Are Liars (1995), [Film]   121
Almodóvar, Pedro   161
alternative sexualities   31, 37
Altman, Dennis   63, 66, 193
Always Greener (2001–3), [TV
        programme]   52
American Psychiatric Association
        (APA)   168
Anderson, Don   44
anti-capitalist gay liberation
        movement   140
anti-gay laws   139
anti-gay murders   139
anti-social behaviour   80
anti-trans lobby   185
Antolovich, Gaby   44
Arcade (1980), [TV programme]   47

Arena Three   108
Are You Being Served? (1972–85),
        [TV programme]   47
Armstrong, Gillian   33
Ashcraft, Catherine   81
audiences   10–13, 21, 36–7, 50–1, 53, 55,
        63–5, 67, 69, 73, 75, 78–9, 81–2,
        85–6, 88, 122, 132–3, 137, 143, 167,
        176, 191
    assumption about   155
    cultural practices   16
    discourse   138
    reception cultures   16
    scholarship   154
    self-esteem of   178
The Aunty Jack Show (1972–3), [TV
        programme]   42
AusQueerScreen study   10, 151
Austin, Ron   68
Australian Department of Health and
        Ageing   40
Australian Film Institute   99
Australian gay liberation movement   67
Australian Idol (2003–24), [TV
        programme]   50
Australian Queer Archives   21
Australian Survivor   51
Australia's Next Top Model (2005–16),
        [TV programme]   52

The Bailey Report   43
Baldwin, Hugh   49
Baltruschat, D.   51
Barry McKenzie Holds His Own (1974),
        [Film]   33
Basic Instinct (1992), [Film]   116, 181
Bassey, Shirley   124
Bendigo Queer Film Festival (BQFF)   97
Benson, Chloe   97
Beresford, Bruce   33
Big Brother Australia (2001–23), [TV
        programme]   50–2

bisexual characters   50
Bitter Springs (1950), [Film]   121
Bittner, Robert   205
Blake, Rachel   49
Blessed Are Those Who Thirst (1997),
    [Film]   115
The Block (2003–), [TV programme]   52
Blood, Warwick   177
Blue Heelers (1994–2006), [TV
    programme]   48
Blundell, Graham   33
Bock, Helen   96
Bonsall-Boone, Peter   43
The Box (1974–7), [TV programme]   45
Boys Don't Cry (1999), [Film]   159, 171
Boys in the Band, The (1970), [Film]   64
Boys in the Trees (2016), [Film]   176
Brisbane Pride Festival   96
Brisbane Queer Film Festival   96
*Broadcasting It: An Encyclopaedia of
    Homosexuality in Film, Radio
    and TV in the UK, 1923–1993*
    (1993)   42
Broadcast Video on Demand (BVOD)
    service   132
Brokeback Mountain (2005), [Film]   183
Brophy, Phillip   35
Brown, Wendy   194
Buffy: The Vampire Slayer (1997–2003),
    [TV programme]   181
The Bulletin   43–4
Burke, Chris   66
Burns, Steve   138, 144
Burstall, Tim   33
'bury your gays' trope   178, 192
Butler, Judith   119, 125
Byatt, Rod   92

cable services   133
Cairns Pride Festival   96
Campaign Against Moral Persecution
    (CAMP)   43, 57, 92
Campbell, Ross   43
CAMP Ink   92
Campion, Jane   7
*Camp TV of the 1960s: Reassessing the Vast
    Wasteland* (2023)   41
Carey, Damien   96
Carlotta (2014), [Film]   123

Carson's Law (1983–4), [TV
    programme]   47
The Cars That Ate Paris (1974),
    [Film]   36
Carswell, Phil   145
Cass, John   51
Cass, Michael   57
casual sexual behaviour   191
The Celluloid Closet (1981)   24, 41
censors   60–2
censorship codes   24
censorship laws   58
Challinor, Ron   45
Chapman, Jan   33
characters cross-dressing   12, 22
Charles, Barry   148
Chasin, Alexandra   101
Chater, Gordon   42
child audiences   129
Ciasullo, Anne M.   116
cinema distributors   6
cisgender heteronormativity   160
cisgender/transgender relationships
    123
civil rights reformism   146
clones and leather sex   145
Club   80 141, 146–7
A Comedy in Six Unnatural Acts (1979),
    [Film]   99
Coming Out (1972), [Film]   93
commercial media   58
community audience   137
community discourse   159
community members   117
community-oriented approach   96
community publications   105
Conigrave, Timothy   179
conservative politics   80
Cooper, Evan   10, 192
Coote, Robert   25
Cop Shop (1977–83), [TV
    programme]   45
Cordoba, Sebastian   134
corporate cultures   101
A Country Practice (1981–93), [TV
    programme]   47, 48, 191
Crawford, Cindy   116
Crawford, Louise   48
Crawley, Jane   98

creative artists   73
Creative Nation policy   95
creative storytelling   79
creative texts   74
creativity   74
Crimes Act   143, 147
criminalization, of gay sex   140
Crowe, Russell   36
Cruising (1980), [Film]   15, 138–44
cultural attitudes   134
cultural change   122, 187
cultural communities   74
cultural generationalism   164
cultural institutions   102
cultural knowledge   176
cultural liberation   92
cultural localization   51
cultural milieu   138
cultural norms   134
cultural patriotism   200
cultural practices   16
cultural representation   190
cultural value   97
cultural vocabularies   76
Curran, James   188
Cutler, Luke   96
Cut Snake (2014), [Film]   176

Dad and Dave Come to Town (1938),
    [Film]   24
Dad Rudd MP (1940), [Film]   25
Daily at Dawn (1981), [TV
    programme]   47
Dangerous Women (1991), [TV
    programme]   *46*
Darwin Pride Festival   96
Daughters of Bilitis   57
Davies, Russell T.   179
Davis, Ken   68
'Decoding *Will and Grace*' (2003)   10
decriminalization   144–7
   of gay sex   140
   of homosexuality   99, 109
   of homosexual sex   143
Deep Water (2016), [TV
    programme]   176
Delamoir, Jeannette   24
D'Emilio, John   191
Dennison, Gary   109

depictions   64–5, 174, 184, 192–3, 209
De Valck, Marijke   90
The Devil's Playground (1976),
    [Film]   *163*
De Waal, Peter   43
digital media   11
digital platforms   132
digital storytelling   53
Division 4 (1969–76), [TV
    programme]   44
documentaries   13, 35, 43, 68, 123
Dooley, Marilyn   21
Doty, Alexander   156
Downriver (2015), [Film]   3, 6, 201
Dowsett, Gary   51
Dow, Stephen   51
The Dreamlife of Georgie Stone (2022),
    [TV programme]   127
Drown (2015), [Film]   *176*
Duncan, Digby   34, 67
Dyer, Richard   75, 177

Eagleton, Terry   180
Eat Carpet (1989–2005), [TV
    programme]   161
economic agenda   97
economic growth   95
electoral bloc   140
Eliza Fraser (1976), [Film]   33
Elsaesser, Thomas   91
emotional repugnance   194
Encounter   43
endemic diversity   120
entertainment   74, 76, 79–83, 87–8
entertainment films   73
Ethereal Queer: Television, Historicity,
    Desire (2014)   9
Europe   94
European film festival   91
The Everlasting Secret Family (1988),
    [Film]   31
Everything Will Be Fine (1998),
    [Film]   115
experimental filmmaking   58

Falassi, Alessandro   90
The Family Law (2016–19), [TV
    programme]   174
family members   162

A Farewell to Charms (1979), [Film]   99
Fast Forward (1989–92), [TV
      programme]   121
Feed Them to the Cannibals (1993),
      [Film]   35
fictional programmes   44
fictional texts   121
Film Comment magazine   107
film co-operatives   33–5, 37
film festival   14, 32, 89
      cultural event   90
      early Australian queer film
         festivals   91–3
      Melbourne Queer Film Festival
         (MQFF)   97–8
      mutual viewership   90
      professionalization of   93–6
      Queer Screen, Sydney   99–100
      self-celebration of community   91
film representation   8, 81
Film Victoria   98
Fire (1995–6), [TV programme]   48
First Day (2020–2), [TV
      programme]   15, 120, 128–9
Fischer, Margie   96
Fitzpatrick, Kate   52
Flagg, Fannie   64
Foolish Things (1981), [Film]   33
Ford, Akkadia   96
Fortune and Men's Eyes (1971), [Film]   92
Foss, Paul   64
Franklyn, Lee   67
French, Robert   147
Friedkin, William   137, 141
Fuller, Benjamin   21

Gay and Lesbian Alliance Against
      Defamation (GLAAD)   9, 40
Gay and Lesbian Film Week   99
gay audiences   39
gay bar culture   145
gay bar scene   147
gay characters   44, 50
gay community   101, 140–2, 144, 146–7
gay critics   143
Gay Film Fund   34
gay identities   58
gay liberation   64, 193

gay liberationists   2, 58
gay liberation movement   69, 107, 110,
      131, 145
gay man   64
Gay Mardi Gras (1978)   99
gay protagonist   12
gay rights movement   8, 78
gay sex   16, 139–40
gay sex clubs   16
gay sexual cultures   146, 148
gay sexual pleasure   141
Geelong Pride Film Festival (GPFF)   97
gender affirmation   123, 125–6
gender and sexual diversity   1–2, 55, 84,
      94
gender and sexuality   5, 82–4, 86, 88,
      119, 130, 133, 168, 186, 209
gender appearance   24
gender critique   121
gender-diverse contestants   50
gender-diverse representation   129
gender-diverse subjectivity   134
gender diversity   11, 15, 120, 122–3, 126,
      134
gender play   120–6, 135
gender representations   37
gender subjectivity   134–5
gender theory   185
genealogy   120–6
Gerbner, George   39
The Getting of Wisdom (1977), [Film]   3,
      31
Giroux, Henry   80
Gluyas, Sophia   31
Glynn, Michael   145–6
Gold Coast Queer Film Festival   96
government policy   95
Gowland, Lance   68
Graham, David   52
Grey, Zane   25
Griffin, F. Hollis   77
Gross, Larry   8, 39, 75
Grubb, Robert   48

Halberstam, Jack   97
Hall, Ken G.   25
Hannah Gadsby: Nanette (2018), [TV
      programme]   172

Hart, Kyle-Patrick R.   203
Hasham, Joe   45
Hasluck, Annette   96
Haynes, Todd   161
Head On (1998), [Film]   3, 36, 163, 172, 205
Heartbreak High (1994–9), [TV programme]   49
Heartbreak High (2022–5), [TV programme]   15, 132, 133, 181, 195
Heartstopper (2022–), [TV programme]   3
heterosexual audiences   171, 192
heterosexual romance   23, 25
heterosexual stereotypes   66
Hewson, Liv   53
High Art (1998), [Film]   115
Hill, Robert F.   22
Hills, Matthew   52
Hinter Gittern – Der Fraukenast (1997–2007), [TV programme]   46
Holding (1970), [Film]   93
Holding the Man (2015), [Film]   179, 194
Home and Away (1988–), [TV programme]   48, 121
Homecoming Queens (2018), [TV programme]   53, 55, 132
Homicide (1964–77), [TV programme]   44
homophobia   32–3, 50, 143
homophobic cultures   92
homophobic jokes   33
homophobic oppression   69
homosexual characters   63, 176
homosexuality   15, 24, 31–2, 44, 47, 58, 63–4, 67–8, 94, 99, 147, 168
Homosexuality: A Film for Discussion (1975), [Film]   35
homosexual law reform   144
homosexual people   140
homosexual relationships   66
homosexuals   44, 58, 63–4, 143
homosexual sex   138, 143
homosexual stereotypes   64
Horton, David   196
Hotel Story (1977–8), [TV programme]   45

Housekeeping for Beginners (2023), [Film]   96
Howes, Keith   8, 39, 42, 46, 48, 75, 107
Howson, John-Michael   42
human sexuality   83
Humphries, Barry   42, 122
The Hunger (1983), [Film]   182

Images of Gays film festival   66
Inman, John   47
international audiences   6
internet access   152
intersectionality   41, 86
Inventing Australia   25
It's a Sin (2021), [TV programme]   179

Janet King (2014–17), [TV programme]   172
Jewelled Nights (1925), [Film]   23, 121
Johnson, Derek   52
Johnston, Lawrence   5
Jones, Adam   54
Jory, Victor   25
Junkeer, Paul   127

Kalceff, Julie   129
Kennedy, Graham   42
Klick! 145
Kral, Michael   177

Lacan, Jacques   159
Lake, Gayle   93
Lamond, Toni   45
The Last of the Australians (1975–6), [TV programme]   *45*
The Last Wave (1977), [Film]   *36*
law reform   139
Lee, John   64, 110
Lee, Mark   32
lesbian community   112
lesbian culture and identity   116
lesbian identity   58
Lesbian Mardi Gras   54, 99
lesbians   43, 65
Lesbians on the Loose (*LOTL*) magazine   15, 112–17
Les Biches (1968), [Film]   92
LGBTQ+ 105

linear causality   177
Loist, Skadi   93–4
Love and Other Catastrophes (1996),
      [Film]   36, 170
Love Lies Bleeding (2024), [Film]   96
Lovers and Luggers (1937), [Film]   24
Lovett, Ken   146
Lumby, Catherine   114
The L Word (2004–9), [TV
      programme]   182

MacKay, Barry   21
The Mad King of Bavaria (1972),
      [Film]   92
Maidens (1978), [Film]   33
Majoos, James   133
male homosexuals   43, 177
Marché du Film   100
Mardi Gras Film Festival   21, 48, 67–8,
      92, 99–100, 115
Mariposa Film Group   65
marriage equality   186
masculinity   33
Maselli, Louise   48
mass-circulation media   123
Mattachine Society   108
The Mavis Bramston Show (1964–8),
      [TV programme]   42
McElroy, Hal   36
McIntyre, Joanna   22, 24
McKee, Alan   76, 128, 200, 202
McMann, Marg   68
McNab, Duncan   143
McNichol, Kristy   3
Meatpacking District clubs   147
media culture   4, 115
media effects models   185, 187
media representation   15, 57, 117, 192
Melbourne Gay Liberation Film
      Society   92
Melbourne International Film
      Festival   98
Melbourne Queer Film Festival
      (MQFF)   97–8
In Melbourne Tonight (1957–70), [TV
      programme]   42
Melbourne University Gay Society
      (GaySoc)   92
Meldrum, Molly   162

mental health, of LGBTQ+ young people
      167
   death   175–80
   public awareness of   169
   queer representation   170–5
   screen media   180–3
   socio-cultural causes   168
Mercado, Andrew   45, 49, 111
Mercurio, Paul   127
Meyrowitz, Joshua   196
Miller, Quinlan   41
minority communities   73, 86, 88
minority screen representation   16
minority sexuality   81, 86, 178
Monster Pies (2013), [Film]   101, 176
Morris, Nathan   52
motivation   76
Muriel's Wedding (1994), [Film]   3, 35

The Naked Bunyip (1970), [Film]   31
National Gay and Lesbian Film
      Festival   99
Naughton, Tish   96
negative stereotypes   8
Neighbours (1985–), [TV
      programme]   15, 126
Neighbours: Erinsborough High (2019),
      [TV programme]   127
Nelson, Margaret   32
neoliberalism   80
Netflix   172
Newcastle (2008), [Film]   201
New Farm Queer Film Festival   96
New Queer Cinema   106
New South Wales Crimes Act   139
New York magazine   116
Night Out (1990), [Film]   5
non-binary identities   135
non-fictional character   122
non-heterosexual intimacy   32
non-heterosexuality   133
non-normative sexuality   164
NSW Crimes Act   140, 148
Number 96 (1972–7), [TV
      programme]   45, 158

O'Brien, Gabrielle   68
ocker comedies   33
Olympic Follies   42

O'Meara, Damien   10, 50
online dating sites   131
on-screen gender diversity   134
on-screen narrative   121
on-screen representation   2, 13, 50, 60, 69, 77, 185, 209
organized communality   32
Outland (2012), [TV programme]   53
The Overlanders (1946), [Film]   26
Oxford Street   143

Pacella, Jess   96
Page, Peter   66
para-social relationality   196
Peach, Ricardo   35, 93
Perth Queer Film Festival   96
Petersen (1974), [Film]   33
Petersen, Marie Bjelke   23
Phillips, Wyatt D.   41
Picnic at Hanging Rock (1975), [Film]   31–2, 36
Pinedo, Isabel Cristina   41
The Pirate Movie (1982), [Film]   3
Pirkis, Jane   177
Pizzey, Jack   47
Please Like Me (2013–16), [TV programme]   171–2, 174
Point of Departure (1975), [Film]   35
police violence   138, 143
policy change   95
political activism   138
political freedom   92
political identities   58
Poll, Christabel   57
post-binary identities   55, 130–5
poststructuralist theory   2
The Power of the Dog (2021), [Film]   7
Price, Thomas   180
PrideFest Western Australia   96
Prisoner (1979–86), [TV programme]   174
production   73
professional organization   14, 89
psychiatric discourses   167
psychoanalytic Marxism   130
psychological distress   180
public attitudes   167
public discourse   36, 73, 162, 167, 187
public funding   95

public opinion   139

Q! Film Festival   94
Queer as Folk (1999–2000), [TV programme]   161, 182
queer character arc   47–9
queer characters   57
queer-coded characters   42
queer communities   53
queer contestants   52
queer culture   101, 167
queer, defined   2
QueerDOC   100
Queer Fruits Film Festival   96
queer masculinity   145
Queer Screen   98–100
queer screen scholarship   7–10, 41

racial diversity   69
racist stereotypes   122
Rafferty, Chips   26
Rand, Erin J.   116
Rand, Frances   112, 116
Rangle River (1936), [Film]   7, 25
Raw FM (1997–8), [TV programme]   49
reception practices   147–8
Reece, Anna   90
Reeves, Jimmie L.   6, 133, 204
reformism   139
Reid, Fiona Cunningham   35
Reid, Mark   96
Relax, It's Just Sex (1998), [Film]   115
renaissances   4–7
representation   32–3, 39, 50, 55, 63, 65, 69, 75, 88, 209
    asexual/intersex representation   41
    of gender diversity   120
    of gender/sexual minorities   177
    of homosexual desires on-screen   138
    of homosexual lives   69
    lesbian and gay characters in 'mainstream' film   152
    LGBTIQ+ representation   41
    of non-heteronormative characters   33
    on public agenda   40
    of queer characters on film and television   57
    queer screen representation   151, 176

Reynolds, Robert   58
Rhyne, Ragan   93
Rice, Damien   49
Richards, Stuart   92, 96, 106
Rich, B. Ruby   106
Robinson, Denise   100
Rodriga, Melanie   67
Russo, Vito   24, 41, 75, 78

same-sex couple   63
San Francisco   92
San Francisco Frameline International
　　LGBTQ Film Festival   92–3
Sargent, Dave P.   68
Satdee Night (1973), [Film]   33, 93
scandalous conduct   147
Scanlan, Toni   49
Scardino, Don   138
Scherer, Jackie   112
Scobie Malone (1975), [Film]   33
screen affordances   17
Screen Australia   41, 55
screen content   174
screen creativity   73
screen cultural content   14
screen culture   105
　　critic   106–8
　　Lesbians on the Loose (lesbian
　　　magazine)   112–16
　　LGBTQ+ print media   108–11
screen documentaries   65
screen entertainment   131, 189, 193
screen media   57, 76, 82, 134, 137,
　　210
screen media and social change   186
　　allyship and belonging   198–9
　　audience engagement   195–7
　　audience members' agency   187
　　cultural pedagogy   189
　　'media effects' model   187
　　palatability and tolerance   192–5
　　psychoanalytic film theory   187
　　queer and trans representation   189
　　queer screen representation   202–6
　　visibility and invisibility, concepts
　　　of   190–1
　　visual and audio framing   200–2
screen narratives   121

screen representation   9, 32, 69, 87, 151,
　　169, 190, 207
screen stakeholders   74
　　audiences, for social change   83–7
　　entertainment   79–83
　　production site   75–6
　　representation and visibility   76–9
　　scholarship   73
screen texts   83, 209
SeaChange (1998–2000), [TV
　　programme]   48
The Secret Life of Us (2001–5), [TV
　　programme]   3, 50, 173–4
*Seeing Ourselves: Reflections on Diversity
　　in TV Drama* (2016)   40–1
self-expression   95
self-identification   171
self-identity   152
self-perception   173
Sender, Katherine   101
The Set (1970), [Film]   12, 21, 26–30, 32
sexploitation films   26–30, 37
sex scenes   162
sexual content   182
sexual cultures   148
sexual identity   64, 178
sexuality   40, 44, 49–50
sexually explicit   161
sexual pleasure   146
sexual practices   148
sexual revolution   139
sexual subculture   146
Shannon's Mob (1975–6), [TV
　　programme]   45
Showtime (1978), [Film]   33
Sight and Sound (magazine)   106
Silent Number (1974), [TV
　　programme]   45
Silks and Saddles (1921), [Film]   22
Six Feet Under (2001–5), [TV
　　programme]   204
Skyways (1979–81), [TV programme]   45
The Slap (2011), [TV programme]
　　176
social activism   101
social altruism   98
social attitudes   207
social belonging   198–9

social change 10, 14, 17, 35, 69, 73–4, 117, 119, 185
social empowerment 14, 89
social engagement 174
social generation 165
social impact 85
social influence 83
social issues 73
social logic 177
social media 131, 152
social norms 158
social stereotypes 82
societal movements 93
socio-economic equality 180
sociopathic personality disturbance 168
Some of My Best Friends Are... (1971), [Film] 63–4, 110
Spencer, Carol 123
Staiger, Janet 156
The Star 145
Stark, Boaz 54
Starting From Now (2014–16), [Web series] 132
stereotypes 9, 43, 82, 85, 114, 131, 168, 177, 191
Steven, David 36
St Kilda Film Festival 98
Stokes, Terry 145
Stone, Georgie 53, 120, 127
Stork (1971), [Film] 33
Straayer, Chris 121
Strange World (2022), [Film] 96
streaming services 132–3
Strictly Ballroom (1992), [Film] 35
Submerge (2012), [Film] 101
Subscription Video on Demand (SVOD) services 132
suicide 176–7
Summer Heights High (2007), [TV programme] 122
The Sum of Us (1994), [Film] 3, 36, 171, 183
Sundance Film Festival 125
Sunday, Bloody Sunday (1971), [Film] 92
The Sun-Herald 43
Sunshine Coast Mardi Gras 96
Sunshine Sally (1922), [Film] 23
Swain, Madeline 97

Sweat (1996), [TV programme] 48
Sydney Film Co-operative 33, 93
Sydney Film Festival 115
Sydney Gay 54, 99
Sydney Mardi Gras parade 162
Sylvania Waters (1992), [TV programme] 52
symbolic annihilation 40

Tamagne, Florence 108
Tanner, Libby 49
TasPride Festival 96
Taylor, Noah 161
temporary transvestite 121
textual representation 10
'The Gay Festival' 99
This Day Tonight (1967–78), [TV programme] 43
Thompson, Jack 33, 36
Thornley, Jeni 33
trans and gender diverse (TGD) 169
trans-cis relationship 199
transgender character 40, 53
transgender contestants 50
transgender representation 23–4
trans identities 167, 185
Transparent (2014–19), [TV programme] 133
trans subjectivity 135, 167
Triple Oh! (2024), [TV programme] 55
Tropiano, Stephen 40
Tropical Fruits 96
Tucker, Abi 50
Tudor, Deborah 25–6
Turkish Baths (1975), [Film] 35

Uninvited: Classical Hollywood Cinema and Lesbian Representability (1999) 9
United States 119
Up from Invisibility: Lesbians, Gay Men, and the Media in America (2001) 40
urban gay community 138

Vanity Fair 116
Veenstra, Anton 92
Venkatesh, Vinodh 200

Verhoeven, Deb   10, 120
Victorian State Government   98
video cassette recorder (VCR)   162
Villarejo, Amy   9
visual storytellers   83

Wake in Fright (1971), [Film]   32
Walker, Gerald   137
Walking on Water (2002), [Film]   173
Ware, John   57
Water Rats (1996–2001), [TV
      programme]   49
Watson, Lex   147
Weaver, Jacki   33
Web 2.0 internet   152
web series   53–4
Weiss, Peter   64
The Well (1997), [Film]   36
Wells, Peter   33
Wenger, Etienne   197
Wentworth (2013–21), [TV
      programme]   53
White, Patricia   9

White, Richard   25
Will & Grace (1998–2006; 2017–20), [TV
      programme]   101, 192
Williams, Kathleen   163
Williams, Raymond   196
Wills, Sue   44
Witches and Faggots, Dykes and Poofters
      (1980), [Film]   34, 67–8
Wohl, Richard   196
women's fashion   24
Wood, Robin   107, 110
Word Is Out: Stories of Some of Our Lives
      (1977), [Film]   65–7
Wotherspoon, G.   24
Wran, Neville   143

The Year My Voice Broke (1987),
      [Film]   161
Young Royals (2021–4), [TV
      programme]   3
youth transitionalism   164
youth vulnerability   11
YouTube   53–4